AF343507

UFO
The 12 files that the Pentagon cannot explain

To Colette and James,
My blond and precious constellations.
To Armande.

Quotes

"The light of the mysteries penetrates better to those who do not expect it."
Saint Ambrose of Milan

"One is quick to say: it is childish. What is childish is to imagine that by blindfolding oneself in front of the Unknown, one suppresses the Unknown."
Victor Hugo, *Supreme Contemplation.*

"Under the guise of secrecy, the United States Air Force has engaged in a dangerous game. They are discrediting the UFOs which, despite the denials of the general staff, are operating in our skies.
From the 1970s onwards, these demonstrations have multiplied.
At the same time, interceptor aircraft, under orders from the Aerospace Defense Command (ADC), were attempting to shoot down these unknown objects."
Major Donald Keyhoe (formerly assigned to the Pentagon, Naval Aviation Training Division).

Contents

concrete natural phenomena, atmospheric or astronomical (meteors, planets, ball lightning...). Others see them as post-war fables, a barely pubescent, contemporary myth. Or dreams a little crazy straight from speculative fictions. Everyone will pick and choose as they see fit.

It moves in the sky UFO

Acting since always in a space of appearance, the UFOs gain however, recently, a more "official" status. It moves in the UFO sky!

Let's summarize the facts.

On December 16, 2017, the *New York Times* newspaper revealed that the Pentagon acknowledges the existence of a covert program to investigate UFOs. The U.S. Department of Defense confirms that this program, called the *Advanced Aerospace Threat Identification Program* or *ATIP*, began in 2007 and ended in 2012. Its purpose: to investigate in-flight encounters between combat aircraft and unknown flying objects moving at high speed without visible propulsion or in a stationary position without apparent means of lift.

However, *The New York Times* drops a scud: it maintains that investigations into incidents involving these UFOs continue. It points out that between 2007 and 2012, the program, known only to a small number of officials, had a budget of $22 million, out of the $600 billion allocated annually to the military. It was set up by former Nevada Democratic Senator Harry Reid, then Senate Majority Leader, who is interested in these unexplained phenomena.

According to *The New York Times*, most of the money for the program went to an aerospace research company run by Robert Bigelow, a billionaire entrepreneur and longtime friend of Harry Reid. "We don't have the answers, but we have plenty of evidence to justify asking questions," the senator explained on his Twitter account after the *New York Times* investigation was published. "This is a scientific and national security issue. If America doesn't step up to the plate and answer these questions, others will."

The New York Times also published three videos from the US military. One of these documents, which quickly went viral, raises real questions. It shows, in November 2004, an American fighter plane (an F/A-18 Super Hornet) chasing an oval, Tic Tac candy-shaped object the size of an airliner, off the coast of San Diego, near the California coast. The pilot claimed to have first observed a large submerged object causing an eddy on the surface of the water. And above it, moving erratically and performing maneuvers that defied all logic, this 40-foot-long (12-meter) Tic Tac.

This news, made public, created a great stir in the corridors of power in Washington. Highly influential senators, members of the Pentagon and former CIA directors suddenly began to talk about UFOs in a calm and serious manner. No more jeers, no more threats, no more "move along, there's nothing to see". John Podesta, former chief of staff to President Clinton, said, "It used to be a career-ender. You didn't want to be caught talking about it..." That all seems to be changing. Suddenly, these UFOs that have long embarrassed the Pentagon brass are being made official.

A report that changes everything!

Following a request from the Senate, on June 25, 2021, a preliminary report, issued by the ODNI, the Office of the Director of National Intelligence, was made public. This 9-page document, called *Preliminary Assessment:* Unidentified *Aerial Phenomena*, concerns UAPs. It is mainly intended for US military officials (land, air and sea).

The document is based on 144 cases recorded between 2004 and 2021. We learn that 80 of them were confirmed by several means of detection: radar, infrared and electro-optical equipment. Most of these incidents involve "probably" *physical* objects, as corroborated by the detectors in question. The majority of these phenomena, we are told, have interrupted military maneuvers or activities!

Of these 144 cases, 18 incidents were the subject of 21 reports, because the observed phenomena behaved in an astonishing way, outside of known flight characteristics. Stationary in strong winds at altitude, they could move against these winds and reach considerable speeds, without any means of propulsion. Most of these data come from the United States. Only one of these cases was formally identified: it was a deflating balloon.

"Are we dealing with hypersonic technologies tested by China or Russia?

Following the submission of this report, influential figures finally dared to speak out. Like John Ratcliffe - Director of National Intelligence under Donald Trump who oversaw the 18 American intelligence agencies. He declared on Fox News: "Frankly, there are many more observations than have been made public. Some of them have been declassified. We're talking about objects that have been seen by

Navy or Air Force pilots, or that have been spotted by satellite imagery, that frankly engage in actions that are difficult to explain, that have movements that are difficult to replicate, that we don't have the technology for, or that move at speeds beyond the sound barrier without a sonic boom."

In a deafening din of communications, the xxi^e century never ceases to boast of its victories, its technical advances. But from the periphery of the universe to its center, what have we learned? And what do we know? Not much, obviously. We try to tame atoms and viruses, without really mastering them. While the real unfolds its wonders far beyond us, our perceptions and understandings.

And what about UFOs in all this, which defy our pilots, violate our airspace and dance, unmolested, under the noses of the superpowers? Since their advent in June 1947, the question remains the same for the military who do not know what to do with them and for the civilians that we are. In the end, what are they really? Manifestations of another world, extravagance at the very heart of matter, mirages or tangible realities?

Reading these stories, let's bet that for the time being, their main virtue consists in asking us about the "who" of "who are we?", because Epicureans and Stoics agree on one point: only "others", from a very distinct exterior, seem able to provide us with the answer.

I. The hairy cone of Vins-sur-Caramy

We are all from a country. Mine runs along the garrigues, from forested areas to hills, under a beautiful sky devoid of rain. Rare showers, that's for sure, but a capricious wind, the great *master*, this mistral with its thick neck, which raises waves and dust. And slaps pines and mimosas.

My country, spangled with ochre, is Provence. The trains that carry tourists on hot days do not warn them of the mysteries to be found there. For my land, unusual and secret, has "as many as a pope can bless". As we say in our country.

As a child, in this land of light, everything prepares you for the marvelous: the grotto of Mary Magdalene and its prodigies, the arm of Saint Peter in Cuers or the door of the Pardon in the church of Correns. But it is towards the sky - on the other side of a schoolboy's life - that I raised my eyes very early. I was still playing marbles when I was told about lights, about extraordinary machines flying over Carcès, Vins-sur-Caramy and Toulon... At 13, I went camping in Valensole, pitching my tent in the middle of the lavender fields. No UFOs, but the idea was there. Scrutinize, as much as possible our skies of a fertile blue. And to track down singular lights which dance there.

Since then, the years have passed. I knew my Provence was rich in mysteries. I used to talk about it in a low voice. But today, it is no longer me who says so. The very serious daily newspaper *Var-Matin* displayed on its front page, on March 15, 2015 (this is not so old), the apparitions of UFOs in the four corners of the Midi. In the introduction to this paper, the journalist Eric Marmottans asked the following question: "Does the attractiveness of the first tourist department of France extend beyond the borders of our solar system?"

Yes, this Provence of cicadas and devouring fire, much coveted by the summer people, even troubled the high authorities of America... with a UFO of singular form which disconcerted them. Here is its history.

Date: April 14, 1957.

Location: Vins-sur-Caramy in the Var, a small village near Brignoles.

It is 3 pm. It is a very pleasant day. Marie Garcin is walking with her friend, Julia Rami, near the Château de Vins, on the departmental road 24.

Suddenly, at a hundred meters, they see a curious metallic object which loses altitude and practically lands on the road. The object is of conical shape, its point directed downwards. As its upper part is convex, it looks a bit like a big top. It is about 1.5 meters high. Strange... it is bristling with metal-looking tigers animated by rapid vibrations. These rods," says Julia Rami, "looked like car antennas. They were multicolored.

The two walkers observe the object for a good ten minutes. At the moment when this strange "top" maneuvers to land, our two witnesses perceive a deafening noise. In fact, this noise is produced by a road sign located at 5 meters, which starts to oscillate and vibrate brutally, as if someone shook it energetically. Mrs. Rami and Garcin then push cries of fright.

Alerted by this tumult, Jules Boglio, city councilor of Vins - who was taking care of his beehives, 200 meters higher on the hill -, rushes over. He thinks that a car accident has just occurred. Interloqué, he discovers a completely different spectacle: a conical object takes off by making great jumps above the road, then goes to land on a small road very close.

I rushed to the presumed site of the accident," says Jules Boglio, "and there I saw a machine making a huge jump. It came down into a field where it stopped. It stayed there for a few seconds, then went to land on a small dirt road.It was gray and bristling with antennae.

To perform this maneuver, the "hairy cone" flew over a second sign. This panel, in its turn, started to vibrate. And subjected to brutal oscillations, emitted a strong resonance. Our three witnesses did not believe their ears or their eyes.

Finally, the machine moved away towards the south-east at a moderate speed, totally silent, strangely swaying. Before disappearing at the level of the hills.

Our three witnesses return home somewhat shaken. At first, they prefer to keep silent, fearing the ridicule. It is only the next morning that Julia Rami - who did not sleep a wink during the night!- decides to tell everything to her husband, the gardener. Then in the stride, will confide in Mr. Ventre, mayor of the village.

　　UFO: The 12 files that the Pentagon cannot explain

The mayor then alerted the Brignoles gendarmerie, who quickly went to the scene. At the precise location of the landing, the gendarmes noticed that, on the side of the road, the earth had been violently swept away, "as if under the effect of a powerful blast". Same thing on the small road where the earth is scattered on a diameter of approximately 1,5 meter. And the grass is scorched.

48 hours after the observation, the viscountess Marie-Laure de Noailles, passing through Vins, picked up a piece of metal "as big as an olive and of tormented shape, as if it had been brought to a very high temperature".

She presents it successively to the personnel of the nearby electrochemical mine, then to a friend, captain of the Palyvestre base in Hyères. She then entrusted him to Mr. Roteley, a dentist friend who tried in vain to saw him, and to Mr. Rouiller, a plumber in the town. None of these people is able to say what it is about.

After analysis, Mr. Cartoux, head of the electrothermal laboratory of the Pechiney Company, believes that the metallic fragment in question is a by-product of corundum, an unusual alloy manufactured in Paris. What would such a fragment of corundum from a factory located some 600 kilometers away be doing in Provence?

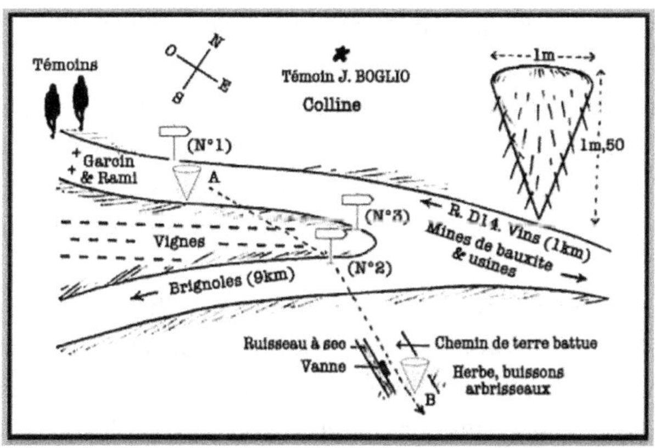

Reconstruction of the observation of the "hairy cone" of Vins-sur-Caramy

Jimmy Guieu[2] leads the investigation

On April 17, 1957, Jimmy Guieu went to the scene. He was accompanied by Pierre Ayraud, sound engineer of the Radio Monte Carlo studio.

The two men are received by a gendarmerie adjutant. The man of law, very courteously, summarizes the case to them, specifying that the witnesses are "people of good faith, above any suspicion of deception".

However, the investigation proved difficult. It was impossible to locate the witnesses who, fearing any media coverage, had "gone underground". The villagers are hardly more cooperative. Doors and shutters are slammed in the face of our investigators.

A Citroën pulls up in the village square, with a policeman and a gendarme on board. The brigadier declares, peremptorily, that the case is solved. The "remote-controlled" machine certainly came from the base on the Ile du Levant. A lively exchange began. Jimmy Guieu contested this hypothesis. "No nation has a silently moving aircraft! he retorted. Moreover, if the road signs began to vibrate with such a din, it is because they must have been caught in the magnetic field propelling the craft. The gendarmes, somewhat overwhelmed by these considerations, remain speechless.

"Let's see if there are magnetic remanences on the spot!", proposed Jimmy Guieu. Perplexed but still intrigued, the gendarmes complied.

There," said Jimmy Guieu, "in the presence of the police who, at my request, carefully monitored my experiment, I brought my compass close to the body of my 4CV and had the amplitude of the needle's deviation noted: 3 to 4 degrees maximum. Then I put my compass on the exact spot where I had landed: negative result, no magnetic remanence.

"However, 5 meters away, the signpost made the compass needle jump (approached at 5 cm), marking a deviation of 15 degrees! A moment later, we followed on the road the "line of flight" of the machine which, at about 100 meters from there, passed above another signpost. This sign (indicating Brignoles) was also "magnetized" and made the compass needle deviate by 15 degrees.

---

2. Jimmy Guieu (1926-2000) : at the same time science fiction novelist, radio man and ufologist, he integrated the Ouranos Commission founded in 1951, one of the first French research groups on UFOs. He wrote many articles for the magazine *Ouranos*, of which he was the head of the investigation department. Then, in 1980, he co-founded the IMSA (World Institute of Advanced Sciences).

UFO: The 12 files that the Pentagon cannot explain

The gendarmes are bluffed. What technology - in the 1950s - could cause such magnetic disturbances, they ask themselves?

Back in the village, Jimmy Guieu met Mr. Rami, the village guard. After discussion, he agrees to go and find his wife and Marie Garcin who are hiding in the hill! This was a godsend, because the two women finally agreed to talk. The interview is then recorded by Pierre Ayraud and broadcast the same evening - April 17 - at 7 pm on Radio Monte Carlo. The listeners are dumbfounded. The flying saucers have definitely a predilection for this beautiful region that is Provence!

The regional press seized on the story. It announces that all the intelligence services of the country are on the teeth. The prefecture of Toulon, the scientific services of Lyon and Paris have indeed dispatched investigators. And the air police went to the scene (Inspector Rochu, from this formation, confirmed that one of their men went to the scene on April 18).

In the end, the Brignoles gendarmerie wrote a precise and detailed report that it gave to the air police, the Ministry of the Interior, the command of the IVe air region as well as to several official organizations. Conclusion: unknown object "not coming from any French or foreign power"!

The US military is interested in it

This surprisingly solid case also had an international impact. It landed in the US Air Force archives, including those of Project *Blue Book* (the largest official UFO investigation ever launched)! It was recorded in a 60-page report written by the Foreign Technology Division of Wright-Patterson Air Force Base.

Dr. J. Allen Hynek, astronomer and father of scientific ufology, states that this French case interested the American military. But they officially concluded that it was a "hoax". According to Hynek, the high degree of strangeness and the unprecedented appearance of the craft disconcerted the US Air Force personnel who, for this reason, gave up on conducting an on-site investigation.

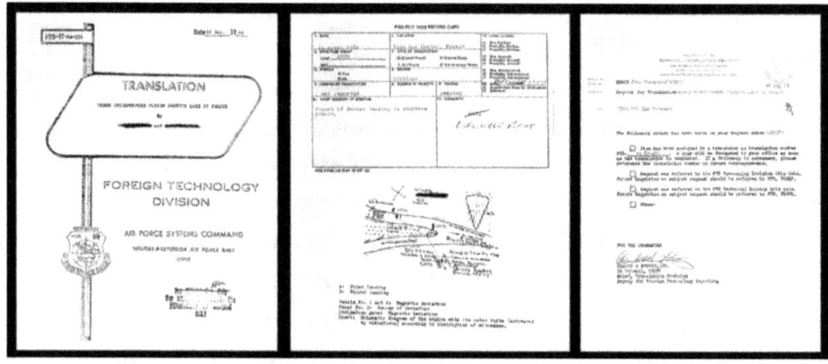

US Air Force document concerning the case of Vins-sur-Caramy

Steven Spielberg enters the scene

By reopening, years later, the file of Vins-sur-Caramy, an investigator put forward the hypothesis that the UFO seen in April 1957 was in fact a small helicopter. To which the ufologist René Fouéré retorted: "We also note that, according to information taken from the best sources, at the moment when the "top" began to rise, the witnesses saw a whirlwind of dust also rise. Rene Hardy points out that a helicopter would have, on the contrary, thrown the dust in all directions."

In spite of these debates, the Provençal "hairy cone" received a late and unprecedented recognition since it inspired one of the masterpieces of American cinema. In the 1970's, when Jacques Vallée met the director Steven Spielberg, he told him in detail the story of Mrs. Rami and Garcin in 1957. Later, when the director made his iconic film *Encounters of the Third Kind*, he used a very precise detail. During a scene that has become cult, when a UFO appears, he made one of the signposts on the side of the road vibrate!

Sources

Var-Matin, April 18, 1957 - *Var-Matin*, April 26, 1957 - *Ouranos* n° 21, 3e quarter 1957, pp. 50-52 - *Ouranos* n° 28, September 1961, pp. 17-18 - *Three Unidentified Flying Objects Land in France*, report of the Foreign Technology Division, Wright-Patterson US Air Force base, December 22, 1964 - TV report " Actualités de Provence ", broadcasted on April 22, 1965 - Aimé Michel, *À propos des soucoupes volantes, Planète*, 1966, pp. 247-248 - *Phénomènes spatiaux* n∞ 17, 3e quarter 1968, pp. 6-7 - *Lumières dans la nuit* n∞ 104, February 1970, pp. 8-9 - *Var-Matin La République*, Draguignan, January 15, 1972 - J. Allen Hynek, *Les Objets volants non identifiés, mythe ou réalité ?* J'ai Lu, 1972, pp. 215-217 - *Inforespace* n° 12, 1973, p. 4 - *Fenómenos Aéreos* n∞ 3, July-September 1980, p. 13 - *Awareness*, vol. 14, n° 4, season 1985-6, pp. 20-22 - *MUFON UFO Journal* n∞ 288, April 1992, p. 17 - Henri Julien and Michel Figuet, *Ovni en Provence*, Éditions de Haute-Provence, 1993, pp. 186-188 - *Les Mystères de l'Est* n∞ 5, year 1999, pp. 21-23 - *Var-Matin*, March 15, 2015 - *El Ojo Critico* n∞ 85-86, December 2017, p. 67.

II. The wave of *foo fighters* of the Second World War

1er September 1939: the Second World War is declared, mobilizing for 6 years 61 nations and more than 100 million combatants.

Aviation has undergone enormous progress. The invention of radar, on-board weaponry, the power of fighter engines, and radio communications made aeronautics an essential component of this conflict.

In the summer of 1939, the German air force was unparalleled. They had 4,021 operational aircraft, including 1,191 bombers, all maintained and flown by 2 million men. In comparison, France and England had only half that number.

During these war years, 850,000 aircraft were produced. It is not surprising that humans discovered uncharted spaces and colonized the sky! During offensive raids, these pioneers came across some strange phenomena. If we are to believe the pilots of the Second World War, strange things are happening in these skies of confrontation. As early as 1940, fluorescent spheres, "endowed with reason", escorted fighter planes and bombers. With extraordinary speed, these unknown "machines" approached military aircraft without causing any damage. And no belligerent claims to have designed or used them.

Portrait of the phenomenon

The pilots describe luminous balls of rather modest size. Of red, orange, green or white color, their brightness is very intense. The military speak of "crystal balls", "golden phosphorescent spheres" or "Christmas balls". Their appearance varies: some appear metallic, silver, while others are described as translucent "like glass".

They can be seen over Europe (France, Germany, Belgium, Italy, Sicily), but also over Norway, Tunisia, the Pacific Ocean, Japan, Ceylon, the Indian Ocean, Burma... This is undoubtedly a global phenomenon.

The origin of the name

The Germans call them *Kraut Bolids*. The English pilots called them *The Light* or *The Thing*. The French called them *ghost fighters*.

But it was the Americans who were to make history with this phenomenon. The 415ᵉ night fighter squadron called these "fireballs" *foo fighters*. They were inspired by the comic strip *Smokey Stover, which* was very popular at the time and featured a rather crazy fireman. The term *foo* derives from the French word "feu" (the phenomenon is often described as "a ball of fire").

Other pilots dispute this origin and claim that the name comes from the exclamation *Phooey!* which means: "Oh no! Gee!" While the military in Korea prefer to call them *Gremlins*.

Copy of the North American comic strip Smokey Stover

Behavior of the phenomenon

With an extraordinary velocity, these luminous spheres sometimes rise from the ground to meet the planes. Or appear from nowhere. They then escort the bombers, changing color, from orange to red and then to white.

UFO: The 12 files that the Pentagon cannot explain

They are never offensive and pose no threat to aircraft in flight. Since they seem to "observe" and "play" with pilots, pilots attribute "intelligent behavior" to them. Most of them are not detected by radar. They can be observed day and night.

What disconcerts and worries the military is that they are, by far, faster and more agile than British, German, Japanese or French aircraft.

A veteran ex-B-17 pilot sums up their modus operandi perfectly: "Suddenly, they would appear against the wing of your plane. There were six or eight of them. They would fly in perfect formation. You would turn, they would turn with you. You gained altitude, they gained altitude. You would dive, they would dive together. You couldn't get rid of them. They were small aluminum objects, of a dirty gray. They measured between 2 and 3 meters in diameter... No cockpit, no window, no sign of life. When these things got tired of playing, they would fly off into space and disappear at a prodigious speed."

A first demonstration

June 25, 1942. Lieutenant Roman Sabinski, later commander of the 301ᵉ bomber squadron of the British Royal Air Force (RAF), reported the sighting of a spherical object over Holland.

That evening, the weather was mild, the sky perfectly clear. Lieutenant Sabinski - a soldier of the Polish division attached to the RAF - was returning from a mission. He had participated in the bombing of strategic German sites in the Ruhr Valley. Suddenly, the tail gunner informed him that an enemy plane had just chased them. Sabinski left his seat to observe the intruder. He saw "a very bright light" on their tail. "If it gets any closer, open fire," he tells the gunner on duty. Sabinski is worried. He thought it was a German fighter that had placed a light on his nose. This was unusual, as enemy aircraft were usually equipped with lights on their wings.

The "object" is getting closer and closer. And it is not a plane. It is a round "thing", about the size of a full moon as seen from the ground. It is not white, and seems to be made of shiny copper, "rather dull like a setting sun". Its contours are imprecise, vaporous. "Take it down!", Sabinski orders. Four machine guns then fire in concert.

The tracer bullets hit their target perfectly. But "they penetrate the object without coming out. And instead of falling back to the ground, they vanish! The crew is appalled. The strange phenomenon does not seem to be affected at all by the heavy fire it has just suffered. Still intact, the sphere then moves at a prodigious speed and comes to position itself at 180 meters of the wing of the bomber. The gunners of head and tail empty again their weapons on the intruder. Without any result. Sabinski recalls: "I went back to the cockpit, took over the controls and tried to avoid the intruder because I was really worried about it. I also had no idea what it was. I maneuvered quite violently, but the object remained stuck to the wing of my aircraft. That means it was moving extremely fast so it wouldn't let go of us."

Then suddenly, the object leaps and precedes the bomber. "It sped by at a prodigious speed, at an angle of 45 degrees, to merge among the stars."

Once he had landed, Roman Sabinski reported his observation to his unit's intelligence office. He was greeted with loud laughter. "How many beers have you had?" he was asked.

Later, while talking with a captain of the Wellington bomber unit, Sabinski learned that other pilots had experienced the same phenomenon. But these men preferred to keep quiet to avoid the mocking and humiliating remarks of their superiors.

Sources

UFO NYT, September 1962, p. 186 - Henry Durrant, *The Black Book of Flying Saucers*, Robert Laffont, 1970, p. 76 - *UFODATA Magazine*, September-October 2007, p. 35 - Keith Chester, *Strange Company*, Anomalist Books, 2007

A fleet of 150

August 12, 1942, 10 a.m.

Not all sightings of mysterious celestial objects are made only by pilots. Thus a soldier of the 1re Marine Division, in bivouac with his squad on the island of Tulagi (south of the Solomon Islands), was able to observe metallic objects from the ground. On watch west of Guadalcanal, Sgt. Stephen J. Brickner reports:

"It was a bright tropical morning, with high banks of white, woolly clouds. I was cleaning my rifle on the edge of my trench, when suddenly the siren announcing an air raid sounded.

"I immediately ducked into my trench with my back to the ground and my face to the sky. I heard the formation before I saw it. And the sound I perceived intrigued me. It was a loud roar that seemed to echo in the sky. It did not sound at all like the "sewing machine" sound of Japanese air formations. A few seconds later, I saw a fleet of silver objects appear directly above my head.

"I was very tense because it was my 5[e] day of combat in the Marines. So it was easy to mistake anything that crossed at altitude for Japanese aircraft. At first, I thought that was the case. But these objects were flying high above the clouds, too high to be a squadron coming to bomb our little island. Someone in a nearby trench shouted that they were Japanese planes looking for our fleet. I accepted this explanation with some reservations. First, the formation was huge. I would say there were over 150 objects there. Instead of the usual tight "V" of 25 aircraft, this formation was moving in straight lines of 10 to 12 objects, one behind the other. Their speed was a little faster than that of the Japanese planes. In fact, they were soon out of sight.

"I was puzzled by some of the details. I could not make out any wings or tails on these objects. They seemed to fly with a slight wobble. Every time they wobbled, they glinted in the sunlight. Their color was like polished silver. Of course, no bombs were dropped. It was the most impressive and frightening sight I have ever seen in my life.

We will find, in future UFO observations, this "oscillatory" mode of displacement (*cf.* the observation of Kenneth Arnold in 1947 and many others).

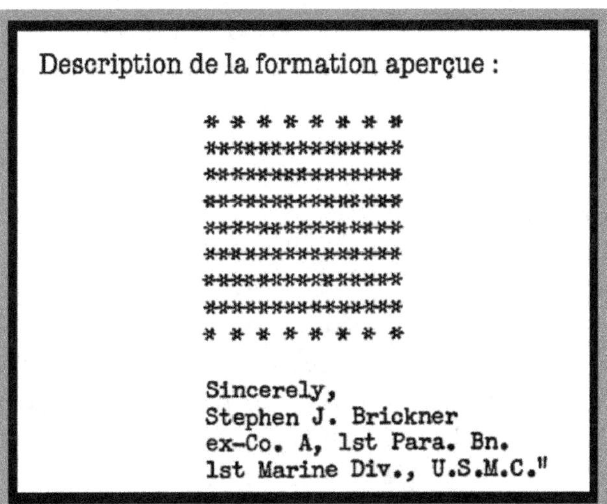

Description de la formation aperçue :

Sincerely,
Stephen J. Brickner
ex-Co. A, 1st Para. Bn.
1st Marine Div., U.S.M.C."

Reconstruction by Stephen J. Brickner

Sources

Civilian Saucer Intelligence of New York No. 22, December 15, 1957, p. 28 - Timothy Good, *Above Top Secret*, Quill William Morrow 1988, p. 18 - *MUFON UFO Journal* No. 476, December 2007, p. 12

The Air Ministry is concerned

A day in December 1942. 7 p.m.

B.C. Lumsden took the controls of his Hurricane and took off from England. This British pilot of the RAF had to carry out a control mission over the French coast.

20 hours. Lumsden flew over the mouth of the Somme at an altitude of 2,000 meters. The flight is going smoothly. Suddenly, our pilot saw 2 orange lights coming up from the ground to meet him... and they started to follow him!

At first, Lumsden thinks it's a tracer shot from a flak gun. But he quickly changes his mind. These projectiles are moving too slowly. He then begins a tight turn. To port, the lights suddenly appear larger and more intense. They stop their ascent and stay level with the aircraft. Our pilot panics. He negotiated a second sharp turn. No use, the lights are right on his tail! Lumsden then starts a dive, diving to 1,200 meters. The lights are still there, sticking to his wake. When he straightened his aircraft, the two spheres were 300 meters below him, then in one go, they caught up with the aircraft, resuming their stalking. In desperation, Lumsden accelerates. And ends up losing this curious phenomenon.

"I had a hard time convincing my unit members," Lumsden later said, "but the next night one of the squadron commanders had a similar experience in the same area with a green light."

Lumsden's report was given to the Air Ministry. It was added to a number of similar statements. Witnesses were unaware that three months earlier, on September 23, 1942, concerned about the increasing number of sightings, the Department's Operational Research Section had written an official, classified report entitled "Note on Recent Enemy Pyrotechnic Activity over Germany. A first investigation was launched.

Source

Dr. David Clarke and Andy Roberts, *Out Of The Shadows*, Piatkus, 2002, pp. 9-10.

A shimmering golden ball

The following astonishing testimony came to us many years later. Louis Kiss, now living in Connecticut, belatedly informed *Citizens Against UFO Secrecy* (CAUS) of his encounter with a *foo fighter* while fighting in Europe during World War II. Kiss, then a staff sergeant, was at the time a tail gunner on the *Phyllis Marie*, a B-17 bomber owned by the 390th Bombardment Group, 3rd Division of the 8th U.S. Air Force.

In late 1943, while on a daytime mission over Germany, he observed a strange sphere approaching his plane from behind. The thing, about the size of a basketball, was a shimmering golden color. It caught up with the bomber and hovered over his wing. Then, passing over the plane, it settled for a while on the other wing. Sergeant Kiss was tempted to open fire with his machine gun. But since the strange device was close to the B-17's fuel tank, he changed his mind.

As Kiss watched, the golden ball moved backwards. Then, caught in the wake and turbulence of the aircraft, it quickly disappeared.

Louis Kiss still does not know if another crew member observed this phenomenon as he did. But he reported the incident to his intelligence officer.

Curiously, until then, Louis Kiss had never heard of *foo fighters*. So it was a ufologist who told him about them. While some question the credibility of the witness, CAUS published, along with the testimony of this former soldier, an excerpt from the 390[e] newsletter of the Veterans Association Foundation, Fall-Winter 1991 issue, attesting to his excellent record as a combat pilot.

Source
Australian UFO Bulletin, December 1992, pp. 8-9.

North of Strasbourg

December 22, 1944.

Lieutenants David L. McFalls and Edward Baker (radar operator) fly over Haguenau, a French town 28 kilometers north of Strasbourg. Both pilots are members of the 415[e] fighter squadron based in Dijon. At the controls of their aircraft, they witnessed a strange phenomenon. Here is their report:

"At 6 p.m., near Haguenau, while we were flying at an altitude of 3,000 meters, we saw two lights coming from the ground towards us. When they reached our level, they stabilized and stayed close to the tail of our plane. They were two big lights of an intense orange. They followed us for 2 minutes, without ever leaving the tail of the aircraft. They flew in a perfectly controlled way. Then they negotiated a turn, moved away and their glow seemed to fade."

On December 24, 1944, Christmas Eve, McFalls and Baker made the same observation. They tell us: "A ball of red light came straight up at us. Suddenly it turned into an airplane which performed an acrobatic maneuver, climbing straight up into the sky, followed by a vertical flat turn. Then the phenomenon plunged toward the ground and disappeared."

When Jo Chamberlin, a reporter for *The American Legion* magazine, went to Germany to interview the pilots of 415ᵉ squadron, he said, impressed, that he encountered pragmatic, "normal soldiers, primarily concerned with their combat mission, and interested, in descending order, in pretty girls, poker, doughnuts, and all liquid derivatives of grapes."

Sources

The American Legion Magazine, vol. 39, No. 6, December 1945, p. 44 - Harold T. Wilkins, *Flying Saucers on the Attack,* Citadel Press 1954, p. 25 - Gordon I. R. Lore and Harold H. Deneault, *Mysteries of the Skies: UFOs in Perspective*, Prentice Hall, 1968, p. 116 - Michel Bougard, *La Chronique des Ovni*, Jean-Pierre Delarge, 1977, pp. 271-272.

Testimony of George Barton

In November 1998, George Barton, an ex-British pilot, now living in South Africa, sent a letter to the English magazine *UFO* concerning an incident dating from June 1944. Here is his account:

"Starting from Elsham Wolds, Lincolnshire, I was flying with 576 Squadron, 1ᵉʳ Tactical Air Command Group. I remember this incident vividly. This particular flight took place just after D-Day in June 1944. It was the second of three raids we made on Stuttgart, Ruhr, Germany. Our bombers never flew in a straight line to the target. They flew in hooks so the Germans could not guess where we were going. But that night was special. The enemy seemed to anticipate our every move. They sent up *flares at* regular intervals, which illuminated our planes despite our detours. And we suffered heavy losses.

Back at the base, for the *debriefing*, I was exhausted. I wasn't paying much attention to the guy who was supposed to take my report. My mind was wandering. That's why I picked up on the conversation at the next table. One guy, in particular, was very excited and talking loudly. I realized that he was a tail gunner. And here's what he was talking about: as they were approaching their target, they suddenly realized that their plane was being followed by glowing spheres. It was as if they were caught in the plane's wake. Believing that this was a new German secret weapon, he asked the pilot to perform a rather violent stall, just to outrun them. And at the same time, he shot at these spheres. All this without any result. These objects remained stuck to the bomber. They were the size of a large football. At that time, I had no idea what they were. It was only after the war that I heard about these *foo fighters*. And it was only then that I made the connection."

Source

UFO, November-December 1998, p. 12.

On the Indian Ocean

August 1944.

Flying a U.S. Army B-29 Superfortress bomber, Captain Alvah M. Reida has a strange encounter over the Indian Ocean. Based in Kharagpur, India, he is a member of the 486ᵉ bomber group, 792ᵉ squadron, 20ᵉ air tactical command. Here is his account:

"I was from Sri Lanka, flying a bombing mission over Palembang in South Sumatra. It was August 10, 1944. It was after midnight. We were a formation of 50 planes and had to drop our bombs every 3 minutes. As my plane was the very last of the group, my mission was to drop a bomb and then circle the target and take some pictures to assess the damage caused by my predecessors. The weather was cloudy with an overcast sky above us. We were flying at an altitude of 4,200 meters and our speed was 330 km/h. As we flew over the target, we were exposed to flak. But as we moved away, the threat ceased.

"About 20 or 30 minutes into our mission, the gunner and my co-pilot suddenly reported that a strange object was following us. It was flying about 450 yards off our wing. From where we were, it looked like a spherical object 1 to 2 meters in diameter, a dense orange-red color and very bright. It was surrounded by a sort of halo. My gunner then told me that it was moving from a "5 o'clock" [right rear] position to keep up with us. It seemed to pulse or vibrate continuously. I thought it was a radio-controlled object that was launched to find us. I tried to lose it by changing direction, making 90-degree turns, descending to an altitude of 600 meters. For 8 minutes, he stuck to each of our maneuvers, always at a distance of 450 meters and at a position of "2 o'clock" [right front]. Then suddenly he initiated an abrupt 90-degree turn, accelerated rapidly and disappeared into the clouds."

Sources

NICAP, *The UFO Evidence*, Richard H. Hall Editor, May 1964, p. 23 - Jerome Clark and Lucius Farish, "*The Mysterious 'Foo Fighters' of World War II*," *UFO Report*, Spring 1975, p. 44 - Timothy Good, *Above Top Secret*, Quill William Morrow 1988, p. 19

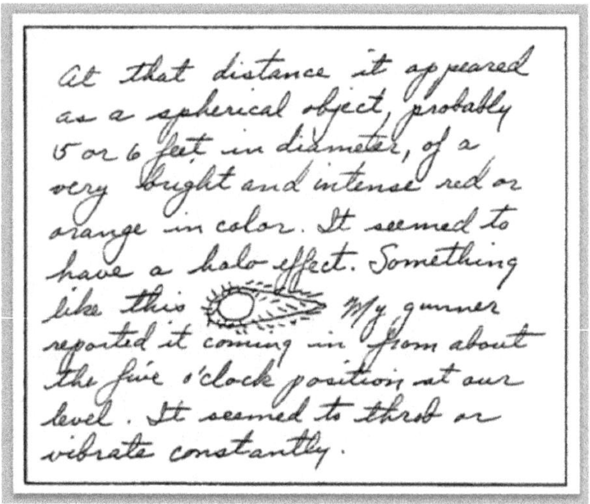

At that distance it appeared as a spherical object, probably 5 or 6 feet in diameter, of a very bright and intense red or orange in color. It seemed to have a halo effect. Something like this. My gunner reported it coming in from about the five o'clock position at our level. It seemed to throb or vibrate constantly.

Description and drawing of Captain Alvah M. Reida

Major Augspurger's testimony

Commander of the 415[e] American night fighter squadron, this soldier saw a *foo fighter* during the winter of 1944-45. At the time, he thought it must be a secret Nazi weapon. But once the war was over, he realized that this phenomenon was neither a plane, nor a jet, nor a rocket. And even less a weapon! He looked for other explanations. But neither a flare, nor a weather balloon, nor the moon or any visible star that evening could explain this observation.

In 2003, investigator and author Keith Chester asked Augspurger for his theory on the nature of the sighting. He replied bluntly, "Well, I think it was an extraterrestrial object. At the time, I didn›t think anything of it. But time has passed, and I now think it was something from outer space. I believe in these things. What we saw… is to me extraterrestrial, from somewhere else. Today, I tend to think that they had come down to Earth to see what was going on.*"

Major Augspurger said he said he said little about his observation with his superior, Captain Ringwald, chief of intelligence. "We didn't discuss much about what it might be, and the rest for that matter. We just stated what we saw. The other soldiers did the same. I really didn't know what it was. There must be, somewhere, a report of my observation in the intelligence files."

Source

Keith Chester, *Strange Company*, Anomalist Books, 2007, p. 207.

Testimony of Lieutenant Meiers

In the *Morning Avalanche* (Lubbock, Texas) of January 2, 1945, an American officer testifies. Under the headline "Sinister German *foo fighters* stalk Yankees over Nazi country," it reads:

"The Nazis have launched something new into the night sky over Germany. They are the strange and mysterious *foo fighters*, the fireballs that fly close to the wings of American Beaufighters then on intrusion missions over the Reich."For more than a month, American pilots have been encountering the strange *foo fighters* during these night flights. And no one knows exactly what this heavenly weapon is.

"These fireballs appear suddenly and follow the planes for miles. They appear to be radio-controlled from the ground and, according to official intelligence reports, are able to follow planes flying at 480 km/h.

"Lt. Donald Meiers of Chicago, Illinois says, "There are three types of these lights that we call *foo fighters*. The first type is red fireballs that position themselves at the tips of our wings and escort us. The second type is a vertical row of three fireballs that fly In front of our aircraft. And the third type is a group of about 15 lights that appear in the distance - like a Christmas tree in the air - and flash."

"The pilots of this night fighter squadron - in operation since September 1943 - find these fireballs the strangest thing they have ever encountered. They are convinced that these *foo fighters* are designed to be a psychological as well as a military weapon. Although it is not in the nature of these devices to attack aircraft.

"Meiers continued, "*Foo fighters* appeared 200 meters from my plane and chased me for more than 30 kilometers over the Rhine Valley. I turned to starboard and two fireballs turned with me. I then turned to port and they also turned with me. We were flying at 420 km/h and these balls were on our tail.

"Another time, when a *foo fighter* popped up beside me, I did a 580 mph dive. Despite this, he held on to my wingtips for a while. Then he went up into the sky in a candle.

"The first time I saw these things on my wingtips, I had this terrible thought that some German on the ground was ready to push a button and blow them up. But they never explode. Nor do they attack. They only escort us like will-o'-the-wisps."

A coincidence?

March 1945.

While flying over the Brenner Pass (which separates Austria from Italy), a pilot at the controls of his B-25 spotted a *foo fighter*. The object, which appeared from nowhere, like a shooting star, came to rest 1 meter from the right wing of the aircraft. It is a luminous white sphere, the size of a basketball. The *foo fighter* escorts the aircraft for 2 to 3 minutes, then suddenly stalls and disappears into the sky.

The next day, our pilot was again on mission (mission n° 38). But his plane was shot down over the Brenner. All the crew lost their lives... except for him who miraculously escaped. Coincidence?

Source

Michel Bougard, *La Chronique des Ovni*, Jean-Pierre Delarge, 1977, p. 273.

Testimony of Major Paul A. Duich

July 1945.

A B-29 bomber is followed, during a night flight over Japan, by a *foo fighter*. The entire crew witnesses the phenomenon. Major Paul A. Duich, then a flight engineer and now retired, testifies:

"The *foo fighter* that my crew first saw was orange in color. It followed our plane for miles and miles.It was close to the tail of the aircraft, on the left. It was hard to tell how far away it was because it was a night flight. Around us, it was total darkness except for the lights that could be seen further down on the ground. Our mission was to bomb the city of Sasebo, Japan. The chief gunner who was in charge of the artillery of our B-29 bomber, and who was positioned in the tail, finally fired! We saw the tracer bullets heading straight for the object. But nothing happened.

"And then quickly, this thing stalled. It made a kind of dive, slid under our camera and came to our right. We, who were in front of it, could see it. That's where I could see it. It was a big ball... like ionized gas, at least that›s the term we would use today. It gave us the creeps. At the time, we thought it was a secret Japanese device, probably designed by the Germans. I should point out that our colleagues in Europe also thought it was a German weapon, while the German pilots were convinced it was an Allied weapon. With each side accusing the other, no one ever really knew what it was. "

Source

Double vinyl album *Factual Eyewitness Testimony of UFO Encounters*, Investigative Research Associates 1978.

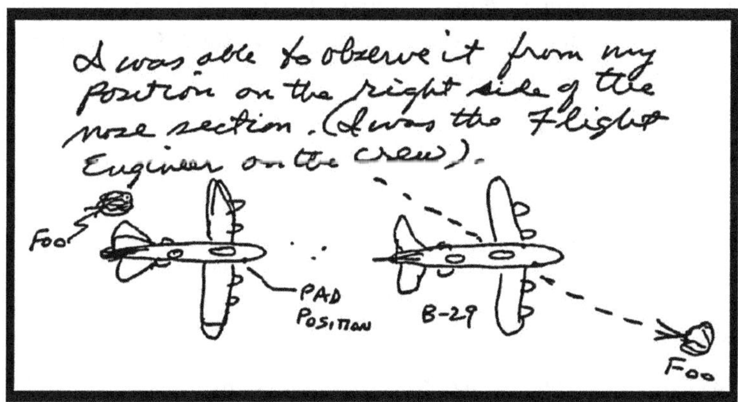

Description and drawing of Major Paul A. Duich

Disruptions in flight

August 28, 1945.

A C-46 aircraft flies over the Pacific Ocean, towards Tokyo. Three weeks earlier, the first two atomic bombs were dropped on Hiroshima (August 6, 1945) and Nagasaki (August 9, 1945). One of the occupants, Sergeant Leonard Stringfield, recounts:

"I was one of twelve specialists from the 5e air force aboard a C-46 going from Shima to Iwo Jima where we were to make a technical stop... [...] We were flying at 3,000 meters, in a bright sunny sky, when I saw through a starboard window, and to my amazement, 3 pear-shaped objects. They were bright white, like burning magnesium. They were approaching the C-46 while flying parallel. Suddenly the left engine failed. I was to learn later that the magnetic needles of the navigation devices had gone crazy. The C-46 was sinking. Oil was gushing out of the failing engine. The pilot raised the alarm. The *crew and passengers were* warned *to be ready to dive. I don't remember what I* thought or did during the next few horrific minutes. The last fleeting vision I had of the 3 craft was that they were about 20 degrees above us. Then, still in tight formation, they disappeared into a cloud bank. Immediately our failing engine started to run again. The plane gained altitude again and flew us safely to Iwo Jima."

Marked by this episode, Leonard Stringfield became a renowned ufologist. He collaborated in particular with the CRIFO, the CUFOS, the NICAP and the MUFON, four American study groups studying the phenomenon. And he wrote several books on the subject.

Sources

Leonard Stringfield, *General Alert: UFOs*, France Empire, 1978, pp. 27-28 - *UFODATA Magazine*, September-October 2007, pp. 34-35.

A crushed beer can

In the October 30, 1966 issue of *Nashville Tennessean Magazine*, Joe Thompson Jr. recounts his experiences as a pilot during World War II and his encounter with the *foo fighters.*

A major in the 109e static reconnaissance squadron, Thompson commanded nearly 45 pilots, all of whom flew P-51 Mustangs.

"When the weather was too bad to take off, I would go around and talk to the men. I would ask them what they had seen on their mission. More than once, they admitted to running into *foo fighters*."

Everyone had their own description. Captain Frank Robinson of California said his looked like "a crushed beer can. Other pilots described them as "tennis balls" or "footballs," but of a larger size. Captain Robinson saw them coming towards him from the ground. All these pilots were convinced that it was a German weapon.

"We thought the enemy was using them to detect the altitude of our aircraft, so they could accurately adjust their defensive fire. "

Then one day, Major Thompson spotted them over the Rhine Valley. They didn't look like a crushed beer can," he recalls. Our pilot's job was to take reconnaissance photos. After taking a few shots, we were heading to a new strategic point to photograph when my teammate called out, "Bogeys at 9 o'clock!"[3] At my wing level, a little below us, towards Cologne, I spotted 4 or 5 objects that looked like silver balloons. I had the impression that they were motionless. But they must have been moving forward because they were not letting go of us. For a moment I thought it was an enemy device. I watched them, wondering what they were going to do. But they just followed us. When we turned around, I figured they were of little use to the German army."

Back at the base, Thompson reported his observation to the intelligence officer. Then he stopped thinking about it. The war was raging, and with one raid after another, the urgency to survive was the main concern of the soldiers. The pilots of the 109e squadron never tried to pursue these *foo fighters* because, they said, they "never bothered" them.

Source
UFO monthly.com n° 37, June 2007, pp. 25-26.

The press takes hold of the phenomenon

The British press has exercised a certain censorship concerning these *foo fighters*. It is therefore necessary to go across the Atlantic to find the first articles concerning the phenomenon. On January 2, 1945, *The New York Times* published an article entitled "Fireballs Stalk American Fighters in Night Assaults Over

---

3. "Bogey", term used by the military to designate an unknown flying object.

Germany. The *Post Dispatch* of January 2 reported the observation of Captain Fred E. Ringwald, who was on a flight after hearing numerous reports of these *foo fighters*. He said, "I saw lights on my right and told my pilot. He said, *"That's* just the lights on the hill. I looked in that direction for several minutes and said, "Well, that hill is considerably closer to us now.

January 15, 1945, the *Times* declared: "If this is not a hoax or an optical illusion, it is certainly the most mysterious and secret weapon the Allies could ever encounter. [No one seems to know what these glowing balls are for. The pilots think that it is a new psychological weapon..."

Also on January 15, *Newsweek* reported the observation of one of the pilots of the 415e squadron and concluded: "Probably related to the sightings of silver balls seen by day by pilots (article in our December 25, 1944 issue), the *foo fighters are* confusing intelligence officers. They may be an anti-radar device developed by the Germans."

On January 22, 1945, the American journal *Current Science and Aviation* wrote about these phenomena: "The latest Nazi air weapon is called a *foo fighter*. These mysterious red or silver balls follow Allied aircraft at speeds of up to 480 km/h. We still haven't determined what their exact function is. These balls do not hit our planes, but accompany their flights and then vanish in a flash, far from sight. Obviously radio-controlled, they would be a weapon of psychological intimidation.

Finally, we must mention *The American Legion Magazine*, dated December 1945, which published, under the pen of Jo Chamberlin, a 4-page article entitled "The mystery of the *foo fighters*", which remains the ultimate reference on the subject.

It is interesting to note here that each belligerent believes that these mysterious balls are a new weapon developed by the enemy. For America, there is no doubt, it is a Nazi weapon. For the Germans, it is an American weapon. For the Japanese, a Russian weapon. These flying spheres caused confusion everywhere.

Header for Jo Chamberlin's article in The American Legion Magazine.

An enduring mystery

It is known that the subject questioned the high authorities of the army. The first official American study of UFOs began in 1943, when World War II pilots reported that luminous objects were following their aircraft during night flights. In the archives of the US Air Force, dated February 21, 1952, a letter written by a certain Albert Rosenthal and addressed to the Air Force Intelligence Service, reports the following: "During the winter of 1944-45, I was a tactical controller in the 64^e fighter wing, reinforcement for the 7^e army based in France and Germany. The 415^e night fighter squadron, flying Beaufighters, flew under our control. When there was no air-to-air combat with the enemy, they were scouting for intruders in southwest Germany. On several occasions we received reports from the crews of these Beaufighters about strange phenomena, which they called *foo fighters*. Sometimes these craft seemed to be associated with anti-aircraft fire, at other times they exploded when pursued. It was reported that they were sometimes detected by automatic identification radar.

"We never solved the problem, nor did we discover what they were. Theories included St. Elmo's fire (a phenomenon of static electricity), German barrage balloons, meteors, or Gremlins[4] from the nearby Black Forest. And of course, we suspected the possibility of a new secret weapon."

There is also a letter dated April 23, 1952, from Lieutenant Colonel W. W. Ottinger of the *Intelligence Evaluation Division*, which states that an evaluation of the phenomenon was conducted at the end of the war. This study was never made public.

Even in 1952, although they had disappeared several years earlier, there were still questions about the nature of these *foo fighters*.

Some explanations

Many attempts have been made to explain the nature of these phenomena. Here are some suggested hypotheses.

1. Lightning in a ball

Unlikely, because ball lightning is a natural phenomenon that lasts a short time. However, some testimonies specify that these "incandescent balls" followed the planes over many kilometers, during 40 minutes. And how to explain that this phenomenon appeared so often during these years of hostility? Whereas it did not really appear before or after the Second World War.

2. Flares or positioning rockets launched by the enemy to locate the planes

To this, the 415e U.S. fighter squadron replied with a laugh, "Impossible, we've never seen *flares* dive, break away at high speed from aircraft in flight or negotiate impressive turns."

3. Flying bombs

No *foo fighters* exploded or caused any losses to squadrons of any nationality. Moreover, these "objects" had no fins or fuselage.

4. Fires of Saint Elmo

---

4. Pilots in the RAF, and later in the US Air Force, attributed mechanical problems with their engines or unexpected aircraft crashes to Gremlins, goblin-like creatures. These mischievous goblins, sitting on the wings of the aircraft, were said to be able to change the pitch of the propeller, blow particles into the intake pipes, mix liquids incompatible with the fuel, prevent the landing gear from lowering, perforate the empennages or accumulate ice on the wings... An astonishing survival of ancient beliefs.

Dr. Martin D. Altschuler mentioned the hypothesis of St. Elmo's fires, a plasma created by a corona effect. In chapter 7 of the *Condon Report*[5] (p. 1173), he noted: "The difference between ball lightning and St. Elmo's lights is that the latter always remain attached to their conductive surface. However, they have been seen to move, pulsating, along cables or on the body of aircraft. The *foo fighters* are probably one of their manifestations. However, this is unlikely, because these plasma effects are unstable and have an ultra-short life span. Moreover, being fixed, they can be seen, motionless, around boat masts, church spires, airplane wings... How then can we explain that *foo fighters* flew at prodigious speeds, alone or in perfect formation, independently of any driver? Finally, the Saint-Elme fires presuppose quite exceptional conditions of formation (meteorological or other).

5. Hallucinations

Not very credible, because entire crews saw them. One also spoke about reflections on the windows, which is not very defensible either, because they were observed under different angles and sometimes by two bombers at the same time.

6. A retinal persistence effect

This can happen after perceiving flak or flashes from an enemy aircraft. But many pilots have observed this phenomenon in a calm, deserted sky. Also, any phenomenon that attributes to the eye an afterimage is very brief (about $1/25^e$ of a second on the retina).

7. A secret Nazi weapon

This was the most cited hypothesis. If it was really a weapon, the first thing we can say is that it was not very effective. This raises a big doubt. However, authors like Renato Vesco persist. In his book *Man-Made UFOs: World War II's Secret Legacy*, he states that during the Second World War, one of the most successful Nazi projects was precisely this *Feuerball*, in other words the *foo fighter* that so often escorted

---

5. This "scientific study of unidentified flying objects" was supervised by the physicist Edward U. Condon. It resulted from a contract signed on October 6, 1966 between the vice-president of the University of Colorado and the US Air Force. A final file of 965 pages was submitted on October 31, 1968 to the North American General Staff. This project - which concluded that the study of UFOs could not be justified in the hope of advancing science - was carried out over two years and cost the US Air Force the sum of 500,000 dollars. The computer scientist and astronomer Jacques Vallée called the Condon Commission "the burial of the UFO subject" and its report "a burial permit".

American and British crews. He describes it as follows: "It was circular and armored, looking more or less like the shell of a turtle. It was powered by a special turbojet engine, also flat and circular... which generated a halo of luminous flames. That's why it was named *Feuerball* ("fireball"). It was unarmed and operated without a pilot. It was radio-controlled at the time of take-off and automatically followed enemy aircraft, attracted by the flames of their exhaust. It would then approach the aircraft very closely, without a collision, to destroy their radar equipment." Renato Vesco explains that these *foo fighters* looked like silver disks during the day. And at night they took the shape of spheres.

However, the phenomenon has appeared in too many different places to be reasonably a secret weapon. Moreover, if they were really secret weapons, it is reasonable to think that no war department would have launched so many new prototypes into these skies of confrontation. They could have been easily shot down or intercepted. And their secrets would have been discovered.

Source

Renato Vesco and David Hatcher Childress, *Man-Made UFOs: World War II's Secret Legacy*, Adventures Unlimited Press, 2007.

Fascinating, these *foo fighters* still remain the most neglected field of study in the history of ufology. This independent phenomenon, capable of changing speed and form, disappeared from the skies of confrontation at the end of the conflict, in the last days of 1945. It was believed then that our skies had suddenly found their quietude. We were wrong...

To go further

Gordon I. R. Lore and Harold H. Deneaul, *Mysteries of the Skies*, Prentice Hall, 1968.

Keith Chester, *Strange Company: Military Encounters with UFOs in World War II*, Anomalist Book, 2007.

III. The Belgian wave (1989-1991)

Between 1989 and 1991, Belgium was massively overflown by gigantic unknown objects.This Western European country, bordering France, was the site of a remarkable wave of UFO sightings. Credible witnesses, such as gendarmes and high-ranking military officers, were confronted with these mysterious devices. And they had the courage to speak out. Some even filmed and photographed them.

This Belgian wave remains a dense, solid and exceptional event. All the more so - and this is a first - that the Gendarmerie and the Belgian Air Force collaborated with the local ufological association, the Belgian Society for the Study of Space Phenomena (SOBEPS).

Lucien Clerebaut, co-founder and secretary general of this SOBEPS, remembers: "In almost daily telephone contact with witnesses during eighteen months of a veritable avalanche of observations, and having often had the opportunity to meet them in the field, I obviously tried to identify what they had seen. More than 300 tapes of telephone communications were recorded. The letters of the witnesses and the investigation reports gathered at the secretariat of the SOBEPS form a file which currently counts several tens of thousands of pages. [...] In fact, the whole phenomenology of the Belgian wave seems to be modelled on a clever mix of "I show myself enough for them to be surprised, but not too much, so as not to upset them."

What were these machines that played, in a strange waltz, with cars and stunned citizens?

Profile of the phenomenon

The objects described by the witnesses are mainly platforms in the shape of a triangle. These machines move at low altitude, at less than 50 meters from the ground. And sometimes only 5 or 10 meters from the witnesses. They are generally silent, or emit a very weak noise, like "the hum of an electric turbine".

They measure between 35 and 70 meters in wingspan. According to some witnesses, they can be gigantic, reaching "the size of a soccer field".

A recurring detail: they are equipped with powerful headlights at each angle, producing a white luminosity. These headlights have a diameter estimated between 2 and 4 meters! They illuminate the ground "on a large surface". "It was as if we were in August, at midday, in full sun", reports a witness.

Strange characteristic: these triangles - with broken or rounded corners - are equipped, in their center, with a kind of pulsating red-orange beacon. This light source has the faculty to detach itself sometimes from the machine and to move as it pleases. It seems to be composed of "a cluster of lights" that can scatter in all directions.

These machines generally move slowly. And are capable of hovering. But they can start at breakneck speeds, negotiate tight turns and disappear in a flash.

During these 18 months of observations, contrary to the older international waves, neither landing nor electromagnetic disturbances (stopping of engines, effect on televisions or radios) were reported.

Other forms were observed during the 18 months of this exceptional wave. We will come back to this later.

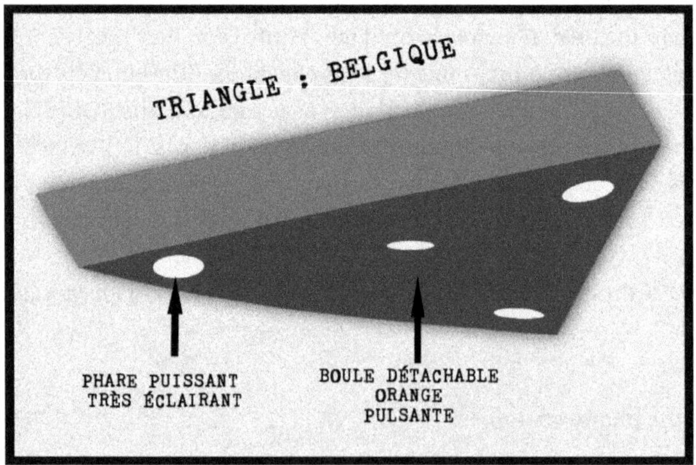

The witnesses

After having drawn up a portrait of the phenomenon, it is interesting to describe the witnesses. The vast majority of them are people considered "trustworthy" by the investigators. On December 6, 1989, Lucien Clerebaut declared to the daily newspaper *Le Soir*: "In general, we have not noted any tendency to exaggerate. Most of the testimonies seem to us to have flagrant accents of truth. *"*

These witnesses are gendarmes, journalists, nurses, lawyers, soldiers, workers, doctors, teachers or engineers... Among the thousands of citizens concerned, we can mention, in no particular order, a major of the Mobilization Division, an unemployed person, a member of NATO, a priest, a deputy inspector of the ministry, a painter, a weather forecaster or an engineer in aeronautical construction.

Professor Auguste Meessen notes that the UFO phenomenon is "eminently democratic". Indeed, it presents itself to all, does not make any sort of selection, cares little about levels of education and social hierarchies. In Belgium, as everywhere, it manifested itself in an ostentatious way to whoever was there.

His "clandestine" side is often mentioned. It is only a step to imagine him as a virtuoso of breaking and entering, quick to flee from the uniform of the men of law... However, nothing could be further from the truth during this Belgian wave. A great number of gendarmes were confronted with these mysterious flying objects and were able to testify. In particular those of the brigades of Eupen, Lasne, Belœil, Namur or Esneux. Here is one of the examples, highly emblematic, which marked the "official" beginning of the Belgian wave.

A first founding meeting

Date: November 29, 1989.
Location: road N68 between the cities of Eupen and Eynatten.

17 h 15.

The night has just fallen. It is a cold end of the day, with clear skies and excellent visibility. Two gendarmes - Heinrich Nicoll and Hubert Von Montigny - are patrolling about 30 kilometers east of the city of Liège.

When they arrived between Kettenis and Merols, at the height of "Grosse Weide", the two men saw, at the edge of the N68, a field lit with such intensity that they were very surprised. One of the gendarmes said that "the light was as bright as a soccer stadium". And so powerful that he could have read the day's newspaper without effort.

The gendarmes slow down. Where does this strange lighting come from? When they look up, they discover a huge triangular machine, a carrying platform to be exact, hovering above the meadow. This "isosceles triangle with a large base" measures between 30 and 35 meters wide and 2 meters thick. It is perfectly motionless, at 120 meters from the ground

The machine is equipped with three large headlights, one in each corner, pointing downwards. And a sort of flashing "red beacon" in the middle. It is these three projectors that shine a blinding beam on the ground. What strikes our gendarmes is that the object is absolutely silent, and does not emit any noise.

Suddenly the object comes to life. It starts to move, "pointing forward", moving parallel to the road, in the same direction as the service van. The two men estimate its speed at 60 km/h. While following it closely, they contact the barracks in Eupen and ask for information from the military camp in Elsenborn. Are there any special maneuvers in progress with unconventional machines? The answer was no.

The object finally came to rest above the city of Eupen. It remained for about 30 minutes in the vicinity of the municipality. Many people saw it, including an official of the city, a school principal, a brigadier of Water and Forests, and a contractor... Then it moves again to stop this time above the lake of Gileppe, "a little to the left of the lit tower". It remains nearly one hour, immobile above the water.

Suddenly, our two witnesses witnessed a very curious spectacle. The machine emits several times, in opposite direction, two horizontal beams of red light, one kilometer long. At the point of these beams, one distinguishes like a red ball. Then these beams disappear and "these balls of fire" return at once in the machine. The gendarmes cannot believe their eyes. One of the men compares it to the arrows that divers shoot into the water. "The arrow goes off very quickly, but held by a thread, the diver can bring it back slowly towards him. The other constable thinks of it more as "balls attached to a bungee cord, thrown with a paddle." All this seems surreal. But our witnesses are not at the end of their surprise!

18 h 45.

Suddenly, from behind the nearby pine forest, a second aircraft appears! This triangle slows down and then tilts forward while initiating a turn. Our witnesses

UFO: The 12 files that the Pentagon cannot explain

distinguish perfectly, on the upper part of the fuselage, a dome, more precisely a dome like a spherical cap in the center of a thin plate. This dome "is provided with rectangular windows, lit from the inside". Finally, the two objects move away, one towards the north and the other towards the southwest.

This observation - even if it was not the very first in 1989 - marks the beginning of what will be called "the Belgian wave". The fact that two gendarmes dared to testify undoubtedly gave credibility to the phenomenon and allowed it to emerge both in the media and with the highest authorities.

During the evening of November 29, 143 sightings of unidentified aerial phenomena (UAP) were reported in the region of Eupen, 30 kilometers from the city of Liege. And 13 gendarmes saw these mysterious devices in 8 different places. It is estimated that a total of 1500 people witnessed these strange flying objects that day!

This observation illustrates the cover of the Italian ufological magazine *UFO* n° 9, published in January 1991.

The press goes wild

November 30, 1989

In its 7:30 pm edition, the RTBF television news broadcasts a first report on the enigmatic triangles of the Belgian sky. SOBEPS is then besieged with calls.

December 1st

The press gets hold of the phenomenon. A first article appeared in *Le Soir* and in *La Libre Belgique*. The next day, *Le Jour* and *L'Avenir*, a daily newspaper in Luxembourg, headlined: "UFOs persist and sign.

December 6

The front page of *Le Soir* reads: "Belgian UFOs: witnesses in spades".

December 8

Testimonies are pouring in. There is now talk of an "epidemic of UFOs". One tries to give an explanation to the phenomenon: prototype plane, laser projection, ULM, AWACS... The journalist Daniel Conraads specifies in the daily newspaper *Le Soir*: "On its side, the Ministry of National Defense has however categorically affirmed that no prototype flight had taken place these last days in Belgium."

SOBEPS obtains an appointment at the Gendarmerie headquarters. It becomes, to its great surprise, the official relay between the witnesses and the authorities. A telex sent in the afternoon to all the French-speaking gendarmerie brigades asked them to forward all information concerning UFOs to the association. It was a first! That day, the wave took on a considerable magnitude, spreading over almost the entire territory.

A testimony taken seriously

Date: December 11, 1989.
Location: between Ernage and Gembloux.

Our witness, Mr. André Amond, is a lieutenant-colonel in the Belgian Land Force. It is therefore understandable why his story was taken seriously from the start.

18 h 45.

Having left Ernage by car where they live, Mr. André Amond and Chantal, his wife, go to the Gembloux train station to pick up their son.

Suddenly, at the level of the farm of Sart Ernage, Mr. Amond saw in the sky "a series of three or four panels of light" which moved along a north-south trajectory. These panels hover at an altitude of about 200 and 300 meters.

Under this series of panels, we can see a surprising red flashing light in the center, which, according to our witness, "does not correspond at all to the red flashing lights found on classic airplanes and which twinkle like stars".

The object - for it is one - is travelling at a speed of 50 km/h. Mr. Amond pulls over to the side of the road. He tells us: "To continue my observation, I stop on the highest point of this country road, located directly after the farm of Sart Ernage. My wife opened the window of the car. The UFO, which moves slowly on my right, passes me and continues its way... This part of the observation lasted between 2 and 4 minutes.

Then, the UFO suddenly headed in our direction. Only a huge white light headlight, bigger than a large air carrier headlight, was visible. Here, a certain appre-hension seizes me. My wife gets scared and asks me to start again. [...] The object, with this enormous luminous abnormal mass, shows itself a little aggressive, more especially as we do not hear any noise of engine... This machine was silent!"

Mr. Amond starts again. On the vehicle, the big light disappears and is replaced by three smaller lights forming an equilateral triangle. In the center, again, the red flashing light reappears. The object then performs a nose-up maneuver. "The maneuver made by the machine is majestic, slow. The turn is tight.

Finally, the three luminous headlights go out. The UFO resumes its attitude. Only the flashing light remains visible for a moment while the machine melts into the depths of the night.

The day after the observation, equipped with a video camera, Mr. Amond returned to the scene. "I went several times in a row to the same place. In vain. After some hesitation, fearing ridicule, I sent a note to the office of the Minister of National Defence, relating the facts. For me, it was clear. It was not an AWACS, nor a microlight, nor a helicopter, nor a hologram."

An educator and her students

This night of December 11 to 12, 1989 will remain marked by an important number of observations. Here is a second one.

Location: south of Malonne.

18 h 45.

Miss Lucie G. is an educator. Three students from the Institut médico-pédagogique Reumonjoie are also present.

The students, suddenly excited, call Ms. G. so that she can observe "a strange thing in the sky". She relates:

"I left the bungalow G. and in the direction of Malonne, towards the north, I saw a mysterious object which flew very low and very slowly above the trees which, in this direction, occupy the whole horizon. My first observation was at azimuth 300. The object was heading from west to east. I thought I could see a dark mass with three very bright headlights arranged in an isosceles triangle, pointing forward, and a kind of light spot in its center, but above. The object was flying low over the trees, so its altitude was about 50 meters and the distance about 1000 meters. The apparent diameter corresponded to that of the full moon. At azimuth 030, where there is a small depression in the woods on the horizon, the object stopped briefly and then turned back to azimuth 300. This maneuver occurred 3 to 4 times during the 10-minute observation.

"I had heard about UFOs through the media, but I didn't realize that it could have been one. In any case, it was not an airplane, nor a microlight, nor a helicopter. It is possible, on reflection, that the light spot above the object had a dome shape. The observation ended when the object disappeared behind the wood at azimuth 030.

The students, aged 14, 17 and 18, corroborated the educator's account. Although the description of the object, according to each, differed somewhat.

Various forms of UFOs

If the most frequently seen UFO resembles a large triangle, it would be reductive to claim that it was the only flying object of the Belgian wave. The range of strangeness of the phenomenon leaves one stunned. Witnesses say that they have seen an array of mysterious devices with totally baroque shapes. Among the thousands of reports, we can count, in no particular order, well rounded "saucers", a "triangular star", a "scallop shell", a "perfect square", an "illuminated cube", "cones", "boomerangs", quadrilaterals, a diamond, rectangles, a "top", an "inverted aircraft carrier", an "iron", a "flying bed", a "profiled helmet of a cyclist", a "brown sphere", a "torpedo", cigars, "a big dirty box", trapezoids, oval machines, a "plate", a "round ashtray"... In short, a protean celestial hardware.

Here is, for example, an astonishing object seen not far from Liege.

An old *Nautilus*

Date: December 11, 1989.

Location: Les Piétresses, a residential area on the heights of the town of Jupille-sur-Meuse, in the suburbs of Liege.

2:05 am.

Our witness, Mr. I. F., a 36 year old engineer, married and father of a little girl, was deeply asleep. Suddenly, an unusual noise woke him up. He thinks that the circulator of his boiler is out of order. He gets up, puts on a jacket because, to check the boiler room, he has to go out into the garden.

After checking, the boiler works perfectly. He realizes that the unusual noise is actually coming from the street.

Our witness returns to his yard. And from there... sees a strange stationary object, right in front of the road that goes up to Beyne-Heusay.

The machine, which measures about twenty meters, leans on a fir tree whose top bends dangerously. It does not look at all like the triangles that the press has been describing for weeks. No, it is "egg-shaped", more rounded towards the front. On its "nose" we can see a kind of dark windshield, unlit, which looks like "a plexiglass window".

The object appears to be made of dull grey metal. The witness specifies that this matt aspect, without any shiny reflection, "resembles a car body which would have been sandblasted before being repainted".

A horizontal band surrounds the UFO. Along this band are distributed several lamps "of a bluish and reddish glow, comparable to the glows produced by arc welding".

At the back of the object, the witness noticed an orifice "in which is planted a kind of fin or oar, of the same matt metallic gray aspect". Under the object, 3 protuberances arranged in triangle shelter projectors.

This strange machine, said our witness, reminds us of "a kind of old *Nautilus* escaped from a Jules Verne novel! At the back of the Plexiglas windshield, there is an inscription, a kind of acronym. It is "three ellipses symmetrically intertwined, reminiscent of the trajectories described by the electrons of an atomic nucleus". A surrealist vision.

The object seems quite material, yet its contours are not really clear. "It was," the witness will say, "as if this object had been behind a light, more or less translucent screen that blurred it, to give it this somewhat melted appearance." However, that night, the sky is perfectly clear. There is neither mist, nor fog.

Then slowly, the UFO starts to move. It slowly moves back to free itself from the branches of the tree. At this moment, it emits a noise which, according to our witness, is comparable to that of "an axis which would have play in a bearing".

Its 3 projectors light up. And when the object flies over the neighboring houses, "the shadows of these grow longer as it moves away and disappears towards the east".

The following day, accompanied by a French television crew, our witness went to the meadow overflown for a moment by the object. There, we note traces: "3 circles where the grass is shorter and well visible" compared to the whole of the surrounding vegetation. Each circle of "mowed grass" measures between 3 meters and 3.50 meters in diameter. Arranged in a triangle, about 15 meters separate each of them.

An investigation is immediately carried out. Two gendarmes from the Wamdre brigade came to question the witness. A member of the judicial police followed. Then a senior army officer, accompanied by his driver and four military vans. Nothing will be known about their final conclusions. Yet it is urgent. Not a day goes by, in this month of December, without the press or television mentioning the subject.

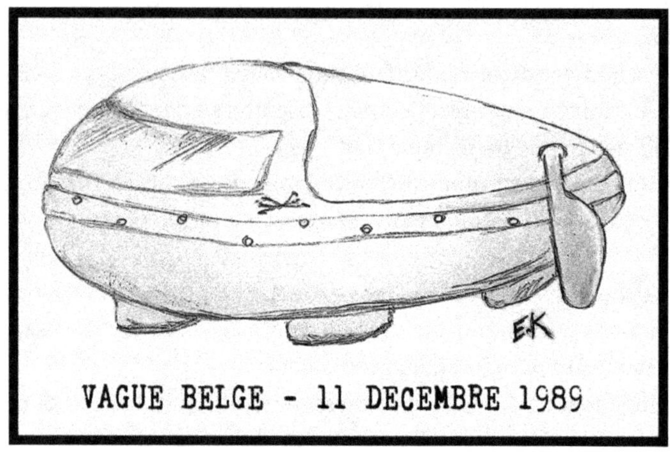

Sketch of the UFO (from a document of the SOBEPS)

The high authorities are snorting

The military comes into play. Colonel Wilfried de Brouwer, Chief of Operations at the Air Force Headquarters, says: "The events of November 29 were widely covered by the media and, naturally, the air force was bombarded with questions. The questions were addressed to the Belgian Minister of Defense but eventually landed on my desk as Chief of Staff Operations... The Belgian Air Force tried to identify the alleged intruder(s)... I was able to determine that the objects seen on November 29 could not have been helicopters, balloons, or any type of fixed wing aircraft. This implied that the reported object or objects had committed a violation of existing aviation rules."

The staff of the Air Force, hard pressed, then turned to the SOBEPS, this civilian ufological association founded in 1971. The military decided to support these few investigators deprived of technical means (they will soon be 111, including the volunteers!). A collaboration is established. And the Belgian Minister of Defense, Guy Coëme, officially recognized SOBEPS as a research partner. Never before seen! Work meetings between civilians and military are organized. Renowned physicists - encouraged by the decision of the officials - agree to collaborate as scientific advisors. They try to approach this great mystery in a reasoned and pragmatic way. One evokes the importance of works of analysis at the same time physical (optics), botanical and chemical (in case of various traces).

At the same time, it was decided to organize repeated vigils because the testimonies were pouring in. In the whole country, at low altitude, the Belgian triangles multiply in an ostentatious way their frightening ballet.

Strange side effects

Date: February 2, 1990.
Location : Gelbressée, near Namur.

That evening, Mrs. M-C. P. experienced a very legitimate fright. "At the end of the evening, she tells us, my 16 year old son saw in the sky a device as described in the article of the newspaper of that day. To the point of having an unusual behavior during several hours. Examination of his eyes, among other things, by the doctor, confirmed the fact "that he saw something bright that scared him. "

But what really happened? After a meticulous investigation, here is a chronology of the facts.

On February 2, the young man first spent the evening in his room with a friend. Nothing exceptional to report. It is only the following day that Mrs. P. discovers him in a worrying state. The teenager is very pale, haggard. His mother thought that he had had a few beers during the night and that he was still under the influence of alcohol. But during the day, his condition worsens. Pupils totally dilated, he speaks incoherently, "in the grip of a real hallucinatory delirium".

Thinking he is talking to his mother, the young man is actually talking to flowers. Then he talks to a coat rack thinking it is his sister. Mrs. P. is now convinced that her son is on drugs. Worried, she consulted two doctors who reassured her that her son had not taken any illicit or psychotropic substances.

As time passed, the young man gradually came to his senses. He tells us that that night, he had to urinate and went to the garden to relieve himself. It was then that he saw in the sky "a strong light". It was in fact an object with three white lights and two small red flashing lights on the side. This object suddenly came closer to him. Terrified, the teenager had the impression "that someone was coming to get him"! There was then a blank in his mind. The rest escaping him completely, he does not know what happened next...

The night the F-116s dance

The colonel-aviator Wilfried de Brouwer shows a remarkable open-mindedness concerning the necessity to identify the nature and the origin of these famous triangles. He decides to send if necessary reconnaissance planes, if and only if: 1/ the observation of a UFO is confirmed by the police, 2/ if this UFO is detected by a radar. In these cases, a *Quick* Reaction Alert procedure will be triggered.

Date: night of March 30 to 31, 1990.
Location: Leuven.

23h00.
The gendarme Renkin alerts the air force and in particular the radar of Glons. He has just spotted lights of changing color (red, green and yellow) in the direction of Thorembais-Gembloux. These lights form an equilateral triangle.

23h15.
Bingo! The radar perceived an "unidentified echo with strange behavior" 5 kilometers north of the Beauvechain air base. The contact moves at a speed of about 46 km/h.

23h38.
Dispatched quickly on the spot, the gendarmes of the brigade of Wavre (Walloon Brabant) confirm the presence in the sky of this luminous phenomenon.

23h45.
3 new lights approach the first observed triangle. They execute a series of disordered movements. Then they also place themselves in triangular formation. The radar of Glons follows all this on its radar.

0h05.

Two F-16 fighters (AL. 17 and AL. 23) took off from the Beauvechain base to try to intercept "these strange things".

0h13.

One of the F-16s blocked its target on an object with astonishing behavior. The object initially passes from a speed of 150 to 970 knots (277 to 1 796 km/h). Initially positioned at an altitude of 9,000 feet (2,743 m), it descends to 5,000 feet (1,524 m), to go back up to 11,000 feet (3,352 m) and finally to come down to the ground level!

0h30.

One of the fighters had a radar contact at 5,000 feet (1,524 m). The object is moving at a speed of 740 knots (1,370 km/h). The lock on the target lasts 6 seconds.

0h32.

The radars of Semmerzake and Glons have again a contact with an "object" moving between 885 and 1277 km/h.

0h45-1h00.

The witnesses on the ground see the last UFO disappear.

1h10.

Return to the base of the first F-16 (AL. 17). Landing.

1h18.

Return to the base of the second F-16 (AL. 23). Landing.

A pilot's testimony

Major Yves Meelbergs is one of the two pilots who, aboard an F-16 fighter, tried to intercept the strange luminous phenomenon in the sky over Leuven. After remaining silent for a long time, he finally gave his testimony. And here is what he tells:

"On Friday, March 30, 1990, as a captain at Beauvechain Air Base, near the small town of Jodoigne, I took my usual alert watch at 8:30 a.m. in the reinforced shelters of the 1er Tactical Wing of the Belgian Air Force. Here are two F-16A Fighting Falcon fighters, armed and capable of taking off within 10 minutes, at any time of the day or night.

"With me was a 25-year-old pilot, Second Lieutenant "Rudy" Verrigt, who was assigned to me as a wingman for the next 24 hours. At about 10 p.m., as we were watching TV, the phone rang, with the base operations center officer on the other end saying, 'Could you take a look outside, we›ve had a report of something funny heading toward Leuven. Let us know if you see anything...'"

"We took off with the two F-16s. I was the patrol leader... Finally, after about 20 minutes of flight, we managed to get close to the object, at about 7 and 8 kilometers. The object in question, we had it at least 3 or 4 times clearly on our radar screen. We managed to hook it with the F-16s. And as we stayed in contact with the ground, we knew that they too were picking up the same echo. The object was accelerating very quickly. It went from 100 km/h to nearly 2,000 km/h. It was soaring and then plunging toward the ground in incredible zigzags. And all this above the speed of sound.

"It was something that was beyond, in those years, the performance that we knew... The accelerations were very fast, much faster than what we were capable of doing then. And even now. There was no sonic bang as the object passed the sound barrier several times... It had different characteristics and much better than what we have now.

"No, it was neither a prototype nor a weather phenomenon. I've been flying for 20 years, and I honestly haven't seen many weather phenomena. Moreover, such phenomena repeating themselves unceasingly, as at the time, it is almost impossible... For me, it was a solid object. This idea has never left me."

Sources

VSD hors-série n∞ 1, " *Ovnis, les preuves scientifiques* ", July 1998, pp. 24-25 - Radio program " *Qui veut savoir ?* ", broadcast in 2004 on Radio Quartz - Radio program " *Entre mystères et secrets : la fascinante histoire des Ovnis* " told by Frank Istasse (episode 4 : " Ovni, les pilotes contre-attaquent "), RTBF, 2020.

A fake photo that goes around the world

On April 4, 1990, in the Walloon region, in Petit-Rechain to be exact, a young man claims to have taken a photo of a triangle flying over his neighborhood. During the development, an exceptional picture was discovered. The military and ufologists could not believe their eyes, this young witness gave them one of the most successful UFO photos in the world!

The color slide was immediately examined by eminent scientists such as Auguste Meessen, professor of physics at the Catholic University of Louvain, Marc Acheroy of the Royal Military School of Brussels, François Louange, space computer engineer and image analysis advisor to the army and the CNES, Richard Haines, ex-NASA scientist, and André Marion, research engineer at the CNRS. For these experts, it is impossible to prove that this picture is a fake.

The providential photo became a reference and went around the world, illustrating articles and many covers of books and magazines. The young photographer even went to a meeting at the military academy in 1997 and maintained his version of events.

Then on July 26, 2011, it is the disappointment. The author of the picture - who is called Patrick Maréchal - decides to speak on Belgian television. He lifts the veil and admits having photographed a model made by him. The photo of Petit-Rechain is therefore in reality a fake, a scandalous deception! Between anger and disappointment, the world of ufology took the blow hard. The skeptics, on the other hand, are having a field day.

Interviewed by *UFOmania* magazine in August 2011, Patrick Maréchal says: "I cut the model out of frigolite, approximately 60 or 70 centimeters long on the large base. I painted it with a can of metallic blue color that I had left. The color melted the frigolite, resulting in a multitude of bumps. I used flashlight bulbs. The middle one I painted with red permanent marker. I connected the whole thing to a 9 volt battery. [...]

"No, I never wanted to disappoint anyone and I apologize for that. And especially not the SOBEPS which did a lot of work [...] in all Belgium. This photo is nothing compared to all the testimonies collected at that time. I just put an image on what thousands of people had seen and, to them, I apologize. They had the chance to see and I took advantage of what they saw. This certainly does not call into question the Belgian wave. It is there and will remain there... "

Mr. Maréchal can beat his chest and ask for forgiveness "to the whole world", but how can we understand this kind of indignity?

A press conference

On July 11, 1990, colonel de Brouwer takes the responsibility of a press conference. He projected to an audience of international journalists the video of the radar signature recorded by the F-16. He commented on the prodigious and unprecedented maneuverability of the intercepted "intruder". He specifies: "If the echo corresponds well to a material object, its passage at this altitude, in the sky of Tubize, should have caused damage on the ground. However, nothing, absolutely nothing, has been reported. He explains that "the electronic capacities of the on-board instruments were exceeded". If in flight, the pilots did not see anything with their own eyes (it is difficult to look down in such an illuminated region), the gendarmes on the ground followed the evolution of the phenomena and some filmed them. Chased, the UFO in question "even seemed to multiply". After this chase, the F-16s had to land, for lack of kerosene. De Brouwer adds that the pilots, extremely qualified, "considered that they had experienced something quite extraordinary".

The questions are flying. What does the army think about the nature of these "devices"? The colonel refuses to decide: "We are very cautious and we do not want to launch hypotheses such as that of extraterrestrial apparitions. He excludes, however, that it could be an airplane, a sounding balloon, a laser beam or a weather phenomenon disrupting the propagation of waves.

The next day, the press and television reported on this unique conference. For the French weekly *Paris Match*: "[The object] cannot be something created by man."

A UFO that answers

Date: night of July 19 to 20, 1990.

Location: freeway ramp connecting Seraing to the E42 freeway, at Grâce-Hollogne.

22h35.

Mr. and Mrs. Marcel H. were driving peacefully when they saw a triangular shape in the sky. They quickly realized that it was a dark-colored device, a large "equilateral triangle", totally immobile, base forward. The object is equipped with a kind of white luminous belt, "similar to a neon tube". On its lower face, one distinguishes 3 headlights also white, "clearly detached from the object". On its upper part, a red light and a green light flash. Each of the 3 sides of the device measures approximately 12 meters.

Both surprised and curious, Mr. H. says to his wife: "We'll have a laugh, I'll call the lights! However Mrs. H. is hardly enthusiastic: "It is a UFO!", she is satisfied prudently to answer.

Mr H. executes and launches 2 consecutive calls of headlight. Total surprise! the 2 lights placed at the front of the UFO swivel in direction of our motorists... and emit in their turn 3 luminous flashes not dazzling! Then the triangle swings, approaches the car and positions itself on its right, at a distance of approximately 100 meters and at an altitude of 60 meters. It does not let go any more our witnesses and, adjusting its speed on that of the vehicle (60 to 70 km/h), accompanies them in the long descent towards Seraing.

At the height of the bridge of Seraing, Mr. H. panics because the UFO follows him while flying over the Meuse. But to the great relief of our witnesses, it ends up moving away, still silent, taking altitude and suddenly running at high speed towards Grâce-Hollogne. A very trying chase...

The year 1990 is coming to an end. The mystery of the Belgian triangles thickens. And the observations continue. There are so many that it is impossible to mention them all. Here are two of them, particularly interesting.

Above a power plant!

Date: March 12, 1991.

Location: at the edge of the Belle Maison road, in Solières, near the Bois de Goesnes.

20h45.

We are in a farm where a family of farmers is still working. Suddenly, Benoît S. saw three large white headlights in the sky, arranged in a triangle. He was surprised to hear "a dull hum, like an airplane, but louder". He soon distinguishes a machine above a large tree, 150 meters away. This object progresses very slowly, parallel to the road. One of its headlights strongly illuminates the road and a part of the adjoining field.

Benoît then shouts to Félicie, his mother: "Come and see! Here are your Martians coming back! She hurriedly leaves the stable and observes the phenomenon. Indeed, it is for her a recurrence, having seen an identical object on November 26, 1990.

The UFO negotiates a sharp turn, without tilting like an airplane would. It is very low, 3 or 4 meters above the roofs! It approaches and flies over our witnesses by emitting an intense noise. There, we distinguish perfectly its structure. The machine is "almost round", ovoid. It stands out perfectly on the night sky. It must measure approximately a dozen meters.

Finally, it moves away towards Solières. Its headlight pointed towards the ground lights successively a low wall, a heap of manure, then an immense chestnut tree before melting in the night.

10 minutes later, Benoît and Albert S., his father, saw the UFO again. Incredible! It is a few meters above the red beacons which crown the top of one of the cooling towers of the nuclear power station of Tihange, very close! It seems to be prospecting... One of its headlights illuminates a part of the building, while a second one, the lowest, projects its light beam, almost vertically, into the chimney itself. Astonishing. Then slowly, the UFO starts again, "crosses the thick column of white vapor spat by the imposing tower", then disappears gradually in the darkness.

It should be noted that this day of March 12 knew a real carousel of these mysterious machines.

An amazing meeting

Date: May 19, 1991.
Location: Highway from Basel to Strasbourg, Baden-Württemberg, Rhine Valley.
22h30.

Axelle Joly, SOBEPS investigator, and her husband come back from a stay in Switzerland. It is raining heavily. In the car's hushed interior, the asphalt is moving to the hypnotic rhythm of the windshield wipers. As the vehicle is loaded and the road is slippery, we drive carefully.

Suddenly a light source appears, straight ahead, very low on the horizon. It looked like "two yellow headlights in the distance", several kilometers away. According to our witnesses, these lights "look like the landing lights of a plane approaching the runway of an airfield".

Suddenly, these lights disappear... and reappear, near the car. At first, our witnesses think that it is a plane. These headlights diffuse all the same a soft light, unusual, of yellow color. Then this phenomenon approaches ostensibly. And when it is almost at the height of the vehicle, our motorists note that it is a large triangle which practically covers the width of the freeway. The object is delimited on its circumference by a series of white and green flashing lights.

While Axelle Joly, stunned, observes the machine, she sees appearing in the heart of the triangle, in a fraction of a second, a completely black shape of plane, bearing no inscription nor identification mark. It is an old twin-engine plane, from the last world war, of the Dakota type. The image of the old propeller plane appears for a brief moment and then disappears. How to explain this?

The fact is all the more disturbing that at the same time, the Belgian daily newspaper *Le Soir* printed a photo of an authentic Dakota for the next day's edition! Indeed, a model of this plane has just been placed in front of the Victory Memorial, a museum dedicated to the Second World War located in Hondelange, along the Ardenne highway, near the Luxembourg border. Coincidence, mirror game, time distortion, provoked synchronism? Or a subtle transfer between energy, matter and information?

As an epilogue

All this, of course, is only a pale sample of the observations of the Belgian wave. For those who would like to go further, it is imperative to read the two books published by the SOBEPS: *Vague d'Ovni sur la Belgique* (1991) and *Vague d'Ovni sur la Belgique, volume 2* (1994). These two essential bibles account for nearly 1,000 pages of exhaustive, demanding work of exemplary rigor.

Then, in the spring of 1991, the triangles suddenly became rarer and deserted the Belgian sky. This cosmic saga nevertheless fascinated the world. One cannot count the number of articles and broadcasts that were devoted to it.

The mysterious triangles continued their rounds elsewhere. They were reported on the banks of the Hudson River (United States), in Colchester or Bakewell (England), in Sagaken (Japan), in Samara (Russia) or on our very French nuclear power plants.

As usual, with these impudent celestials, three small turns... and then come back!

The assumptions

1. THE AWACS

At first, it was said to be confused with the AWACS, the Boeing E-3 Sentry built since 1977. This detection aircraft is however very recognizable because it has a 9 meters rotating radar dome above its fuselage. This explanation was quickly rejected by the army. In the Belgian national daily *La Dernière Heure* of December 14, 1989, a major of the Air Force, a radar specialist, declared under cover of anonymity: "I am absolutely positive that the AWACS hypothesis is excluded and this is one of the reasons why we are interested in the testimonies of military origin, including the observations made by the gendarmes. The military personnel who have seen a UFO know what an AWACS is; they have told me that what they saw had nothing to do with this aircraft. For the Air Force, it is clear that the AWACS trail is one that can be forgotten. In fact, at this point, we have eyewitness accounts and we know that those accounts are credible. And we don't have the first inkling of an explanation."

2. *A Lockheed Martin F-117A Night Hawk*

The second hypothesis was launched by the French magazine *Science & Vie* in its June 1990 issue. Concerned about its rational requirement, one could read on the cover: "A UFO unmasked". According to the author, the mystery of the strange triangles was finally lifted. It was simply the Lockheed Martin F-117A Night Hawk, the flagship of American stealth fighters. However, in the December 15, 1989 edition of *La Dernière Heure*, it was discovered that the Belgian Army had dismissed this explanation. General Terrasson, commander of the Belgian Tactical Air Force, already objected: "I would like to start by excluding the so-called products of the stealth technology developed in the United States, be it the B-2 bomber or the F-117A fighter: I cannot imagine that the Americans could carry out tests in Western Europe, and in particular in Belgian airspace, without informing the top of the military hierarchy. It is absolutely inconceivable. I can tell you that we have not been informed of anything of this kind. For the Air Force, the stealth hypothesis is excluded."

This is corroborated by Jean-Jacques Velasco - former head of SEPRA within the CNES - who noted in his book *Troubles in the Sky*[6] : "The F-117 appeared at the Bourget Air Show, near Paris, and I was able to observe it from all angles and see it

---

6. Jean-Jacques Velasco with Nicolas Montigiani, Troubles in the sky, Presses du Châtelet, 2007.

UFO: The 12 files that the Pentagon cannot explain

fly as it left. I understood, at this precise moment, why it could not be at the origin of the Belgian observations. Its aerodynamic qualities betrayed a total lack of stability at low speed. Its noise, hoarse and powerful, announced it to miles around... Moreover, it is unable to exceed the speed of sound. No, the F-117 was a far cry from silent UFOs at breakneck speeds."

Finally, it should be noted that the three powerful lights of the F-117 are carried by the landing gear and that they are thus visible only during the approach or takeoff phase. Nothing to see, therefore, with the descriptions of the witnesses. Its minimum speed is about 300 km/h. In slower flight, it crashes like an iron! And we end up learning that at that time, in the middle of the Gulf War, these F-117s were in Saudi Arabia.

3. One lighter than air: drone, ULM...

Improbable, because these triangles were seen, on stormy days, maneuvering with ease under heavy rain and against strong winds. Moreover, one of these UFOs was seen hovering over one of the 3 chimneys of the Tihange nuclear power plant. It is important to know that the water vapors of the Meuse, evacuated by the cooling of these towers (600 liters of water per second!), create terrible turbulences which would be fatal to any lighter-than-air aircraft, microlight, but also to helicopters or airships. And who would dare to fly such machines in this highly secured perimeter? A ministerial order prohibits access to these plants to aircraft and civilian machines within 6 kilometers under penalty of sanctions.

4. Helicopters

In a 26-page document entitled *Belgian UFO Wave from 1989 to 1992, a forgotten hypothesis*, the field investigator Renaud Leclet concludes that it must have been helicopters. Witnesses have been flown over or have walked under low-flying machines. They did not perceive any noise or feel any air movement. This is one of the reasons why General de Brouwer, Lieutenant-Colonel André Amond and the investigators of the SOBEPS dismissed this hypothesis very early.

5. Experimental and secret prototypes from the American Black Programs

Very questionable. It would be unwise to fly multi-million dollar prototypes over heavily populated areas for almost two years. In case of damage or crash, the machines would fall into the hands of local civilians and military. Too high a risk. Moreover, it would require impressive logistics: how to move and where to park these huge flying platforms?

Finally, some people have described several objects hovering together. In particular, on May 2, 1990, in Ellezelles, where witnesses counted 13 triangular devices in the sky. When one knows the price that a single experimental prototype costs, which nation could afford to fly so many?

Interviewed by journalist and investigator Bernard Thouanel, Wilfried de Brouwer revealed that he received a visit from Richard D'Amato, an American official working for the NSA and close to the decision-makers of the *Black Programs*. He specified: "It was in 1992 or 1993. [He assured me that there was no *Black Program that had* the characteristics of what had been observed in Belgium. And then we must remain serious: why would the Americans have come to do their tests here? Richard D'Amato, very intrigued, was then given a copy of the F-16 recording.

Conclusion

Even today, we do not know the origin or the intrinsic nature of the large triangles of the Belgian wave. The weekly *Courrier international* of July 24, 2008 concludes: "Unquestionably, they were UFOs, in other words, flying objects that we still cannot identify. In 1997, the Belgian Ministry of Defense closed the case.

As one of the investigators at the time summed it up perfectly, "We know what they are not. But we still don't know what they are."

Sources

Above all, two essential works: *Vague d'Ovni sur la Belgique*, SOBEPS, 1991, and *Vague d'Ovni sur la Belgique*, vol. 2, SOBEPS, 1994 - *Paris Match* n∞ 2145, July 5, 1990, pp. 48-51 - *OVNI Présence* n∞ 45, " Spécial Belgique ", January 1991 - *Phenomena* n° 1, January 1991, pp. 14-19 - *Phenomena* n° 16, "Spécial Belgique ", July-August 1993, pp. 4-18 - *Inforespace* n° 95, October 1997 (issue almost dedicated to the Belgian wave) - *Inforespace* n° 97, December 1998, pp. 9-48 - Bertrand Méheust, *Retour sur l'" Anomalie belge "*, Le Livre Bleu Éditeur, 2000 - Leslie Kean, *Ovnis, des généraux, des pilotes et des officiels parlent*, Dervy, 2010, pp. 23-55 - *UFOmania* n° 68, automne 2011, pp. 12-28 - Radio program "Entre mystères et secrets *: la fascinante histoire des Ovnis* " narrated by Franck Istasse (*episode 3 :* L'anomalie belge), RTBF, 2020.

IV. Kenneth Arnold,
the father of saucers

"In the beginning was the Word", we read in the Gospel according to Saint John. Words have a power. And language has an action on reality. The active force of words, their incredible capacity to create, to designate, to decipher, to underline the functions of all that surrounds us conditions what we are. The philosopher and semiologist Roland Barthes rightly said: "To put words is to shake the meaning of the world."

For decades, even centuries, strange flying objects have been observed in our skies. Considered as a crazy palette of events having no correlation, these events have only been published in the chronicles, without any reflection or concern for synthesis being proposed. It is almost without his knowledge that a young civilian pilot named the phenomenon. An expression, apparently harmless, gave rise to the craziest parascientific controversy of the xx^e century. Ufology gave its first cry, defrosting its lungs, one fine day in June 1947. This is how it all began...

A seasoned pilot

It is Tuesday, June 24, 1947. Our witness is Kenneth Arnold. A 32-year-old civilian pilot from Boise, Idaho, he is also a businessman. He had just delivered firefighting equipment to Chehalis, Washington, and his day was over. He states:

"I used to fly to my customers in five western states...I started out selling sportswear. But since then, I've branched out into firefighting equipment. I sell fire extinguishers because I think it's a useful device for humanity. Plus, it allows me to earn enough money to support my wife, two daughters, and have a partially paid off house, an airplane and several pets."

Having taken his first flying lesson at the age of 16, Arnold is an experienced pilot. As a sheriff's deputy for Ada County, he has flown several rescue missions and regularly transports prisoners to McNeil Island Penitentiary. Flying between 40 and 100 hours a month, he says, "In the type of flying I do, it takes a lot of practice and judgment to be able to land in and take off from the many meadows without damaging your plane. In some of the fields and places I fly to for work, the runways are very short and the altitude very high. To date, I have landed on 823 mountain pastures. And in over 1,000 hours of flying, my most serious glitch was a flat tire."

It is exactly 2:15 pm when our pilot takes off from the small airport of Chehalis to go to Yakima. At the controls of his plane - a small red and white CallAir A-2 -, the trip looks pleasant. The weather is fine, the sky and the air are as clear as crystal. Arnold decided to search for a Curtiss C-46 - the largest transport plane in the U.S. military - that had crashed on December 10, with 32 Marines on board, in the foothills of Mount Rainier. The US Air Force is promising a $5,000 reward for locating the wreckage of the twin-engine plane. A tempting prospect.

Nine singular objects

After an hour of flight, the Cascade Range is finally in sight. Its highest peak, Mount Rainier, a stratovolcano, cuts its imposing silhouette on the blue sky, culminating at 4,392 meters. The visibility is excellent. "We could see almost 80 kilometers," our pilot later confided to US Air Force investigators.

Suddenly something made him flinch.

"As I was negotiating a 180-degree turn over the city of Mineral, an extremely bright flash of light hit my cockpit. I was flying at 9,200 feet *[2,800 meters]* and it really alarmed me. I thought I was about to collide with another aircraft that I hadn't noticed approaching. For 20 or 30 seconds I anxiously scanned the sky, sideways, above and below my aircraft. The only plane I saw was a DC-4, far away, coming from San Francisco and bound for Seattle."

Kenneth Arnold and his CallAir

Where can this flash of bluish light come from? Our witness is circumspect. But then a second flash of lightning struck the plane again. This time," he says, "I could see precisely the direction from which it came. I then saw, far to my left and to the north, a formation of very bright objects coming from Mount Baker, skimming the tops of the mountains and traveling at considerable speed. At first I could not make out their shape because they were still more than 150 kilometers away. However, this formation, flying at about 170 degrees, was about to pass directly in front of me. These objects were rapidly approaching the snow cover of Mount Rainier. I figured it must be a jet formation."

As the objects stand out clearly against the snowy patches of the volcano, Kenneth counts them. "I counted them like one counts cattle or game in flight. There were nine of them. They were flying diagonally..."

Kenneth also distinguishes their shape. Measuring about 15 meters long, they are however without a tail, which is very surprising. "I was sure they were airplanes, so they should have had a tail," says Kenneth. But knowing that the army is very good at camouflage, he thinks that they must be using a new technique to hide the rudder of their machines.

Their way of moving is also atypical. "I was fascinated by this squadron of planes. They did not fly like any aircraft I knew. [...] Sure, they were moving in formation, but erratically. As I said at the time, while flying, they progressed like speedboats bouncing on a rough sea or like the tail of a Chinese kite that I once saw waving in the wind. And to be more precise, they were going like a flight of geese, in a chain and diagonally, as if they were linked to each other."

Their surface being polished like a mirror, our pilot adds: "Another characteristic of these machines disturbed me enormously. I mean by this their way of advancing by tilting alternately. So that they emitted these very luminous blue and white flashes. I didn't get the impression that they were emitting these flashes themselves, but rather that the sun was reflecting off the extremely polished surface of their wings."

Our pilot tries to record as much detail as possible. "These objects," he would later say, "looked like pie dishes cut in half with the back shaped like a convex triangle." The lead craft, different, was shaped like a boomerang.

An incredible speed

As a good pilot, Kenneth Arnold decides to time their speed with his onboard clock. As these objects move from Mount Rainier to Mount Adams, he uses these two mountain peaks as landmarks. He calculates that to cross this distance of 76 kilometers, these machines take 1 minute 42 seconds. A quick equation indicates that they are therefore moving at a speed of more than 2,800 km/h! A speed much higher than all the apparatuses of the time, knowing that the sound barrier will be crossed only on October 14 of this same year by the rocket-plane Bell XS-1, at the speed of Mach 1,06, that is to say 1 297 km/h.

Kenneth Arnold shows an illustration of the head "machine

Arnold's observation lasts 2 minutes and 30 seconds. Then the fleet of machines finally disappeared behind the crest of the mountain ranges. Extremely shaken, our man abandons the search for the C-46, giving up the promised $5,000. But he is too eager to tell his friends about his observation.

"It was about 4 p.m. when I landed in Yakima. I went straight to Al Baxter, the flight center manager. He was at the front desk and I breathlessly asked him to give me a private interview. He dropped what he was doing, we went to his private office and there I told him what I had seen. I also made some sketches of these machines. I remember that he gave me a rather puzzled look, knowing full well that I had not gone crazy and that I was not hallucinating. He then called several pilots and helicopter instructors to hear my testimony. My excitement subsided when one of the helicopter pilots decided, "Bah, it's just a flight of those guided missiles from the secret base at Moses Lake." "

Kenneth took control of his single-engine plane and flew to Pendleton, Oregon.

"When I landed at the big airfield in Pendleton, there were quite a few people there to greet me. But when I got off my plane, they were all silent. They were just standing there looking at me. I don't remember how the subject came up, but I seem to recall that very quickly the entire airfield staff was listening to my story. I mentioned the speed I had calculated, but I made it clear that I was convinced my calculations were poor."

Kenneth spreads out his maps and everyone leans in. We evaluate, we recalculate and the men come to the conclusion that these objects were moving at 2 000 km/h. Never seen before! They think that they must be missiles remotely controlled by robots. No human being could resist such a speed.

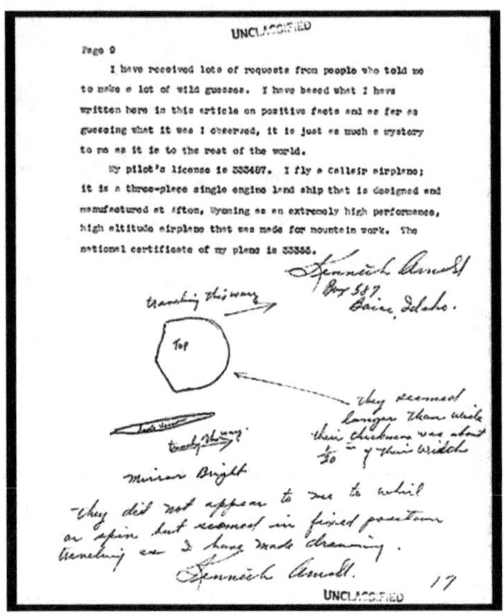

Report written by Kenneth Arnold and drawings of the machines

A media tsunami

Kenneth Arnold spends the night in Pendleton. He is worried. What if these devices were Soviet? In 1947, in the middle of the Cold War, the threat of a Russian invasion worries the population. The next day, our pilot goes to the FBI office. Unfortunately, it is closed. He slips a note under the door, but gets no answer. Determined, he went to the local newspaper, *East Oregonian*. Before lunchtime, he met with two reporters: Nolan Skiff and Bill Bequette. He told them in detail

UFO: The 12 files that the Pentagon cannot explain

about his observation. To describe the trajectory of the craft, he said: "One could compare their irregular movement to the ricochets of a saucer thrown on the surface of the water. This sentence, very harmless, will however prove to have serious consequences.

Touched by the seriousness and sincerity of the witness, the two journalists decided to publish his story in the day's edition. They wrote a small text that they placed at the bottom of the first page and sent it to the printer. At the same time, they wrote a short dispatch to the Associated Press, the country's largest news agency. The Telex begins, "Pendleton, Oregon, June 25 (AP) - Kenneth Arnold, a Boise, Idaho, pilot, reports just today that he observed nine bright saucer-like objects flying at an 'incredible' speed and altitude of 10,000 feet; he says he had no idea what they might be."

When he said that the nine objects Arnold saw were saucer-like *objects*, Bequette had no idea that a media tsunami was about to sweep the country.

After lunch, Nolan Skiff and Bill Bequette return to their office. They are greeted by their distraught and overworked switchboard operator. Newspapers from all over the country and Canada kept calling, asking for more details about the encounter in the sky. Our two reporters contacted Arnold again and this time conducted a longer interview. They wrote a second, more detailed report, which was sent to news agencies and journalists. The next day, our pilot's observation was in all the newspapers! That night," Arnold recalls, "I could have fallen asleep peacefully if all those journalists, reporters and news agencies had left me alone. I didn't share the excitement at all. I can't tell you how many people, letters, telegrams and phone calls I tried to answer. After three days of this brouhaha, I came to the conclusion that I was the only sane person in the whole pack. From that point on, based on the number of sighting reports that were pouring in from all sides and that I was following closely, I figured it wouldn't be long before there was one of these things in every garage. To put an end to what I thought was so much nonsense, and since I couldn't do my job, I went to the airport, got on my plane and flew home to Boise."

An avalanche of testimonies

On July 6, 1947, Arnold's account was published in *The New York Times*, which headlined, "Flying Saucers Mystify Experts. Perhaps Nature's Prank, They Say."

But these journalists are wrong. Like Bequette, they think that the term "saucer" defines the shape of these machines and not the singularity of their flight. Anyway, the damage is done.

A modern epic is born. The word does not only describe a thing, it creates it. The phenomenon suddenly takes shape, it is embodied, it is clothed with a reality that no one - whether skeptical or doubtful - can contest. Real or not, these saucers materialize to fly in the debates. One wonders, one searches, one inquires. All that was needed was a name, the sesame of a sudden epiphany to open an investigation. It is essential to name a phenomenon in order to consider it. And Arnold, unwillingly, has given it an acoustic image, has integrated it into our lexical field. As a result, the expression "flying saucer" soon appeared on the front page of the newspapers. Citizens look up and track down these phantom ships. Popular culture was turned upside down. The shock wave is massive. Crossing the oceans, it quickly reached Europe, Asia, Australia and Russia.

And now tongues are wagging. In Oklahoma City, in Kansas City, in Pueblo in Colorado, people say they see these saucers.The summer of 1947, victim of a UFO epidemic, will be remembered. At the end of June, citizens reported sightings of craft described as "bright", "extremely fast", "with unprecedented maneuverability". Most of them were "round" or "disc-shaped". The reports literally poured in until July 15, 1947. A total of 28 states were visited by these intruders!

By digging into the chronicle, we discover that Arnold was not the first to have seen these objects. For several weeks, some people have seen them dancing in their skies without daring to speak out. The media coverage of Arnold's story encouraged these citizens to suddenly confide in us. On May 17, 1947, Byron Savage, who was also a pilot, saw in the sky over Oklahoma City "a shiny, silvery, silent object, much larger than an airplane. It was "perfectly round and flat". His detailed account was published in the June 26, 1947 issue of the *Oklahoma City Times.*

Two days later, on May 19, in Manitoba Springs (Colorado), 7 employees of the *Pikes Peak Railway* saw, between 12:30 and 1:00 p.m., "a luminous, silvery object" that hovered over them, then began to describe large circles for 20 minutes before speeding off and melting into the blue of a pure sky. This story was published in the June 28, 1947 issue of the *Denver Post.*

In the last days of May 1947, Dr. Coden R. Battey - a physician from Augusta (Georgia) - who was fishing near Beaufort (South Carolina), saw a formation of 4 disc-shaped objects. These objects seemed to rotate on their axis. Silver plated, with an "extremely polished" surface, they then sped off into the sky, completely silent. On July 6, 1947, the Augusta *Chronicle* published this testimony and devoted its first page to the phenomenon of flying saucers.

Let's move on to the next month. There were nearly fifty testimonies between June 1[er] and June 24, from 74 witnesses. But these will only be made public after the declarations of Kenneth Arnold. This wave of 1947 is very interesting because the UFO phenomenon is totally new. There were few *preconceived ideas*, few risks of "imitation" or "contamination". We are just discovering these saucers, and the view we take of them is often surprisingly fresh.

A second disturbing testimony

In this media tumult, Arnold's story remains the most audible. He is the one we want, the one who started it all. If some are fascinated, even interested, the skeptics enter the scene, speaking of a misunderstanding, a set-up or a hallucination. They do not know that on June 24, 1947, after spending the day in this same mountainous region, Fred Johnson, a prospector from Portland (Oregon), back at his mining company's office, told his boss: "I saw some strange machines this afternoon: 5 or 6 discs going south. I only saw them for a few seconds, but I noticed that the magnetized needle of my compass was suddenly flapping quite widely!"

We have an official record of this sighting because Fred Johnson wrote and sent his testimony to the US Air Force on August 20, 1947. He stated: "Since I had a telescope, I can assure you that these objects were real. They were unlike anything I have ever seen in my life. They didn't pass very high, about 300 meters above me. They were round, about 10 meters in diameter, with an extremely bright surface. They didn't make any sound."

Same day, same place and obviously same time. It is likely that Fred Johnson saw part of the formation of the nine objects that Arnold saw. This testimony seems to authenticate the Boise pilot's sighting, knowing that Fred Johnson reported his sighting when neither the press nor the radio had broadcast the news. The official document - an FBI memorandum dated September 17, 1947 - concludes, "This informant seems to us to be very reliable, stating that he has been prospecting in the states of Montana, Washington and Oregon for 40 years."

To see is to believe...

June 26, 1947.

When approached by reporters, a veteran United Airlines pilot, Captain Emil Smith, said, "I've never seen anything like this in the sky, nor have my men... What Mr. Arnold saw was probably the reflection of his instruments."

July 4, 1947.

As he prepares to take off from the Boise, Idaho airport, Smith drives the point home, saying, "I'll believe in these flying disks the day I see them." Little does he know that a big surprise awaits him.

At 9:04 p.m., the DC-3 of flight 105 that he was piloting left the runway. The control tower agent bids him a cordial but ironic farewell, recommending that he "watch out for flying saucers".

8 minutes later, the DC-3 flies over the town of Emmett in Idaho. The co-pilot, Ralph Stevens, saw a formation of 5 aircraft in front of him. Believing they were civilian aircraft, he signaled them with his landing lights. The objects answer at once by changing formation. Stevens caught the attention of Captain Smith. At first," Smith said, "I thought it was a group of light aircraft returning from the Fourth of July celebrations. But I soon realized that they were not airplanes. These objects were flat and circular."

Not believing their eyes, the two men call hostess Marty Morrow to the rescue. "What do you see in the sky in front of you? Glancing through the cockpit windows, she then exclaims, "Oh, but it's a squadron of those flying saucers."

These objects are "huge", dark gray. They stand out perfectly against the clear night sky. They are much larger than a conventional aircraft. With confirmation from the stewardess, Captain Smith contacted the control tower in Ontario, Oregon. As the DC-3 was approaching, he asked the operator to leave the building, scan the sky and report if he saw anything unusual. The employee did not see anything unusual.

The saucers flew away and disappeared towards the northwest. A short respite. The next moment, a squadron of four new UFOs appeared to the left of the DC-3. The aircraft was flying at an altitude of 2,500 meters, and these UFOs were crossing much higher, progressing in single file. They were very high above us," says our pilot, "and they left at a very high speed.

The observation of these 9 objects will have lasted a total of 20 minutes. They were flying 70 kilometers from the plane. Smith insists: "They were not phenomena coming from the ground like fireworks, reflections or things like that. They weren't smoke clouds either. And I know they weren›t planes. They were much larger than known aircraft."

While on a layover in Seattle, Smith and Stevens meet with Kenneth Arnold and discuss their respective observations. A photo of the three men is taken in the offices of the *International News Service* and makes the rounds of newspapers across the country.

July 5, 1947: Captain E. J. Smith, Kenneth Arnold and First Officer Ralph Stevens

A media coverage at the end of its rope

Kenneth Arnold tastes the inconveniences of notoriety. Having become one of the most prominent figures of the summer of 1947, he is constantly hounded, solicited, harassed. But nevertheless he fights, pugnacious, on all fronts.

Arnold receives nearly 10,000 letters from around the world. *Doubleday Book* Publishing offered him a $50,000 advance to write a book about his observation. An enormous sum for the time. But he refused, finding the contract too complex. And because he was demotivated by the fact that the publisher could add fictional touches to the story to make it more commercial.

The editor Ray Palmer and Curtis Fuller decided to create a magazine dedicated to paranormal phenomena. Named *Fate*, this magazine is still today the ultimate reference for subjects that are shunned by orthodoxy. The first issue of the magazine came out in the spring of 1948. Kenneth Arnold's observation is on the cover! Inside, our pilot confides and questions himself. It was a great success and this issue gave the magazine international recognition.

On April 7, 1950, Arnold was interviewed on CBS by the renowned Edward R. Murrow in his radio show entitled *"The Case Of The Flying Saucer"*. Praised for his objectivity and integrity, Edward Murrow is a leading authority. For years, he has built a loyal following of millions of listeners. And the personalities of the century - from Marilyn Monroe to Fidel Castro - follow one another at his microphone. In a brief but beautiful exchange, Arnold says, "I don't really know what these things are. I prefer to be cautious and keep my beliefs to myself. But as an American citizen, if these flying disks are not designed by our science or manufactured by our military air forces, I would be inclined to believe that they are of extraterrestrial origin." Before asserting, a little bitterly: "The only thing I want to add is on behalf of all the pilots who have made strange observations. All these airline pilots don›t appreciate being laughed at. We wrote our reports mainly out of duty. We feel that if our government does not know what these objects are, it is our obligation to report them to our nation and to our Air Force. I believe this is a matter of concern to all citizens of our country. Although it should not in any way trigger mass hysteria. Here's what I think. "

In January 1952, the magazine *Other Worlds*, also edited by Ray Palmer, gave Arnold the opportunity to speak again in a marathon 18-page article entitled *"The Real Flying* Saucer".

There were countless press articles devoted to him during the months of June and July 1947. The *East Oregonian*, the *Montreal Gazette*, the *Tennessean News*, the *Saturday Evening Post*, the *Gazette Times*, the *Chicago Tribune*, the *Los Angeles Times*, the *Arizona Republic*, the *Daily Press*, the *Herald and News*, the *Chicago Sun* and many others reported his testimony. The press echoed the strange encounter but noted that the military had serious doubts. A spokesman for the Army in Washington, D. C., commented, "As far as we know, nothing flies that fast except a V2 rocket, which travels about 3,000 miles an hour - and that's too fast to see. The spokesman added that V2 rockets do not resemble the objects reported by Arnold and that no high-speed experimental tests were being conducted in the area where Arnold made his observation. An inspector with the Civil Aeronautics Administration in Portland, Oregon, added, "I really doubt anything could fly that fast."

An exceptional document

In 1988, in Wisconsin, investigator and author Pierre Lagrange found a previously unreleased recording. He found, in the archives of Raymond Palmer, a large black vinyl record. After listening to it, he realized that it was an exceptional document: the recording of an interview that Kenneth Arnold gave on June 26, 1947 (i.e. 2 days after his observation) to Ted Smith for the radio station KWRC. Considering the historical value of this document, I think it is important to propose a translation. Here is what Kenneth Arnold said at the time:

"It was about 2:15 p.m. when I took off from Chehalis, Washington, on my way to Yakima. Of course, every time one of us flies to Mount Rainier, we spend an hour or two looking for that plane carrying Marines that still hasn't been found and crashed there in the snow southwest of the mountains.

"The average elevation of this area is about 10,000 feet. Over a canyon, I began a turn to get closer to Mount Rainier. I was trying to spot an object that would be the Marine Corps aircraft. I flew over this canyon for 15 minutes. I was about 40 to 45 kilometers from Mount Rainier. I gained altitude, climbed to 9,200 feet *[2,800 meters]*, and suddenly I saw a chain of objects to my left, which looked to me like the tail of a Chinese kite. It was undulating and moving at an incredible speed over the foothills of Mount Rainier.

"At first I thought it was a group of geese, because these objects were progressing like a flight of geese. But in fact their speed was so great that I immediately realized that it was not that. So I changed my mind, I said to myself that it must be a flight of airplanes, completely new, in formation.

"My aircraft was approaching Mount Rainier, flying at about 160 degrees south. I then thought I could calculate their speed. The visibility was perfect, the day was clear. I didn't know where these objects were going, but by tracking to Mount St. Helens and Mount Adams, I could estimate their speed. We pilots spend a lot of time discussing the speed of aircraft.

"These objects seemed to tilt and reflect the sun, like a mirror. As I flew at a particular angle, I could see the sun beating down on the surface of these strange machines. It literally dazzled you, I was almost blinded when I looked at them through my plexiglass windshield.

"It was 2:59 p.m. when I started timing them. I kept looking at my watch without taking my eyes off them. I was trying to catch a glimpse of their tails... and they had no tails! I thought, "Something is wrong with my observation, is it my eyes?" So I positioned my plane on its side, opened my window and looked. In fact, that was it, they had no tails!

"The observation lasted between 2 minutes and 2 minutes and a half. I could make out these objects perfectly. It almost looked like they were tilting their wings... or something. And the sun was reflecting off of them.

"They looked like pie plates cut in half, with a sort of convex triangle at the back. Then I thought: these are military planes and their tails are painted green or brown, that's why you can't see them. And then I stopped thinking and looked at them better. They were not flying in a conventional formation at all, you know the way you learn in the military. They seemed to be undulating, like snaking through the air, over the mountain tops. I even had the impression that they were sometimes descending into the canyon, losing 100 feet of altitude. I could make them out perfectly on the snow, on the flanks of Mount Rainier and Mount Adams. They reflected the sunlight like a flash.

"When I saw the last object pass Mount Adams, I looked at my watch. These objects had taken 1 minute 42 seconds to cross the distance between the two peaks. I thought, 'Wow, they're going pretty damn fast! "I started thinking about the distance between these two mountains.

And then I landed in Yakima, Washington. Al Baxter was there to greet me. When I told him about the speed of the objects I had just seen, he laughed and said, "You should change your watch brand!" And then he looked at me mysteriously, that kind of look... like I had really seen something he didn't know about. And then I forgot all about it until I got to Pendleton. There I took out my map, went back to my calculations, tried to be as accurate as possible. It was amazing, even with a small margin of error, these objects were flying at 1,200 miles per hour *[2,000 km/h]*. In fact, they flew from Mount Rainier to Mount Adams in 2 minutes, so that's 40 kilometers per minute... and if you recalculate their flight time, this time giving them 3 or 4 minutes, their speed is still well over 1,300 km/h... I don't know anything, apart from some German rockets, that goes that fast. These objects were flying at a constant altitude. They did not go up or down. They had a straight line of flight, they followed each other at the same level. So I laughed, and I said to the guys at Pendleton, "Well, they must have a tail!" But hey, none of that was any more enlightening. Based on my knowledge, and being as accurate as possible, this is what I saw. That's what I told the Associated Press and I'm willing to swear to it, my hand on the Bible. Because that's what I saw. And if these things don't have anything to do with our military or our secret service, and if they don't come from a foreign nation, I'm at a loss. I don't know a damn thing about it. The only thing I know for sure is that I saw these things, I timed them, and I was in a perfect position to do so. It's a big mystery to me, as much as it is to all those people who have been calling me for the last 24 hours, wondering what this is all about."

What do the higher authorities think?

As we have seen, the US Air Force expressed important reservations from the beginning. Pierre Lagrange, in an article entitled "The Kenneth Arnold Affair", aptly summarizes this sterile stalemate between a witness hoping for an explanation from the higher authorities... and military and intelligence offices seeking to evacuate the problem. Thus, on July 10, 1947, a document reports an interview between General Schulgen and a special agent named Reynolds, concerning these flying saucers. It states: "General Schulgen advised Mr. [Reynolds] that it was possible that the first reported sightings of the so-called flying disks were spurious and initiated by publicity-seeking individuals, or reported for political reasons. He stated that, if this was the case, the subsequent sightings could be the result of mass hysteria. He speculated that the first reported sightings could have been made by individuals with communist sympathies in order to create hysteria and fear of Russian secret weapons. UFO witnesses thus become, from the beginning, dangerous agitators.

On July 12, two military investigators from Hamilton Field, California, moved to interview Arnold. They are Lieutenant Frank M. Brown and Captain William Davidson. Meeting with the witness changed everything. The military noted in their report dated July 16, 1947, "Arnold is a 32 year old man, married with two children. He has a good reputation in the community where he lives, being a good father who obviously takes good care of his family. [It is the personal opinion of the investigator that Arnold really saw what he said. It is hard to believe that a man of his character and apparent integrity would claim to have seen such objects, and write a report, when he would not in fact have seen any of it."

In spite of this, we can see that the "Arnold affair" is embarrassing the Pentagon brass.

Attempts to explain

The first hypothesis proposed by the press was that Arnold's testimony had triggered a collective psychosis. Fear being contagious, the hysteria of the Cold War would make many citizens lose their reason. Having dropped two bombs on Hiroshima and Nagasaki on August 6 and 9, 1945, America now lived in fear of retaliation.

Second hypothesis: a mistake. Arnold would in fact have seen simple planes in formation. This is what the astronomer J. Allen Hynek defended at the time. Before becoming a convinced ufologist, Hynek was an advisor for various military commissions of inquiry on UFOs. In the 1940s, not believing in the phenomenon at all, he proposed a very prosaic explanation. Kenneth Arnold never forgave him for this interpretation, which he considered dishonest.

A second astronomer, Donald Menzel, took over. He became obsessed with the observation of Mount Rainier. Throughout his life, Menzel proposed 16 different hypotheses: snow clouds, a thin layer of fog, atmospheric turbulence, mountain-top mirages, orographic clouds, moving waves of clouds... Finally, seeing that these meteorological vagaries were unconvincing, he claimed that Arnold had been fooled by drops of water on his windshield. He simply forgot to read the official reports of the pilot who said he had opened his window and removed his sunglasses to better observe this phenomenon.

The English author James Easton then proposed a more than debatable hypothesis. Kenneth Arnold would have seen a flight of pelicans! Easton would have made a poor ornithologist. A pelican, seen on a snowy slope, appears black and not metallic. Moreover, it does not emit intense bluish light reflections, comparable to welding arcs. A ufologist then proposed, not without humor, to speak henceforth of "pelicanization" to designate any such far-fetched explanation.

Finally, the U.S. Air Force and the FBI, who conducted a joint investigation, made their official conclusion on July 12, 1947: Arnold was the victim of a mirage or unexplained optical phenomena.

Even today, no one can explain, in a certain way, the observation of the young pilot of Boise.

UFO: The 12 files that the Pentagon cannot explain

The very first ufologist

Having seen strange things in the sky, this pragmatic man (like many pilots) now sets out to track them down. He is seen in the press, posing next to his single-engine plane and declaring: "From now on, every time I get into my plane to fly, I take a camera with me. He also acquires a latest model camera.

This Sherlock Holmes of the clouds is not content with tracking down saucers. Shortly after his adventure, he hears about a strange case that took place on June 21, 1947, on an island off the coast of Tacoma, on the Pacific coast: Maury Island. On that day, a man making a living selling logs, a man named Harold Dahl, was on his tugboat with his 15-year-old son Charles and two crewmen. It was 2 p.m. Suddenly, these sailors saw 6 objects, hovering in the sky, in the shape of doughnuts about 30 meters in diameter. One of these objects seems to be in difficulty. And vomits on the waves and on the boat an important mass of debris. These substances, which seem hot, cause jets of steam when they touch the sea. The 15 year old son was burned on his arm. And the dog that was on board was killed. During this observation, Harold Dahl tried to take some pictures which turned out to be totally unusable.

The day after the sighting, a man dressed in black and driving a brand new Buick sedan came to Harold Dahl. He told him that he knew about the sighting. Then he became threatening, telling Dahl to keep his mouth shut if he didn't want trouble for his safety and that of his family.

On July 29, 1947, Kenneth Arnold flew to Tacoma. He conducts the first real ufological investigation in history. The debris that looked like pieces of solidified lava or blast furnace slag did not seem to convince him. He calls the military intelligence to the rescue. Old acquaintances arrived: Lieutenant Frank Brown and Captain William Davidson. These military men were cautious and thought it was a hoax. On August 1[er], 1947, they returned to their California base aboard a twin-engine B-25 Mitchell bomber that crashed at 2:50 am. The two soldiers, who were carrying the debris with them, were killed on the spot! Two weeks later, the journalist Paul Lantz, who was investigating the case, died suddenly. And Dahl's son mysteriously disappears. He is found in the small village of Lusk, Wyoming, 1,800 kilometers from his family home, with total amnesia. So many twists and turns! Kenneth Arnold is shaken. All the more so when, while leaving Tacoma, the engine of his plane suddenly stalls. He barely escapes with his flying skills. Then he realizes that the fuel intake valve of his CallAir has been closed and Arnold is convinced that it is sabotage.

Here is a founding investigation, the very first one, comprising all the ingredients, the related, archetypal phenomena, that we will find, thereafter, in the world ufological gesture. We will mention: the appearance of one or more UFOs, as brief as it was spectacular. The photos taken on the sly do not reveal anything about the development. The secret services that quickly point their nose. The army enters the dance and, skeptical in appearance, tries to stifle the affair. The almost supernatural appearance of men in black, always threatening. And a tragic event, in this case the crash of a bomber, the indispensable leaven in any conspiracy scenario.

What can we say today about this "Maury Island case"? Hoax or real case? Very quickly, the rumor of a set-up circulated, carried by the US Air Force, the press and certain investigators. But there are still serious grey areas to explore. The debate is still raging...

A heavy toll

Observing a UFO and daring to talk about it is not without risk. In his report dated July 16, 1947, Army officer Frank Brown notes, "Arnold is very open, and somewhat bitter about the Air Force and FBI officials who did not investigate the matter sooner. [...] Arnold says, to quote him directly, 'From now on, if I saw a 10-story building flying through the air, I wouldn›t say a word about it,' since he has been ridiculed by the press to the point where he now looks like an idiot to the majority of the population of the United States."

Kenneth Arnold has complained repeatedly about the abuse he suffered as a result of his public testimony: "I reported what I saw and anyone would have done the same. If I had not done so, in the name of our patriotic principles, I would have been rightly considered disloyal to my country. My observations were not caused by any particular deficiency in my sight, nor by any abnormal or supernatural phenomenon. I am certain that any pilot, in the same place and at the same time, would have seen the same thing I did. I refuse to attribute my observation to explanations such as illusion, hallucination, apparition, or certain vision disorders.

"Since that day, I have been investigated. I have been questioned many times by agencies such as military intelligence, the FBI, the IRS, the CIA, maritime security intelligence, private investigators, private citizens, or nuisance investigators.

"I was subjected to ridicule, I lost a lot of time and money. Newspapers and press articles have given me some notoriety, but I have had to face many questions, questions about my honesty, my character, my business relationships. All the real persecution I suffered (whether intentional or not) - and that because of my accidental involvement in what became the strangest story ever told - was a continual source of amazement to me.

"However, the research is not finished. [...] An answer to this phenomenon should be obtained with certainty. I am convinced that the facts we have accumulated should not be buried under a mass of official nonsense and masked by a smoke screen of all kinds of nonsense. It is time to separate truth from untruth, fact from falsification, real flying saucer from fantasy. This is perhaps the most important event of our time!"

Epilogue

It was Ranger William J. Butler who finally located the wreckage of the twin-engine plane in the foothills of Mount Rainier. He was offered the $5,000 reward, but as a gentleman and good servant of the nation, he refused. The National Park Service placed a bronze plaque with the 32 names of the deceased soldiers. And every year on the same date, a church service is held in memory of these men who died too soon.

The press frenzy subsided in July 1947 when the Air Force announced that it had recovered the remains of a flying disk in Roswell, New Mexico. The same evening, it denied that it was the debris of a sounding balloon. This denial," writes the ufologist Gildas Bourdais, "was a decisive turning point in the attitude of the press. From that day on, the watchword became the systematic denigration of flying saucers."

Kenneth Arnold later moved to Idaho. Settled in Meridian, now a father of four, with his wife Doris, he lived a secluded life away from the hustle and bustle of the media. Reading Charles Fort's books[7] , he said, "I was amazed when I discovered his

---

7. Charles Fort (1874-1932) was an American writer who was passionate about all the strange facts and unexplained phenomena rejected by orthodoxy and science. An absolute pioneer, this "angel of the bizarre" published four works, including the famous "Book of the Damned", a bible of the supernatural that scandalized scientific circles at the time. Rain of frogs, rain of blood, footprints of giants, crying statues and other prodigies haunt his works. He was the first to evoke the presence of mysterious marine and celestial objects, thus laying the foundations of contemporary world ufology.

works. There are many similarities between my investigations and the facts he has patiently collected. The major difference is that by naming this phenomenon, Arnold inscribed it in our vocabulary. And made these UFOs a component of our reality.

Invited by ufologist and investigator Paola Harris, on January 16, 2012, on the *"Coast to Coast"* program, Kim Arnold, the pilot's third daughter, revealed that her father had made several sightings of unusual flying objects: *"His second sighting,"* she confided, *"took place, if I remember correctly, in July 1947 [July 29 to be exact]. He was flying toward the city of Tacoma and saw 25 bronze-colored objects, very bright, moving in formation. His last sighting is rather fascinating. It was in 1952, over Susanville, California. He saw 2 objects flying under his plane. One was as solid as a Chevrolet. The other was transparent, and my father could see, through the center of the object, the pine trees of a forest he was flying over. He then realized that these machines had the possibility of changing density... Concerning the first machines that he saw in June 1947, he repeated that at first sight, he believed that they reflected the sunlight. It was like a pulse. But he soon realized that it was their entire surface that was pulsating and beating like a human heart. To him, these things were alive. Everyone thought that these things were manufactured, made of sheet metal and bolts. That was never his opinion... In 1982, two years before his death, he thought that these devices were in fact the missing link that unites the living and the dead. Indeed, regarding his last sighting, Arnold confided in 1981 to journalist Gregory Long: "These things looked alive. I had the impression that they were quite aware of my presence. But they made no effort to approach me."*

Kenneth Arnold never stopped investigating, questioning this phenomenon. He spent nearly $30,000 to carry out his investigations throughout the country. With the help of publisher Ray Palmer, he wrote his account under the title *The Coming* of *the* Saucers. "Not to get rich," he said. In fact, the modest profits from his sales were used to finance new investigations or were distributed to charities.

He died on January 16, 1984 at the age of 68. Nicknamed "the man who started *it all*", he became a legend, and is now on a par with the angels and the stars.

Sources

Fate, vol. 1, no. 1, Spring 1948, pp. 4-10, then 19-48 - Kenneth Arnold and Ray Palmer, *The Coming of the Saucers*, Amherst (Wisconsin), 1952 - *Other Worlds*, January 1952, pp. 75-92 (long article signed by Kenneth Arnold) - Ted Bloecher, *"Report on the UFO Wave of 1947 "*, 1967 - *MUFON UFO Journal* no. 165, November

1981, pp. 7-10 (Kenneth Arnold is on the cover) - *Flying Saucer Review*, vol. 32, n° 5, 1987, pp. 2-12 - Gildas Bourdais, " Arnold et les sceptiques ", *Lumières dans la nuit* n∞ 359, pp. 17-26 - Pierre Lagrange, "L'affaire Kenneth Arnold ", in *Communications* n° 52, 1990 - *Special Edition of Science & Vie*, " 50 ans d'Ovnis ", 1997, pp. 16-21 - Interview of Kim Arnold by Paola Harris, June 21, 2008.

V. The Flatwoods Monster

Among the most emblematic cases dealing with disturbing confrontations, the so-called "Flatwoods Monster" case remains a must in the ufology chronicle of the 1950s. It is true that this affair was little treated in France. Jacques Bergier[8] briefly mentioned it. As well as the late Jimmy Guieu. But on the whole, French ufologists and mystery lovers did not seem to take this story too seriously. Or rather they did not know what to do with it.

On the other hand, around the world, this affair made a lot of noise. And it had an unprecedented impact on both our North American and Japanese friends, for whom the "Flatwoods Monster" remains one of the most iconic aliens in our history.

A real star in the United States and an essential figure in the land of the Rising Sun, he is seasoned with all kinds of sauces. He is regularly featured in comics, manga, television series and video games.

The Facts

But what exactly happened in this remote corner of the United States?

Date: September 12, 1952.

Location: Flatwoods, a small town of 300 souls located in Braxton County, West Virginia.

---

8. Of French-Polish origin, Jacques Bergier (1912-1978) was a chemical engineer, journalist, writer, spy and resistance fighter. Known as the "Mirandole Peak of the Strange", he co-authored with Louis Pauwels *The Morning of the Magicians,* a work of more than 500 pages, a true publishing phenomenon, which sold more than one million copies. This essay, at the frontiers of science and the occult, was the breviary of "fantastic realism", mixing scientific advances, alchemy, esotericism, religions and unusual facts. In 1961, still with Louis Pauwels, he founded the magazine *Planète.* Speaking 14 languages, this colorful character liked to define himself as "Amateur of the unusual and scribe of miracles".

19 h 15.

It is a very mild end of day, typical of these Indian summers so pleasant in the region. The evening falls softly on the neighbouring hills. Their work day is over, the adults are resting. And some children play ball on the playground of the local school. There are two brothers there: Freddie and Eddie May, who are 12 and 13 years old respectively. And their friend Tommy Hyer, 10 years old.

Suddenly, one of the boys freezes and points his finger at the sky. His classmates immediately looked up and saw a strange luminous object rising from the mountains, slowly flying over them, gradually losing altitude... and landing on the top of a nearby hill, on a piece of land belonging to Bailey Fisher, a neighboring farmer. The children agree: "It looks like a silver dollar coin that just flew across the sky with a trail of fire behind it," says Freddie. One thing is certain: this object seems very strange to them. It doesn't look like an airplane or any other flying machine they know.

Their curiosity piqued, Eddie and Freddie immediately rush to their mother's house: "Mom, mom, we just saw a flying saucer land on Mr. Fisher's field!" they shout, out of breath.

Drawings by Freddie and Eddie May

A night scouting

Their mother's name is Kathleen May. She was born on November 20, 1920 and was 32 years old at the time. It is a former teacher who works from now on in her own beauty institute: *Kathy's Beauty Shop*. She is a rational, pragmatic and very religious woman. A typical American woman of the 1950s.

Kathleen May, rather incredulous, listens to the children's disjointed talk. It all seems fanciful to her. But measuring their state of excitement, she decides all the same to throw a glance outside, on the nearby hill where the supposed flying saucer would have landed. And there, surprise! She sees in the falling night, a red glow that pulses between the trees.

At Kathleen May's house that night is a cousin, Eugene Lemon, a reservist in the U.S. National Guard. Seventeen years old, Eugene is practical. He is a responsive boy. When he sees this unusual glow, he thinks that a plane may have crashed and that potential victims need help.

Without missing a beat, our little troupe sets off. Eugene takes the lead, followed by Kathleen, her two sons (Eddie and Freddie), their friend Tommy Hyer, as well as two young neighbors: Neil Nunley (14) and Ronnie Shaver (10). With a single impulse, they decide, in spite of the darkness which settles, to go to see closely this "thing" fallen from the sky. Kathleen and Eugene take a flashlight. Eugene also whistles to his dog who joins them. And here they are left in night expedition.

The dog runs away

When our scouts arrive on the spot, they notice that a light mist floats at ground level. And a strange smell seizes them in the throat, acrid, unpleasant. They also see on their right, hardly 15 meters away, an enormous mass which seems to rest on the ground. "It was like a big fireball. How big was it? As big as a house!" This "object", resting on the clearing, is silent. It blinks, changes color. A bit like a piece of ember on which one would blow, temporarily reviving its incandescence.

This strange mist that floats on the ground is not reassuring. An ideal setting for a horror film. And all around, a pestilential smell rises more and more violently, which will make them say: "It was a mixture of sulfur and molten metal. It burned our throats, our eyes watered, we *almost* suffocated..."

You have to imagine all this, on an isolated hill, in the middle of the night. Worrying then. And to make it worse, the dog starts to bark, he seems very disturbed. He advances, hair bristling, towards the object. But when he enters this singular mist, he freezes, suddenly terrified, then runs away screaming, tail between his legs. It runs down the hill, leaving the group totally stunned. What did the animal see or feel to be in such a state?

A terrifying creature

Suddenly, under a large oak tree, to the left of the clearing, something comes to life. And two eyes start to glow in the darkness. Eugene immediately shines his torch. A hunter like all the locals, and therefore a connoisseur of the local fauna, Eugene thinks at first that it is a raccoon or a possum. But the light of the lamp reveals something else.

Standing over them is a terrifying creature that is almost 3 meters tall, with - in the center of a scarlet head surrounded by a dark cap in the shape of an ace of spades - two large luminous eyes. When we speak of "eyes", it is rather two openings that project rays of "orange and green" light. The body of the "monster" - because for our witnesses this vision is purely monstrous - seems draped of a kind of long pleated "skirt", of dark green color. Terrified, Eugene falls backwards.

Kathy and the children are also frozen with fright. And then this creature starts to move. It makes a kind of hissing sound, "like bacon being thrown into a hot pan. It moves uniformly, slowly, smoothly, so that our witnesses think it is floating above the ground and heading straight for them. In panic, the group fled without asking for help, running down the hill screaming. It is said that Kathy May, in a panic, jumped over a six-foot fence. She was not very athletic.

Drawings done separately by Ronnie Shaver, Tommy Hyer and Freddie May. Despite slight diffe-rences, the sketches are very similar.

UFO: The 12 files that the Pentagon cannot explain

Scarier than Frankenstein's creature

Later, Eugene would describe this apparition by saying, "This creature was very tall. As it stood under this branch, we concluded that it was about 10 feet tall. I wasn't even half its height. It was very tall.To me, it was mechanical, not alive. Maybe inside there was something living, but what I saw was either a spaceship or some kind of suit. Something that a creature was wearing. Either way, it was mechanical!"

Kathleen May said, "I was very close to this thing, close enough that it sprayed oil all over my uniform. But it didn't have arms. A drawing showed arms, but it didn't have any. It looked more like antennae between the body and the head. You know...it was scarier than Frankenstein›s creature.It couldn›t have been human."

Freddie May added: "My mother said the creature was wearing a green pleated skirt. I think the pleats were more like vertically arranged tubes. They were made of metal and actually reflected the vegetation around it. These tubes were as thick as my arm. And the monster's eyes were more like portholes."

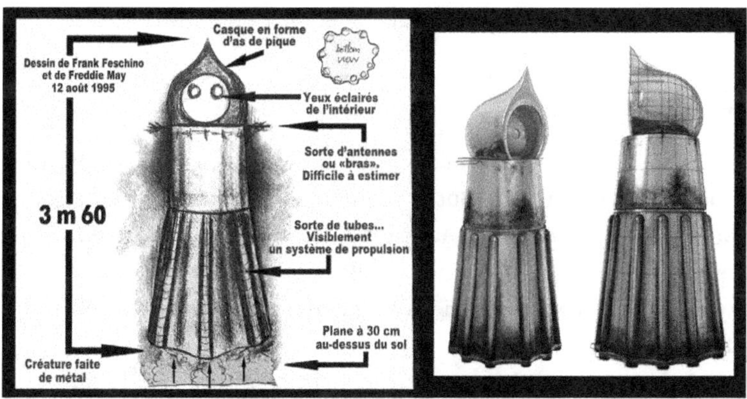

Left: drawing of the "monster" by Frank Feschino and Freddie May, made in 1995.
Right: metal reconstruction

Too shocked...

Back home, our witnesses discover that the dog that came home before them has vomited on the terrace. He was lying in a corner, with his tail between his legs, and was moaning. The investigator Ivan Terence Sanderson, who quickly went to the scene, revealed on November 25, 1956, on WOR radio, that the poor animal died shortly after.

The May brothers have some kind of oily liquid on their faces that their grandmother tries to wipe off. Everyone is in shock.

Kathleen May then calls the local sheriff: Robert Carr. And some close friends. The story quickly makes the turn of the village.

Kathleen then contacted the journalist of the *Braxton Democrat* - the local daily newspaper -, a certain Lee Stewart Junior who arrived at once. The reporter tries to interview the witnesses. But the boys, too shocked, are unable to express themselves. They remained silent for more than an hour and a half.

Eugene Lemon, the young national guard, was by far the most upset. Stewart would later note in his column, "Certainly these people saw something that totally terrified them. They weren't acting, they weren't lying, it was obvious."

A group of neighbors armed with guns decide to go, without delay, to take a look at the hill. Eugene (who is "shaking like a leaf") and the reporter join the expedition. But alas, there is no trace of the "monster" and the luminous UFO.

Two long parallel tracks

Alerted about the crash of an "object" or a small plane several miles away, Sheriff Robert Carr was absent. But as soon as he returned, he decided to go to the place haunted by the "monster". A mist fell, too thick, and the sheriff had to give up. Moreover, as he approaches the fateful spot, his two dogs, suddenly terrified, run away screaming. The sheriff tried twice that night to reach the hill. But nothing makes it.

The next morning, at 7:00 a.m., journalist Lee Stewart went back to the scene. He noticed two long parallel tracks on the ground, like sled tracks. These tracks start from the tree where "the monster" would have been seen and lead to the place where "the machine" would have landed. The grass is packed on a good surface. These marks will be attributed, by more skeptical investigators, to the pick-up truck of Max Lockard, a very curious neighbor who would have visited the site before Stewart. But once questioned, Max Lockard denies it. He confirms, during a telephone discussion, that he only approached the site because it was impossible to reach the crest of the hill with his vehicle. The slope "is much too steep".

At first, Lee Stewart did not perceive any suspicious odors described by witnesses. But as he bent low to the ground, he smelled "a pungent, irritating odor that stung his nose and throat. Stewart, a US Air Force veteran, is familiar with gases used for military purposes. However, he says he has never smelled anything like it.

Sheriff Carr and his deputy Burnell Long searched the area extensively. But, disappointed, they come back empty-handed.

A monster that breathed fire

Of course, the local press was quick to pick up on the story. The headlines followed: "As they turned a corner, they saw a pair of bulging eyes", "A fire-breathing monster routed seven people", "Braxton residents fainted and fell ill after being chased by a strange 10-foot *tall* monster"...

Sick, that's exactly right. For our witnesses, this encounter is not without damage. Their throats are so inflamed that they cannot swallow anything for several days. Eugene Lemon is, the same night, at his worst. He has convulsions and vomits constantly. 15 days after this disastrous encounter, he is still unable to drink without feeling terrible pain in his throat. A doctor came to examine the children and concluded that they had all the symptoms of "mustard gas poisoning".

Witnesses come out of the silence. They begin to tell that, that evening, they saw strange lights in the sky of Flatwoods. Mr. A. J. Jordan claims that a strange object landed on the hill in a surprising way. It came from the southeast. Its top was a rather dark red while its base was a deep red. An airplane? Impossible, it had no wings. And strangest of all, it hovered over the hill for a while before landing. A certain Bailey Frame, from Birch River, also confided that he had seen that evening an orange, circular and luminous object at the place where the monster appeared.

A week earlier, 17 kilometers away, a woman and her 21-year-old daughter were driving to church in Weston when they reported encountering a similar creature. The "thing" had a "stench". The girl was so shocked that she had to be admitted to *Clarksburg Hospital* where she stayed for 3 weeks. This case was not reported in the press, but was reported by two investigators of the *Civilian Saucer Investigation* of Los Angeles: William and Donna Smith.

Equally intriguing, Eugene Lemon's mother confided that at the time of the crash, her house began to shake. And the radio she was listening to stopped for 45 minutes.

A similar "monster

It is also worth mentioning an incident that occurred the next day, on September 13, 1952, in the same area, in Stuton exactly. Mr. George Snitowsky was driving his car when he saw a strange object. Stopping his car, he perceived a strong and unpleasant odor "like ether mixed with burnt sulfur". He thought "that a sulfur factory had just burned the residues of its production and that the wind was pushing the effluvia in its direction". The witness would discover that the smell emanated from a luminous sphere from which a giant creature was about to emerge, which bore a striking resemblance to the Flatwoods "monster".

Source

Male, vol. 5, no. 7, July 1955, pp. 39, 78-79.

A new cryptid

A second investigator and famous ufologist is then dispatched on the scene. It is Gray Barker. This one tells: "At first I did not believe in this story. But I said to myself that such an event should be either explained or condemned to oblivion. I asked *Fate* magazine if they were interested. I immediately received the following telegram: "Story probably bogus but to be investigated thoroughly - No speculation, just facts - 3 or 4 photos and 3,000 signs due Monday at the latest." The paper I gave them met the philosophical requirement of that telegram perfectly."

Barker wrote the first report of the incident in the prestigious magazine *Fate*. Kathleen May and Eugene Lemon were invited to testify on television, in the program *"We The People"*, broadcast on September 19, 1952.

This is how the Flatwoods Monster became a resounding success. It joined Bigfoot, Ogopogo and other mysterious creatures in the North American cryptozoological bestiary. This incident will become one of the most famous encounters of the third kind in the United States. Since then, a plethora of works evoke it: science fiction novels, comic books and popular magazines... As well as a reference book, signed by Frank Feschino, which recounts this emblematic case.

Kathy May and the drawing of the "monster" made for the show "We The People

The assumptions

Concerning the "Flatwood Monster" (the "Braxton County Monster" or the "Green Monster" as the press calls it), several explanations have been put forward.

1. The Sanderson-Schoenenberger report

After being among the first investigators on the scene, Ivan Sanderson and his assistant Eddie Schoenenberger wrote a detailed 26-page report. This report was sent to the entire American press. An English magazine even dared to publish it. According to Sanderson, at least 5 flying objects crossed the states of Maryland, Pennsylvania and West Virginia in a straight line that evening. They would have been seen, on the evening of the facts, by a great number of people. But two of these objects (the one in Flatwoods and the one in Sugar Creek) would have made an unexpected U-turn in straight flight. This would exclude the hypothesis of meteorites. For him, it would be a group of UFOs all flying in the same direction. One of them would have crashed near Flatwoods and its occupant would have come out in a spacesuit. Sanderson definitively dismisses the meteor hypothesis by concluding: "It took the boys 20 minutes to reach the hill. When they arrived, the object was still there. No meteorite fragment would burn up glowing like that so long after it crashed."

2. For Gray Barker

Gray Barker corroborates Sanderson's findings. After interviewing the seven witnesses separately, he said, "Many people told me that they saw objects crossing the sky that night. It would have taken me a month to interview them all. According to them, these objects were round, red or orange, and they spat flames. The mayor of Sutton, Mr. J. Holt Byrne, asked me what my conclusion was. I would have liked to answer: "A misinterpretation of a natural phenomenon." But I told him that the descriptions were consistent with other flying saucer sightings. The monster could be a robot escaped from a ship, or an entity inside a suit that allows it to withstand the earth's atmosphere. This, of course, is only speculation. But what I do know is that there was a great deal of honesty and fear in the eyes of the seven witnesses when they told me their stories. These people really saw something. And what they saw seems to totally match what they are describing."

3. For the police

For the state police, on the other hand, there was nothing abnormal. No doubt a phenomenon of collective hysteria after the group had seen a meteorite that had fallen on the hill.

4. According to Joe Nickel's research

This member of the "Committee of Skeptical Investigators" claims that the flying objects observed in different states that night were in fact one and the same: a single meteor. The Maryland Academy of Sciences seems to agree, reporting that a meteor headed for West Virginia passed over Baltimore that night at 7 p.m. This, according to Nickel, would be the origin of the May brothers' and Tommy Hyer's 7:15 p.m. observation.

At the time of the events, 3 aviation beacons were visible from the top of the hill (a fact also reported by Sanderson), which would explain for Nickel the observation of a "pulsating red ball of light" by the witnesses and the red complexion of the monster.

Regarding the latter, Joe Nickel agrees with the opinion of the US Air Force investigators who looked into the matter. He concludes that it must have been an animal perched on a branch, giving the impression of being a much larger creature. He thinks more specifically of a barn owl: head in the shape of an inverted ace of spades, talons that could match Kathleen May's description and a piercing cry similar to that described by some witnesses. This is the animal that best fits the appearance of the Flatwoods "monster". However, this does not eliminate many questions, which remain unanswered. Any self-respecting ornithologist knows that a barn owl is, at best, about 40 centimeters long. So, even on a branch, we are far from the imposing 3 meters of the creature. Moreover, no naturalist has ever reported that this nocturnal raptor was capable of projecting an oily substance on a group of too intrusive walkers. Or to emit orange and green light rays. Finally, the most amazing thing is the dog's attitude. None of these professional investigators took it into account. Let's start again: we are in 1954, in a village of 300 souls, in the middle of nature. It is therefore a rural, preserved territory. The dogs live in a semi-wild way, used to hunt, to run freely, knowing perfectly the hosts of the forest. It would be unreasonable to imagine that a dog would be terrified by a peaceful nocturnal bird of prey that it knows very well. And that to the point of dying...

5. The fall of a meteorite

Other hypotheses have also been proposed, such as the fall of a meteorite near the hill, which would have caused a cloud of smoke of almost human shape. Not very credible.

6. An inflatable cow?

A cheese company in Wisconsin speculated that it might be a huge inflatable cow, advertising their company, that they had launched a few days earlier into the air and that it had strayed into the hills of Flatwoods.

7. The counter-inquiry of Renaud Leclet

Renaud Leclet, an aeronautics enthusiast, proposed a counter-investigation in 2016. For him, the luminous object was an agricultural machine equipped with a red orange flashing light, the "monster", a barn owl. The flashes of light coming out of the eyes? The reflection of the witnesses' flashlights. The stench? The prey stored in the nest of the raptor, therefore in decomposition. The physiological effects of the witnesses? An allergy to bird feathers, wood dust, mushroom spores. Or more simply hysterical reactions due to fear.

It is however easy to consult the first sketches made by Gray Barker with the help of the 7 witnesses, drawings made on the spot and made public in 1953. The "monster" is represented on the ground, floating a few centimeters above the grass, its head almost reaching the first branch of the tree. The witnesses are therefore formal: this creature has never been seen perched on a branch. Why then this theory of a perched bird of prey?

The attitude of the US Air Force

This case was documented by Project *Blue Book*, a commission created by the US Air Force to study the UFO phenomenon.

Investigators reported that there was a strange smell at the scene. Some said some trees in the vicinity were scorched. Others said that the branches of nearby trees had been broken off. This would suggest that something did land there... Looking into this case, J. Allen Hynek (Project *Blue Book* advisor between 1951 and 1969) found it very intriguing, but could not draw any conclusions.

For the *Air Technical Intelligence Center* (ATIC), this is simply a misunderstanding with an owl.

As you can see, the US Air Force was very embarrassed by this atypical monster that fell from the stars...

Epilogue

As an epilogue, let's talk to the main witness of this case, Mrs. Kathleen May herself, who passed away on June 13, 2009, taking her secret with her... Shortly before she passed away, she said: "This is all real and God knows I would never have made up such a story to deceive people. We had one of those scares, we were really terrified."

"The Flatwoods Monster" was the eleventh most covered story in the North American press during 1952. Still unsolved, this case remains one of the most mysterious of the modern ufological era.

In October 2017, a museum honoring the "monster" was established in Flatwoods. And a festival called *The Flatwoods Monster Festival* offers an annual weekend of music, food, and sales of specialty items depicting this chilling true story. The small town, the scene of an unprecedented apparition, has become a tourist attraction over the years.

Sources

Fate, January 1953, pp. 12-17 - *The Saucerian*, vol. 1, no. 1, September 1953, pp. 8-21 (this case is on the cover) - *Charleston Gazette*, October 31, 1954 - Jimmy Guieu, *Les Soucoupes volantes viennent d'un autre monde*, Fleuve Noir, 1954, pp. 243-245 - Jacques Lob et Robert Gigi, *Le Dossier des soucoupes volantes* (bande dessinée), Dargaud, 1972, pp. 55-58 - Brad Steiger, *Project Blue Book*, Ballantine Books, 1976, pp. 101-102 - *International UFO Reporter*, no. 6, vol. 17, November-December 1992 - *Skeptical Inquirer*, November-December 2000, pp. 15-19 - Bernard Thouanel, *Objets volants non identifiés*, Michel Lafon, 2003, pp. 50-52 - *MidState Star Gassaway*, September 9, 2002 - *La Nave de los Locos*, no. 25, November 2003, pp. 3-8 (case illustrates cover) - Renaud Leclet, *Flatwoods, une méprise influente trop vite oubliée*, contre-enquête, CNEGU website, 2016.

VI. Malmstrom: Disabled missiles!

Before tackling one of the most astonishing cases of the United States of America, it is important, by way of introduction, to briefly evoke this existing tropism between UFOs and nuclear sites.

In 1945, an international struggle began, dividing the world into two opposing forces: the United States and its allies (the Western bloc) and the Union of Soviet Socialist Republics (the Eastern bloc). This episode of strong geopolitical tensions has gone down in history as the Cold War. It is characterized by a mad nuclear arms race in which the two superpowers engaged.

A crazy race

In his book entitled *Troubles in the Sky*, Jean-Jacques Velasco, former director of GEPAN and then of SEPRA within CNES, draws up a gloomy assessment: "Atmospheric nuclear tests and firings began in July 1945. They ended in 1981. The total power released was 440 megatons (the power of the two bombs on Hiroshima and Nagasaki was 15 and 21 kilotons - the most powerful explosion ever carried out was Soviet with a 50 megaton bomb). The total number of explosions in the atmosphere amounted to 543 air tests. [...] At the height of atmospheric testing, in the years 1961 and 1963, up to one explosion was recorded every three days! These figures, which are very real, are unknown to the ordinary citizen. It is a pity..."

This bipolar and global conflict generated, according to the definition of the philosopher Raymond Aron, a "bellicose peace" during which an impressive arsenal of weapons accumulated. America opened the celebrations by creating the Manhattan Project, whose objective was to create a weapon of mass destruction. This highly secret program employed 130,000 people and cost several billion dollars.

And here is a singular fact: as soon as the Manhattan Project was launched and the first atomic bomb was detonated in 1945, UFOs were regularly seen above the installations of the military-industrial complex, with a predilection for nuclear sites.

Documents attest to this

A large number of documents, both official and secret, now declassified, prove that the high authorities took this seriously. An FBI memorandum, dated January 31, 1949, refers to numerous overflights over Los Alamos National Laboratory in New Mexico. This facility, established in 1943, was responsible for designing nuclear weapons for the Manhattan Project. This document, in the form of a warning, points out that UFOs were specifically "targeting" this highly sensitive facility. The memorandum - which sets out to study the issue of "unidentified aircraft," otherwise known as "flying disks," "flying saucers" and "fireballs" - states in part:

"This matter is considered top secret by Army and Air Force intelligence officers. [...] During the past two months, various sightings of unexplained phenomena have been reported in the vicinity of the Los Alamos, New Mexico facility, where these phenomena now seem to be concentrated. In December 1948, on the 5th, 6th, 7th, 8th, 11th, 13th, 14th, 20th, and 28th, sightings of unexplained phenomena were made near Los Alamos by special agents of the Office of Special Investigations, airline pilots, military pilots, Los Alamos safety inspectors, and private citizens. On January 6, 1949, another similar object was sighted in the same area."

A second document, coming from Project *Sign* - the first official scientific study of the US Air Force on UFOs - proves that the military seriously considered that these devices were of non-terrestrial origin. And that they were very interested in the country's offensive technologies. An appendix to this document, written by Dr. George E. Walley - then a member of the Science Board of the Office of the Chief of Staff of the U.S. Air Force - is entitled "Some Considerations in the Interpretation of Unidentified Flying Object Reports. It states, "If there is an extraterrestrial civilization capable of producing such craft...then we should, therefore, expect to receive such visits. Since the most easily observable human actions at a distance are the explosions of nuclear bombs, we should realize that there are certain correlations between the dates of explosion of these bombs and the dates when spaceships are observed..."

A festival of appearances

It is true that between 1947 and 1952, there was a festival of sightings. There were 37 sightings of mysterious flying objects over the Oak Ridge complex in

Tennessee (built to enrich uranium for the first atomic bombs) and Clarksville Air Force Base (a 20 km complex^2 at Fort Campbell, Tennessee, the second of 13 nuclear weapons storage sites established during the Cold War). Other New Mexico nuclear research hot spots - such as White Sands Rocket Test Center, Roswell (the largest *Strategic Air Command* base), Kirtland, Holloman and Sandia complexes - are also visited.

On December 2, 1952, H. Marshall Chadwell, Assistant Director of the CIA's Office of Scientific Intelligence, sent a secret memorandum to Walter Bedell Smith, its Director. This document, in paragraph 4, reports the following: "Reports of incidents have convinced us that there is something going on that deserves our full attention now. [The sightings of unidentified craft flying at high altitudes and moving at high speeds in the vicinity of major U.S. defense installations are neither attributable to natural phenomena nor to known craft."

For his part, John Edgar Hoover, head of the FBI, is concerned about the protection of the country's "vital installations".

The US Air Force commissioned Dr. Lincoln LaPaz to write an official report that inventoried UFO sightings between 1948 and 1950. This report, dated May 25, 1950, is 37 pages long. The mathematician and astronomer concludes that most of these phenomena occur near sensitive government and military installations: Roswell, Los Alamos, Killeen, Sandia, Kirtland, White Sands, Alamogardo, Trinity Site or Oak Ridge. According to the 209 observations studied by Lincoln LaPaz, 74.4% of them concern military nuclear research, manufacturing or storage sites.

Incredible but true: if a belligerent had obtained this report, he could have located one by one all the strategic nuclear and secret places of America at that time!

Sources

Jean-Jacques Velasco with Nicolas Montigiani, *Troubles in the Sky*, Presses du Châtelet, 2007 - Robert Hastings, *UFO & Nukes, Extraordinary Encounters at Nuclear Weapons Sites*, Independent Editions, 2017 - Daniel Harran, *UFOs and Nuclear Power, the Shock of an Ignored Reality*, Temps Présent, 2017 - Stéphane Royer and Didier Gomez, *UFOs and Nuclear Power, Are We Under Surveillance?* JMG Editions, 2021.

Out of sight

Of all the flyovers of strategic locations related to nuclear power, Malmstrom is undoubtedly one of the most spectacular.

Date: March 16, 1967.

Location: Malmstrom Base, 5 kilometers from the small town of Roy, near Great Falls, Montana, USA.

It is still early. The day is late to dawn. The sky is still dark, cluttered with stars. It reigns an icy cold. In appearance, everything is very calm. Nothing moves. The landscape, almost naked, of a heavy solitude - except for some scattered shelters with the inoffensive airs of agricultural barracks -, is powdered of a fine layer of snow.

No one would believe that we are in a strategic location of American military defense. Malmstrom Air Force Base, with its fake desolate look, is actually home to 120 Minuteman intercontinental missiles. These *Strategic Air Command* missiles are one of the main components of the country's nuclear deterrent forces.

At Malmstrom, everything happens underground, out of sight. In his capsule - an underground shelter plunging to a depth of nearly 20 meters - a young officer, First Lieutenant Robert Salas, watches over 10 missiles in their armored silo. These guided projectiles, carrying a formidable thermonuclear warhead, are ready to take off at the slightest alert.

Used between 1965 and 1967, these solid-fuel ballistic missiles, known as Minuteman II, are three-stage missiles, each weighing 30 tons and capable of reaching a speed of 23,000 km/h.

This shooting officer has no idea that he is about to live a unique adventure. I had the chance to meet him, on March 24, 2018, in Hyères, during a conference organized by the CROPS of ufologist Gilbert Attard. Robert Salas then told me about his amazing adventure.

Robert Salas at the time of the events

Egon Kragel: Mr. Salas, by way of introduction, could you remind us of your civilian and military background?

Roberto Salas: I started my career by entering the U.S. Air Force Military Academy. I graduated in 1964. In 1965-66, I began training as a missile officer. And in August 1966, I was assigned to Malmstrom AFB in Montana. I served on that base, as a firing officer, from 1966 to 1969. Then I got a master's degree in aerospace engineering. And I worked on the Titan 3 missile program, liquid-fueled rockets that the US Air Force uses to put secret military satellites into orbit. After that, I left the military in 1971 with the rank of captain. I then worked for Martin-Marietta and Rockwell International in Los Angeles. Then I joined the FAA *[the government agency responsible for civil aviation regulations and controls in the United States]* as an aircraft structures engineer. I was in that position for almost 22 years, until 1995.

I then decided to change my occupation, and went into teaching. I graduated from the University of Washington with a teaching degree and taught mathematics for 17 years. It was also in 1995 that I decided to speak publicly about my UFO experience in Montana. Until then, I was bound to secrecy. But in 1995, I was in a bookstore when I came across a book written by Timothy Good, entitled *Above Top Secret*. On page 301 of the book, the author reported that UFOs had been observed in 1967 over the Malmstrom military base and that they had disabled the missiles there. As I read this, I thought, "This is it. The US Air Force has declassified this incident!"

EK: Can you tell us what happened on this military base in 1967?

RS: It was March 24, 1967. I was on duty at Malmstrom that day. It was late at night or very early in the morning, I don't remember the exact time. I suddenly got a call from a guard who was on the surface... Our team consisted of 6 surface sentries, while my superior and I were on duty in an underground capsule. We were confined for 24 hours without the possibility of leaving this room located 20 meters below ground. So one of the guards who was outside called me and told me that strange lights had just appeared in the sky. They were silent and moving very fast. These lights were moving, stopping abruptly and turning around and negotiating 90 degree turns... The guard told me that no known aircraft was capable of doing this. It was a surprising, disconcerting call. I wasn›t sure what to make of it. I thought he must be joking with me, that it wasn›t really serious. So I stopped paying attention. And I hung up. I was still intrigued because these guards are serious, professional guys. Not the type to make jokes during official communications.

And then, five minutes later, the guard calls me back. This time he was screaming on the phone, he was terrified. You could hear the panic in his voice. He told me that an oval-shaped, orange, pulsating object was flying over the base. The other guards had arrived, weapons drawn. They were waiting for my instructions, asking me what to do. I was in shock. What was I to make of all this? Given the panic of that call, I thought we must be under terrorist attack. And then the guard cut me off by telling me that one of the men was injured, that he had to go check it out. And he hung up.

Without missing a beat, I decided to notify my station chief, 1er Lieutenant Frederick C. Meiwald, who was on break. We had a bed in our capsule to recuperate in. You know, spending 24 hours straight underground is exhausting. So I woke him up and while I was telling him what was going on up there, our missiles were deactivated, one after another. They went into a *No Go* state. That means we couldn't launch them anymore! 10 missiles in all, 10! They were no longer operational. It was incredible. And above all, technically impossible! Because these 10 missiles were piloted in a totally independent way.

My superior immediately contacted the command post at Malmstrom Base, which was 100 miles away. At the same time, alarms sounded in our capsule. On the surface, our station was equipped with motion detectors. So we were getting reports of an incursion, that someone or something had crossed the secure perimeter of our missiles. I called the guards on the surface again to ask them if the UFO was still in sight. They told me no, that it had just left at breakneck speed!

After I got the headquarters, my commander turned to me and told me that a similar incident had occurred on another post a few miles away. At the time, I thought it had just happened. But I later learned that this incident had actually taken place a week earlier. Our station was called *Oscar Flight*. The other station, having been overflown by a UFO, was called *Echo Flight*. So in one week, a total of 20 missiles were deactivated by a UFO at Malmstrom.

EK: Impossible for you to have visual contact with the UFO...

RS: Yes, I didn't see it. We were not allowed - no matter what happened - to leave our capsule. Imagine a terrorist attack and we suddenly decide to go out, to unlock our door. Then any enemy could have broken into our command post and had access to the missiles. So it was a precaution for the high security of the base. That›s why we stayed underground until a new team took over.

When I reached the surface, I went to the guard and asked him what the UFO looked like. He told me that he could vaguely make out a structure through the lights of the object, but that the lights were too blinding. Then a Special Forces helicopter came and picked us up and took us to headquarters. We then had to report to our squadron commander. There was also a man from AFOSI, the US Air Force Office of Special Investigations. Our commander, who was usually a calm and professional man - he had been a pilot in World War II - was white as a sheet. I asked him, "What happened? He said, "I don't know a damn thing! We were then handed some documents and told to sign them on the spot. I asked, "What are these papers? I was told, "These are non-disclosure forms. You agree never to tell anyone about this incident. Never. Because if you were to tell anyone about this, you could face jail time, a very serious jail time." I objected, "But we are already under a high security restraint!" I was told, "Don't argue and sign!" This is why I never mentioned the Malmstrom incident... Until one day in 1994 when I came across Timothy Good's book.

EK: After this incident, it seems that two investigations were conducted...

RS: That's exactly right! There was an investigation by Boeing and an investigation by the US Air Force. The Boeing investigation was initiated at the request of the US Air Force Major Command Headquarters. And the US Air Force, for its part, conducted its own investigation, but in the greatest secrecy. And that is where the cover-up of what really happened began. They lied. And no technical explanation could be given.

EK: You specified previously that a guard was wounded during the observation of the UFO...

RS: Actually, he cut his hand. I think - I'm not really sure anymore - the security guard who was on the surface told me that he cut his hand on some barbed wire. It wasn't the UFO that hurt him with a beam or anything... Our site was surrounded by barbed wire, the guard was very scared, he tried to run away and grabbed that protective fence. It was a small injury, nothing serious actually. But he was taken to the base hospital anyway. And then watch out! There is one thing that has never been mentioned: the radiation emitted by the object. Maybe these soldiers were contaminated by this radiation. Maybe that's why I never heard from them again. And that they never tried to contact me afterwards.

EK: Having stayed 2 more years on this base, you didn't see these soldiers again?

RS: I never saw them again. I never saw them again, not on duty, not by chance. What the U.S. Air Force had to do to keep the incident quiet was to transfer them elsewhere, disperse them. I think a lot of them had to be sent to Vietnam. And then you know, we have a lot of testimony from around the world about witnesses being irradiated by UFOs. In 1957, for example, a group of UFOs flew over the Palomar Mountain Observatory in California, where there was a large telescope. The scientists had a Geiger counter on site. When the UFOs flew over them, they found a high level of radiation. So the guards, the soldiers of Malmstrom could have died of radiation poisoning. The UFO was very close to them, just above the entrance gate.

EK : As soon as you felt free to evoke publicly this incredible affair, you were on TV, on the radio...

RS: Yes, I immediately wanted to testify. I thought that it was a priority duty to speak on behalf of these men who had seen this UFO. Moreover, the day after my interventions and following these broadcasts, some of these men - essentially the officers - phoned me. We were then able to compare our points of view and we all agreed on what had happened in Malmstrom in 1967. I had signed a non-disclosure agreement at the time, which is why I kept quiet for so long. They too were afraid

UFO: The 12 files that the Pentagon cannot explain

to talk about it, they were scared of it. They didn't know what to think. I myself felt guilty for a long time... So, both for these men and for the public, I decided to testify, to reveal the whole truth about what we had experienced that day.

EK: Since the 1940s, many of these unidentified objects have been seen over strategic nuclear sites. What do you think of them?

RS: I think their message to us is, "Get rid of your nuclear weapons!" That's what they obviously want to tell us. We have to be aware that our nuclear weapons are not weapons of war. They will no longer be used in a conflict. First, because more and more nations have them. In total, today, 9 countries share the world's nuclear arsenal. And these are essentially weapons of mass destruction. They are not used, for example, to invade a country and annex new territories. If we use them, we know that it will ruin our planet for many years. I would say hundreds of years. And then it would be a mistake: that a country uses these weapons, and we would experience a murderous escalation. It would cause the total destruction of our world. It would be the ruin and the end of our civilization. And then I think that the UFOs ask us not to play with nuclear power anymore because it affects them in one way or another. Indeed, UFOs have been seen on several occasions over nuclear test sites, in Nevada and elsewhere. In my opinion, they are asking and advising us to give up our nuclear arsenal. They are asking us to unite to get rid of these weapons. There have been many attempts to do this but we have never succeeded. UFOs were seen over Chernobyl, before and after the nuclear disaster, I saw that in the Russian press. As far as Fukushima is concerned, I don't really know, but it would not be surprising if UFOs appeared. We know that many times UFOs have flown over our nuclear power plants. We have a large number of testimonies on this subject.

EK: In your second book, *Unidentified: The UFO Phenomenon*, you reveal that you were abducted in your California home...

RS: Yes. I decided to speak freely about it after years of silence because these abductions are inseparable from the UFO phenomenon. These mysterious flying objects and their occupants - which I think are of extraterrestrial origin - are visiting us, it is clear, for a precise reason. They pursue a determined goal. The abductions they commit are part of a plan that escapes us, of course... But what is certain is that we can no longer ignore this reality. Millions of abduction cases have been reported for years around the world. As far as I am concerned, in 1985, I was living in a house in Manhattan Beach, California. One night, while I was sleeping with my wife - our two young children were sleeping in their bedroom - I saw a blue light coming from our living room. It was strange, because we didn't have that kind of lighting in the room. I woke up my wife and asked her, "Do you see that blue light? She said, "Yes, I see it." I said, "Wait a minute, I'm going to go take a closer look at it, maybe they are thieves." I wanted to get up, but I realized that I was suddenly paralyzed. I remember, it's still very clear, that I fought hard, I struggled hard to regain my mobility, I tried to move my feet... In vain! When I looked back at my wife, she was unconscious, sleeping deeply, it was really strange. And then suddenly I saw a person, a living being - call it what you will - in my room. He was wearing a kind of hood over his head. I couldn't make out his face. Or I forgot it. So I stopped struggling. And I felt - I didn't see them - I felt the presence of small beings in my room. I told myself that they must be children.

These little beings grabbed me, and they started to carry me to the window. I remember that night I had closed the latch on that window and I thought, "These kids can't lift that latch. And I thought to myself, "These kids can't lift that latch," but against all odds, they carried me *through* the window. I know that sounds crazy and it's hard to believe. But that's what I remember. I then saw a light at the bottom of my garden. And then I found myself on a table. There I was shown a needle, a very long one, and it was held ostensibly in front of my eyes, obviously they wanted me to see it. Then, telepathically, I was told, "We are going to stick this needle into your body. I then asked, "Where are you going to put it?" They said, "We're going to put it in your groin. You will see, it is not painful. But when they plunged that needle into my groin, it was very, very painful... It was excruciating pain! Telepathically, I told them that it was unbearable. Immediately the pain stopped. After that, I sat down on this table. Two beings came to get me and put me on a bench, a curved bench, parallel to the wall of the ship. I glanced to my right and saw a room with glass walls. Inside was a creature wearing a white suit. I was led to this being. He explored, with two fingers, my spine. Then I was taken into a curved tunnel. I was not walking, I was floating. At the end of this tunnel, I saw a white light. Suddenly, I was back in my bed. I can give you all these details because I later decided to undergo four regression hypnosis sessions.

EK: In fact, the day after this kidnapping, you didn't remember anything...

UFO: The 12 files that the Pentagon cannot explain

RS: No, I didn't remember anything. Neither did my wife. You have to wait until 2007. I was giving a conference in Ireland. On that day, there was a woman who told about her abduction. At one point, she said that it all started with a blue light in her room. I turned to my wife and asked her, "Do you remember seeing a blue light in the house in 1985? She replied, "Yes, I remember it very well." It was at that moment that our memories came back, simultaneously. I think that what I experienced then was not a dream. I don›t think I was dreaming because I have never felt such excruciating pain under that needle in my life.

Sources

VSD, hors-série n° 3, " Ovnis USA, les raisons du secret ", July 2001, pp. 24-27 - Bernard Thouanel, *Objets volants non identifiés*, Michel Lafon, 2003, pp. 78-85 - Robert Salas et James Klotz, *Faded Giants*, BookSurge Publishing, 2005 - Joël Mesnard, *Vérités et mensonges sur les Ovnis*, Trajectoire, 2008, pp. 105-111 - Leslie Kean, *UFOs: generals, pilots and officials speak out*, Dervy, 2014, pp. 202-203 - *Robert Salas, Unidentified: The UFO Phenomenon*, New Page Books, 2015.

Robert Salas and the author, Hyères, 2018

VII. The meeting with Herb Schirmer

A real explosion in the world of ufology: one night in September 1961, while returning by car from a stay in Canada, an uneventful couple, Barney and Betty Hill, claimed to have been "abducted" by creatures emerging from a flying saucer. "We're being fished out," warned supernatural pioneer Charles Fort from the depths of his den in 1919. This time, it seemed real.

The UFO dossier already put off a good number of people, by its absurdity, its extravagance, its elusive logic. Suddenly, it has inherited a new disorder: the serial abductions or abductions. The doctrinalists, who only see it as a hoax, consign it to the dustbin of repugnance. The adventurous, on the other hand, question themselves, keeping an open mind, an indispensable virtue for conquering the possible. Nevertheless, how to approach this new "cosmic predation"? The internal criteria of these dark narratives leave one stunned. They speak of space-time manipulation, psycho-sociological distortions, medical tests, absurd dialogues and conscientiously erased memories.

In any case, a new, unprecedented thrill is reaching the general public. Kidnappers from another world" seem to be at work. And they strike without distinction.

If, for the saucerist chronicle, the case of the Hill couple remains inescapable and founding, there is a case no less emblematic, unfortunately less known in our country: the meeting of a young policeman patroller, one night of December 1967, with entities coming from elsewhere. Here is his story, generating in its time embarrassment and anguish.

The witness

Our witness is a police officer named Herbert Schirmer. He is a big, strong, 22 year old man. After serving in the Navy, he made a point of joining the Nebraska police force just a few months ago. In a short period of time, he has gained the trust of the residents. He is seen as serious, responsive, and solves problems with a lot of kindness and diplomacy.

A senior city official said, "Herb loves people. He never alienates anyone. Recently, there was a ruckus in a bar because one of the customers had too much to drink. The guy in question is a worker on one of the city's construction sites. He lives in a trailer with his wife and six kids. If I was married to his shrew, believe me, I'd be drinking every day. Herb got a call about this scuffle. He calmly entered the bar, walked right up to the drunk guy who was looking for a fight. Herb started talking to him nicely, bought him a last beer and calmed him down. Then he loaded him into his company car and drove him home quietly. No confrontation. No confrontation. No tickets."

Herbert Schirmer

The Facts

Date: December 3, 1967.
Location: Ashland, a small town in southeastern Nebraska, USA.
It is past midnight by a few minutes.

That evening, Herb (it is his diminutive) patrols as usual. The night fell, thick, typical of these winter evenings where very quickly, each one calming itself at home, nothing moves any more.

Herb walks tirelessly through the streets of the city. Nothing unusual to report. Yet he has a strange apprehension. Something is bothering him. What exactly? Impossible to define.

Reinforcing his unease, and in a strange way, the local dogs start barking in the dark. Later, our witness will say: "It's a feeling that's hard to explain, but you get it when you know your city well. You know instinctively when something is wrong. And you immediately start looking for someone or something that is a problem."

Herb decides to take a look at the commercial buildings on the other side of town. He walked up Main Street to the cattle sale barn near the corrals where the cattle were kept. He says, "There was a huge bull in a pen. He was furious and kept charging the gate. I wanted to make sure the gates would hold. I examined the place with a flashlight. In the end, I didn't see anything wrong.

Our night patroller then takes the direction of the highway 63, always in periphery of the city.

A metal rugby ball

Just as the officer reaches the intersection of lanes 6 and 63, the headlights of his car shine on something bright, parked on the side of the road a few feet ahead. Herb looks at his watch. It's exactly 2:20 a.m.

At first," Herb says, "I thought it was the cab of a semi-truck. There are a lot of them on these tracks. Then I thought one of those vehicles was broken down. There was a row of flashing lights on this object that might have looked like trucker lights."

But the surprise of our witness is growing.

"These lights were going on and off faster and faster. When I shone my light on this thing, I couldn't believe it. I couldn't believe my eyes. I grabbed my baton, made sure my pepper spray was handy. And as I drove along, I approached this strange contraption."

It is indeed a singular vessel which measures 6 meters long and 4.5 meters thick. The object, crossed by pulsating red lights, takes off at once. At its base, strange feet retract. We can then see its shape clearly. It looks like a metallic and shiny rugby ball, perfectly polished. It hovers about ten meters above the highway. It emits a more and more rapid beep which ends up twisting the eardrums. A beam of light, orange and red, shoots out from its base and illuminates the ground. Then, "in 3 seconds", the UFO melts in the sky, to disappear towards the north.

"I froze. All I could do was watch him go."

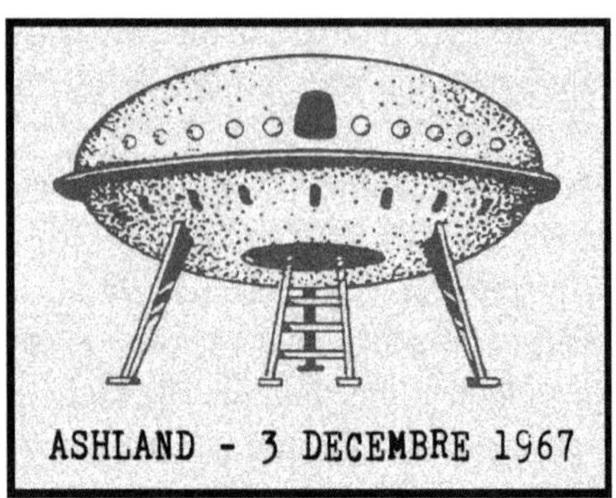

Believe it or not!

As the ship disappears, Herb feels physically ill. He feels hot, starts to sweat and is shaken by nausea. He then decides to return as fast as possible to the police station. Back at his desk, he looks at the wall clock. It is 3 o'clock in the morning. There, something does not stick. The young policeman is persuaded that his observation lasted only a few minutes. There would therefore be a gap of at least 25 minutes in his schedule. An amnesiac interval. What ufologists call a *missing time*, an episode of missing time.

At the time, Herb does not pay much attention. His throat is burning. He has, in priority, an imperative need to drink. He does not deprive himself of it by swallowing large gulps of ice water.

It was," he says, "as if I had been without water for a week. I must say that at that time, I was very agitated, very nervous. Then, after I calmed down a bit, I decided to write my report. And I finally wrote down this: "I saw a flying saucer at the junction of Highways 6 and 63. Believe it or not!"

Herb waits for his shift to end and returns home, still in bad shape.

When the US Air Force recommends hypnosis

A night's rest does nothing to ease his discomfort.

"That morning, I had a headache. And there was a funny buzzing sound in my head. As soon as I started to fall asleep, this noise increased. I also had a red mark on the nerve that runs down my ear. This mark was about 5 centimeters long and 1 centimeter wide. I figured I had bumped into something, and I didn't think anything more of it."

Herb needs peace and quiet more than anything. But since our man is a policeman, the story quickly gets out. The Lincoln and Omaha newspapers picked up the story. TV followed, as well as national radio, reporting on the strange face-to-face encounter with a law enforcement official. This is not a trivial matter.

Following the statement in his logbook, the US Air Force was immediately alerted and decided to investigate. The members of the Condon Committee asked Herb to get on a plane and go to Boulder, to the headquarters of the University of Colorado. He did so. On February 13, 1968, he met with a UFO study group created by the American government. And it was a first because the US Air Force decided to question our witness under hypnosis.

Herb says, "We were brought into room 202 of Woodbury Hall on the University of Colorado campus. Dr. Leo Sprinkle, a psychiatrist at the university, put me under hypnosis. I had no idea what it was all about. Dr. Sprinkle put me in a kind of trance. There, it was discovered that I had done much more than see a UFO."

The National Enquirer, a tabloid newspaper, devoted its cover to the story, with the headline: "US Air Force Asks Doctor to Use Hypnosis to Prove Good Faith of Police Officer Who Reported Flying Saucer". A full-page photo of Herb is shown next to a portrait of Edward Condon, who came to the event.

It is said that Dr. Condon and his team were stunned when they heard our witness, under hypnosis, make incredible revelations.

An amazing encounter

Accompanied and supported by William Wlaschin, his superior, what does our witness reveal?

Plunged under hypnotic regression with the help of a pendulum, the details flow. The 25 missing minutes are gradually reconstituted. A dramatic turn of events! Herb tells of having had a privileged and prolonged contact with the crew members of the UFO. After seeing the saucer, the engine of his car stalled. The headlights on his car dimmed. Then, something extravagant happened. To better appreciate the strangeness, here is an excerpt from the recorded exchanges between Herb and Dr. Sprinkle:

DOCTOR: Did you try to pull out your gun?
HERB: I was prevented from doing so.
Dr: Did you use the car radio?

H: I couldn't turn on the switch. I was prevented from doing so.

Dr: And what happened then?

H: Something approached my vehicle.

Dr: Could you see the features of this being approaching?

H: No, it was all white and very blurry.

Dr: Do you know where they come from?

H: From Venus, Jupiter and other planets. They come from a neighboring galaxy.

Dr: What are their intentions?

H: They don't mean us any harm.

Dr: Why did they land in Ashland?

H: They wanted to get electricity from our high-voltage lines.

Dr: How do they do it?

H (long pause): I can't say at the moment.

Dr: How does their device work?

H: It acts by cancelling gravity.

Dr: How does he do that?

H: I can't say. This is not the time or the place.

Herb is not doing well

After this hypnosis session, Herb is subjected to various psychological tests. Then he is auditioned during long hours.

Herb Schirmer, accompanied by his boss William Wlaschin, shows the pendulum that was used during his hypnosis session

Back in Ashland, since his chief has decided to leave his post, Herb is promoted to head of the local command. He becomes the youngest police chief in the Midwest. But unfortunately, in the days and weeks that followed, his physical and psychological condition deteriorated. He struggles to carry out his police duties for another two months, but eventually resigns.

I wasn't paying attention to what I was doing anymore," he says. It was obsessive, I kept asking myself what really happened to me that night. My migraines were getting worse and worse. I was stuffing myself with aspirin like a person stuffs himself with popcorn. You can't be a good police officer when you have problems like that. That's why I ended up quitting."

A providential help

Concerning this case classified n∞ 42, and very embarrassing for the US Air Force, the Condon report draws a rather laconic conclusion: "The witness said he suffered from 20 minutes of amnesia during which he would have been close to a UFO. However, no evidence was provided that a physical object landed there. Furthermore, tests undergone by the witness - with his consent - did not prove that the object he said he saw was physically real. "

Dr. Leo Sprinkle, on the other hand, states, "There is no doubt that the witness believes in the reality of the events he reports. "

This, of course, does not reassure Herb. What really happened to him? What was the nature of this ship and its strange occupants? Nobody gives him the answers he hopes for. Conclusion: our witness goes more and more badly. His daily life is upset. He then asks for help to ufological associations which, it is a relief, seem to take him seriously. He meets in particular the ufologist Eric Norman (whose real name is Warren Smith). Herb confides to him again: "Before that, I had never thought about these stories of flying saucers. Or the consequences. But when the Condon Committee investigation revealed that I was missing half an hour from my schedule, it shook me. I know a lot happened that night. It's there, somewhere, buried in my brain. But I can't get it out. "

Eric Norman then offers our patrolman a second hypnosis session. It takes place in Des Moines, Iowa. It is Loring G. Williams, a professional, is in charge. The test seems so successful that other sessions will follow... And little by little a strange puzzle is put in place, reporting what Herbert Schirmer claims to have experienced: a singular face-to-face encounter with beings from elsewhere.

New details

What does our witness say, under hypnosis? First of all, he says that this night of December 3, when he sees the UFO at the junction of the expressways, he is very intrigued.At that precise moment, the engine of his car stalled. He tries to call for help, but his radio does not work anymore. As he gets closer, he can see the machine more and more clearly. And it is hardly believable! It is not a truck. It's a flat, elliptical, metal contraption. A flying saucer, sitting there on the side of the road!

Herb panics. He wants to leave the place as soon as possible. But something prevents him from doing so. Then, against all odds, two beings get off the ship and head for his car. Herb is terrified. He tries to grab his gun. He can't. He is as if paralyzed. One of the beings points a small instrument at the car... which is suddenly surrounded by a kind of green gas !

Herb rolls down his window. He doesn't want to, he says, but something forces him to do it. One of the humanoids touches him on the neck, under the ear exactly. It hurts like hell!

Herb leaves his vehicle in spite of himself. The creature stares at him. The eyes of this entity are strange, disturbing, they look like "the eyes of a cat".

The humanoid asks, "Are you the watchman *over* this place?" Herb replies, "I'm a policeman." The creature asks him again: "Would you be able to shoot at our ship?" "No," answers Herb. As if reassured, the ufonaut then invites the policeman to board the saucer.

The ship

The creatures welcome Herb and reveal to him that their vessel is made of pure magnesium. Our witness distinguishes, in a main room, a large console and two small seats of triangular shape facing a vast control screen.

The crew of the machine is composed of 4 members. They are of small size. They measure between 1 meter and 1,30 meter, at most. They are however very muscular, rather dry, having, it seems, "not an ounce of fat". Their torso is large and powerful. They move and move in a rather rigid way, a bit "military".

Their skull is thinner and longer than that of humans. Their gaze is fixed, without any eyelid movement. Their pupils dilate and shrink a bit like a camera lens. Their nose is flat. Their mouth is reduced to a slit that does not move. Their skin is quite pale, of a surprising white gray. They are dressed in a kind of tight silver-gray suit and are wearing boots. On their suit, we can distinguish an emblem, a kind of crest which represents a winged snake (Quetzalcoatl or the Chinese dragon?). These entities wear gloves. And, enclosing their head, a hood. It would be rather a kind of thin and rigid helmet equipped with a small antenna at the level of the left ear.

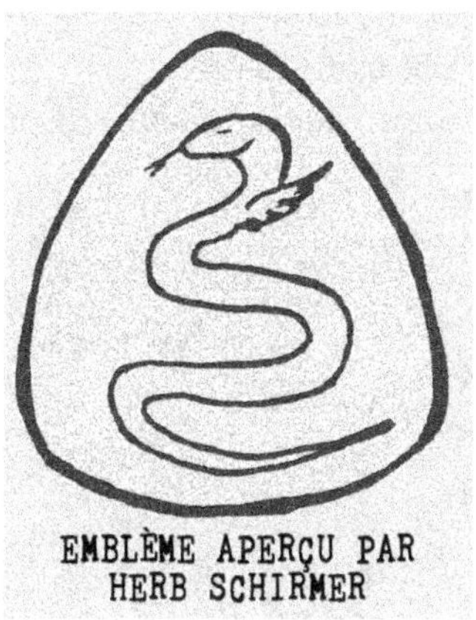

A telepathic dialogue

A long telepathic dialogue is established between Herb and these entities.

Herb sums up this exchange by saying, "They came because we Earthlings handle everything so badly. However, they have no particular message to convey. They have landed in Ashland to get electrical power. They get their power from our high voltage lines. When they decide to address an Earthman, they do so at random. They have no selection criteria. It is luck that decides on the meetings. They collect plant and animal samples on our planet. They carry out a hybridization program, and for this they sometimes use humans. They are also part of an observation mission. They have been visiting us for a long time and have underwater bases, notably off the coast of Florida and Argentina. They have a protective equipment against which we cannot do anything: a force field that surrounds their ships. It is this particular field that stops car engines and turns off radios. They do this because we are a hostile species, very aggressive."

In conclusion, the entities add this cryptic phrase: "Of course, we want you to believe in us. But don't believe everything."

What do they mean by that? In fact, during the exchange, the main entity repeated several times: "We want to keep people confused in front of us..." Or, "We want to maintain some confusion in your public mind." What to understand?

Herb then realizes that it is time to separate. The two entities that appeared at the beginning gallantly walk him to his car. Staring him straight in the eye, they say, "You will not tell anyone that you boarded our ship. You will simply say that the moment you saw it, it took off immediately. You will say that and nothing else. We will come back to see you twice in the future."

Our policeman finds himself in his Plymouth, without really understanding. He feels both bad and lost.

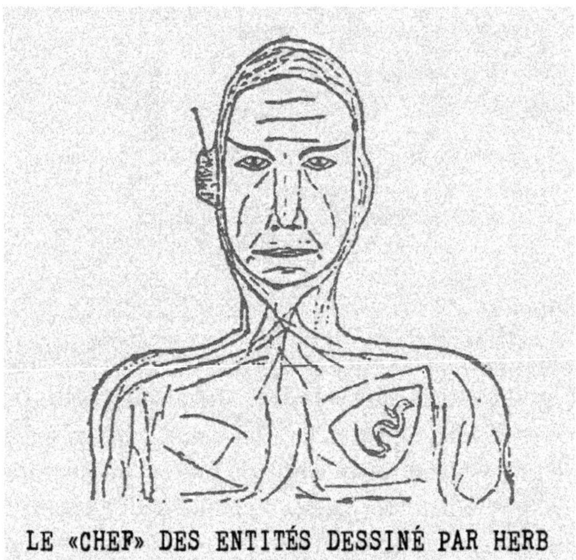

Herb tells

"The minute I left that ship, all of a sudden I was myself again. And I was totally terrified. Inside the ship, I didn't feel much. But when I got out of it, I was suddenly shivering, sweating, hot, nauseous... I got back to my company car, turned around and went back to the police station. During this trip, I must admit that I was speeding! I also tried to reach the Wahoo Sheriff's Office, but the radio was not working.

As soon as I arrived, I jumped out of the car. And there I saw that the wall clock in the police station said that it was 3 o'clock in the morning. I went straight to the bathroom, I went there to drink because I was very hot. Our police station was small, so I went into the main room. I sat down at my desk. I lit a cigarette and thought, "Wow, what happened to me? Did I really see a flying saucer? Did I really experience this?"

I opened my logbook. I thought about those 20 minutes or more that I didn't remember. I had to make a record of what I had just experienced, whatever it was. So I took my pen and wrote simply this: "This December 2, 1967, at 2:00 a.m., I saw a UFO at the junction of Highways 6 and 63. Believe it or not!"

A real way of the cross

Herb Schirmer's name is now splashed across the front pages of newspapers across the country. Week after week, the press is pounding away. It must be said that this story of a policeman having had contact with entities from beyond space is a first! The American public is fascinated by the story. The daily *Omaha World-Herald* published a first article on December 6, 1967 entitled: "Policeman saw a UFO hovering near Ashland". On February 16, 1968, the *Omaha Word-Herald* drove the point home: "Policeman who saw UFO 'remembers' under hypnosis: beings from this saucer said they would return."

As is often the case, seeing a UFO and talking about it publicly is damaging to witnesses. Herb Schirmer is no exception to the rule. Following his deposition, he lived a real nightmare. Mocked, abused, threatened, his life became a living hell. His wife, claiming that he is mentally disturbed, leaves him. And the years which will follow will be a long way of cross. He recounts:

"After my testimony, the TV came. And with it, the press, the newspapers, the radio stations... I was soon inundated with phone calls. Two days later, the ridiculous started to happen. For example, a man ran three blocks to meet me. He was panting. He owned a Goodyear tire store in Nebraska. He said to me, "Herb, if you should happen to see another flying saucer land, try selling them my tires!" My phone would ring and it would say, "Hello, this is Mars!" Stupid stuff like that. One day I was in Florida, at a hotel like this, and a man asked me, "Are you Herb Schirmer?" I told him I was. He said, "My name is Mr. What's-his-name. I was kidnapped too, but in a police van! This time, I thought it was pretty clever.

"The U.S. Air Force, the Condon Committee, Project *Blue Book* came to Nebraska to investigate and interview me. They realized that there were 25 minutes missing from my logbook, 25 minutes that I had no memory of. So they said, "You have to go to Boulder." I agreed. They took me there and I met a team of ufologists and a lot of people. They gave me a lot of tests... When I was in Boulder, the people were courteous, really friendly. But the night I came back to Ashland, it was different. In Ashland, in our beautiful local cemetery, they hung a mannequin from a tree by the neck. They hung a huge star on it and on that star they wrote: HERB. They also put a cowboy hat on him. Then they riddled him with bullets, put red paint like blood. They really did it big. Then they called an ambulance, unhooked the body, put it on a gurney with a sheet over it and took it to the morgue. They thought it would scare me. But they didn't, actually. They wanted to terrify me. It was a failure. I laughed most when I found out about it in the paper and saw the pictures. But when I was in Boulder, they dynamited my car. It made me mad. I had paid for it out of my own pocket. Now, I admit, I was mad.

"As far as my family is concerned, I went to my father. I said to him, "Dad, you who served for 27 years in the US Air Force, do you believe that UFOs exist?" He said neither yes nor no. He just said, "Son, if what you're saying is the truth, stick to it." That's what I've never stopped doing."

Epilogue

This is the amazing story of Herbert Schirmer, one of the most disconcerting ufological encounters in North America. Numerous articles, books and comic strips have been devoted to him. There is even a *coloring book* about his adventure, a coloring book for children.

In 1975, a vinyl record, produced by E. Lee Spiegel, was published by the *Columbia House* label. Its title: *UFOs: The Credibility Factor*. We can hear the great actors of North American ufology, such as Donald Keyhoe or J. Allen Hynek. It also includes the very moving testimony of Herbert Schirmer!

What remains of this strange adventure today? In fact, if you look on the net, you will realize that this case is far from being forgotten. Recently, a young American cartoonist and screenwriter, Michael Jasorka, has created a 56-page comic book entitled *December 3rd 1967*, which details the abduction of our night patroller. The book is sold with a CD where you can hear Herb tell the story of his unique face-to-face encounter. Jasorka had the chance to meet Herb. He says of him: "He was a very authentic person. And I believe in his story."

In 2019, a brewer came up with the idea to create a beer in tribute to Herb. The beer is called *Star, Snake, Dank, IPA* (IPA stands for *India Pale Ale*, a top-fermented beer style of English origin).

Herb Shirmer left us in 2017. Let's dream that in the confines of the stars, he will now toast with his visitors, with plenty of ambrosia.

Sources

Omaha World-Herald, December 6, 1967 - *Ashland Gazette*, December 7, 1967 - *Omaha World-Herald*, February 16, 1968 - *The UFO Investigator*, vol. IV, No. 5, March 1968, p. 1 - *Ashland Gazette*, February 22, 1968 - *Flying Saucer Review*, vol. 4, No. 4, July-August 1968, pp. 18-19 - Dr. Edward U. Condon, *Scientific Study of Unidentified Flying Objects*, Bantam, 1969, p. 389 - Eric Norman, *Gods, Demons and UFOs*, Lancer Books 1970, pp. 169-193 - Ralph and Judy Blum, *Beyond Earth: Man's Contact with UFOs*, Bantam, 1974 - *The Oregonian, Portland*, August 10, 1974 - *The Register*, October 30, 1974 - *The Province, Vancouver*, March 20, 1976 - *Omaha World-Herald*, April 26, 1976 - *CERPI* No. 10, February 1977, pp. 9-11 - D. Scott Rogo (ed.), *Alien Aductions: True Cases of UFO Kidnappings*, Signet Classics, 1980, pp. 112-121 - *Ashland Gazette*, 8 April 2004.

VIII. The UFOs of the Hudson Valley

Among the waves of UFO sightings, this one remains unjustly confidential. However, between 1982 and 1995, 7,000 American citizens declared having seen a strange vessel in the sky of the State of New York. And that is without counting those who - by fear of ridicule or by modesty - chose to remain silent.

It is therefore undeniable that the American East experienced an unprecedented UFO invasion. The regional press of those years reported a mass of testimonies relating to triangular-shaped machines. As a result, civilians, pilots and police officers - a good number of trained observers - demanded an explanation from the authorities. Or at least, an official and detailed investigation. Unfortunately, this was not the case.

However, the number and the coherence of these reports exhort us, still today, to question ourselves, to search the archives. For is this not, as J. Allen Hynek, Philip J. Imbrogno or Bob Pratt - these prestigious ufologists and investigators - have declared, "one of the most important UFO sightings of all time?"

Location of observations

Located north of New York City, the Hudson Valley stretches nearly 250 kilometers from the tip of Manhattan to Albany, the state capital. Described by the *National Geographic* travel guide as one of the world's top 20 must-see destinations, the valley is known for its scenic beauty and the many activities it offers: kayaking, hiking, rock climbing, swimming or skiing in winter. A National Heritage Area and the nation's first wine country, it follows the Hudson River, which marks the border between the states of New York and New Jersey.

It was here that mysterious celestial objects began to appear in the 1980s. These observations took place on a territory of 3 600 km² including the counties of Westchester, Putnam and Dutchess for the State of New York. And the counties of Fairfield, Litchfield and New Haven for Connecticut.

Portrait of the phenomenon

Most witnesses describe a triangular vessel. Or V-shaped and boomerang-shaped. It is very large, even gigantic, as big as a soccer stadium. Some people have compared it to "a flying city". Others, because it obstructed the sky, thought "the sun was going down because it was so big".

It is equipped, along its fuselage, with multicolored lights: red, green and amber. And of big white headlights. Its mass is dark, matt, metallic, and according to some worked of complex structures, traps or various beams. It seems particularly attracted by lakes and ponds.

The UFO is able to remain stationary for a long time. Then to move away at a dizzying speed. It is completely silent or emits a weak "electric motor hum". It sometimes seems to interact telepathically with the witnesses, which seems insane.

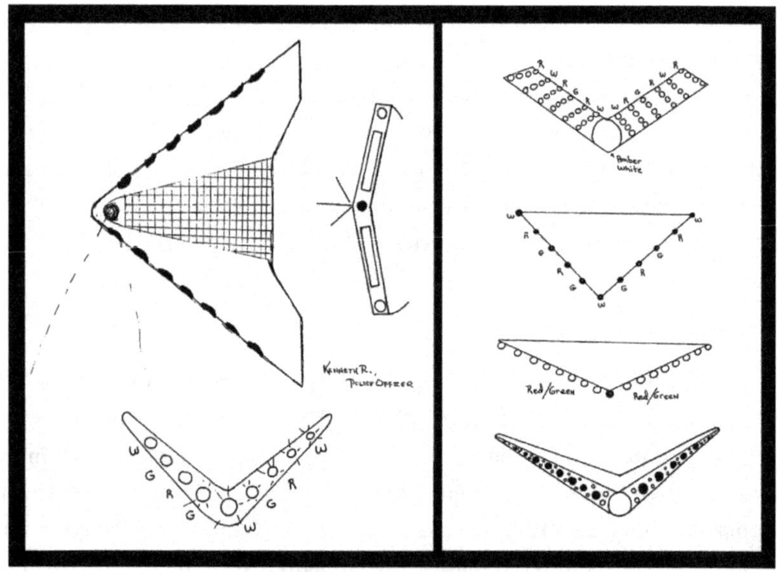

Drawings of flying objects seen by witnesses

An initial observation

Date: 1ᵉʳ January 1982.
Location: Kent, a city in Putnam County, USA.

Our witness, in his forties, is a retired New York City police officer. He has just moved into a new house with his wife and two children. As a "baptism", he throws a bottle of champagne which breaks on the walls of the new house. His wife is worried that the children will get hurt by the shards of glass. Forced to do some cleaning, our policeman returns to collect the scattered shards. Then, looking up, he saw a group of red and green lights in the sky. Here is what he says:

"These lights looked like they were connected by some kind of structure. The thing was boomerang or V-shaped. I could hear a slight deep hum. It sounded like a factory with many machines running in the distance."

The former policeman felt a strange vibration in his chest. Equipped with a camera, he films the UFO hovering 50 meters above the house. Suddenly its multicolored lights go out. And in their place, three big white headlights delimit a triangle. Then these headlights go out in their turn... And the initial lights reappear.

"The lights were so powerful that I could see the ground around me... I had never seen anything like that before. And I could tell it wasn't a device I know."

The same evening...

That same evening, at midnight, a 55-year-old warehouse manager came across the same vehicle, not without emotion. This witness is named Edwin Hansen and lives in Kent Cliffs, New York. As he was driving along the highway, he saw a group of stationary lights in front of him.

"At first," he says, "I thought it was a helicopter examining the ground with its searchlight." Intrigued, he scans the sky. And at the same time, he noticed that several cars parked on the side of the road to observe this phenomenon. The object then starts to describe, all up there, tight flips.

"It projected a beam of white light to the ground. And then I saw that it wasn't a helicopter because it was right in front of me and I couldn't hear any noise. I thought to myself, "I wish it was coming closer so I could get a better look at it." As soon as that thought crossed my mind, the object started to descend and headed straight for my car! It turned off its searchlight and hovered about 100 feet above the road. It was shaped like a boomerang, with lights moving along its wings. A sort of long triangular tail appeared behind the boomerang lights. It was so huge that it completely filled the sky."

The object progresses slowly towards our witness who, terrorized, starts to honk frantically, in the hope of making it flee. Moreover, blinded by the intense lights of the machine, Edwin must protect his eyes with his hand. But the UFO gets closer, projecting a ray of light on the road. Our witness, giving in to panic, starts to scream, begging that this damned thing disappear. Nothing makes it, the UFO is very close from now on. Suddenly, our man feels like a form of communication is established between this object and him. "I felt thoughts that were not mine, and a kind of voice told me not to be afraid. Then suddenly the object moved away and the beam of light went out."

Without asking for anything else, Edwin started the car and hurried home. He did not want to tell anyone about his strange adventure. His wife said that the following nights, he stayed outside for long periods of time, walking and scanning the sky intensely.

Miss O'Driscoll's observation

A year goes by and our machine is rather discreet. But in February 1983, it reappeared. And this time, it gives a breathtaking demonstration.

Date: February 26, 1983.
Location: Kent, a city in New York State and Putnam County.

Our 38-year-old witness is Monique O'Driscoll, an employee of the Brewster City Psychiatric Clinic in Lake Carmel. That evening, accompanied by her 17-year-old daughter, Monique was driving home. The sky is clear despite the night. Suddenly, the car radio began to crackle loudly. Here is what our witness says:

"My mother lives in Kent, near Route 52. After having dinner at her house, my daughter and I went home. We hit the road around 8:30 p.m... Suddenly, my daughter said, "Mom, look at those lights on the hill!" I replied, "Well, there are some partying up there!" Those lights were flashing like a strobe light, but more intensely than a disco. Then suddenly they started moving. My daughter said, "Actually, there are no houses up there. That hill is deserted." "

The two women discover that it is in fact a gigantic object progressing slowly in the sky. As they drove onto *White Pond*, a road with little traffic, the object came into view in front of their car. "These lights were intense and impossible to describe. They were red, blue and gold..."

Monique then leaves her vehicle and finds herself directly under the machine. Her daughter, terrified, yells: "Mom, come back, they are going to take you away!" But our witness does not listen to anyone from now on, she will admit to having been as if hypnotized. "The object was very low, 4 meters above the telephone poles. After 3 or 4 minutes, it started to move away. I thought, "Oh no, don't go away! I still want to watch you." This may sound crazy, but I'm sure he heard me. The moment I thought that, he stopped, turned around and came back to me. It was shaped like a boomerang. Its lights were flashing in a definite sequence, like a computer. It was floating in the air, huge. My daughter tried to make contact on the car›s CB radio, but it was impossible because of static interference. The thing was completely silent. If a monster of this size had been equipped with an engine, many a window would have been shaking. I could see its lower part perfectly. It was very solid. There was a whole mechanism there, criss-crossing, tubular and long elements protruding, all covered by a heavy metal grid. I was so close that if I had thrown a ball, I would have hit it. It was as big as a soccer stadium, much bigger than my mother's house! Between sixty and a hundred meters from one end to the other. I followed it for a short while, then pfft! it was gone. Just as quickly as that."

Monique then returns to her vehicle. Her daughter is scared to death: "Mom, you're completely crazy," she says reproachfully. If the machine had kidnapped you, what would I have done?" Imperturbable, Monique answers: "Don›t worry, I have a good life insurance."

Our witnesses set out again in pursuit of the boomerang. They caught up with it on *Farmers Mill Road*. "I got out of the car again," confided Monique, "and I looked at it... We could see it and suddenly it was gone."

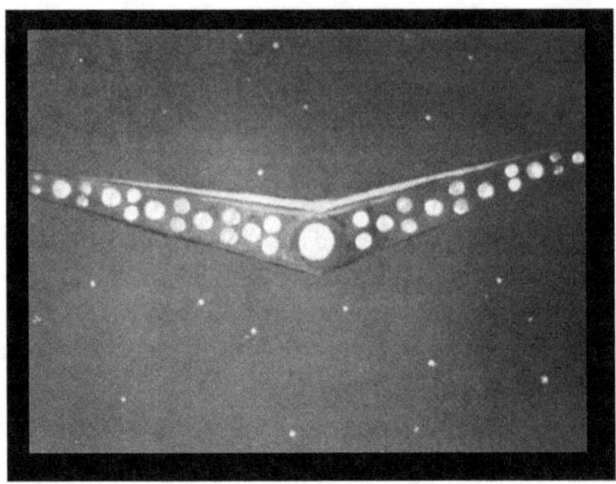

The machine seen and drawn by Monique O'Driscoll

Sources

Reporter Dispatch, White Plains, September 11, 1983 - *Inquirer,* Philadelphia, September 28, 1984 - *UFO Review #20,* 1984, pp. 1, 10.

Dennis Sant's observation

Date: March 17, 1983.
Location: Brewster, New York, in Putnam County.

The witness, Dennis Sant, is in his thirties and holds an important position in local government. Fearing the reaction of his superiors, this assistant to the Putnam County clerk hesitated before confiding in him. However, out of a sense of civic duty, he finally agreed to testify.

Coming back from a religious meeting and accompanied by his two children (6 and 9 years old), this thirty-year-old returned home. It was then that he saw a large triangular object flying over the garden of his house. I noticed," he says, "over the backyard of my home a large L-shaped object. It looked like a tractor trailer parked in the sky. It was there for about five minutes. From one end to the other, it was at least 100 feet long and made no noise."

It's almost 9 p.m. By the time the kids are settled in for the night, Dennis suddenly feels the urgent need to get out, a powerful and pressing desire to go back outside "with the visceral feeling that something is waiting for him outside.

Our witness then sees the machine above the road 84. A garland of lights flickers on its hull, which seems metallic. He warns his father and his children who join him at once.

"The object was hovering over a truck... And I was jealous of those truckers who, parked on the side of the road, could see it up close. I felt a crazy, extreme desire to observe this UFO more closely. At that precise moment, the object negotiated a 360 degree turn, as if it was pivoting on a wheel. I saw that it was in a V-shape and it started to move towards me. Then it stopped about 200 feet from the house. And about 30 or 40 feet above the trees. It stayed stationary for at least 5 minutes. My father and I walked towards the object. I had, in the past, read some articles about UFOs. And I had told myself that the day I would see one, I would probably be very afraid. However, this encounter was far from being frightening. For me, it was a spiritual experience, rich in emotions. The 19 to 20 minutes during which I observed this machine were like a kind of self-examination, an introspection to know who I was. By approaching us, we could distinguish perfectly the shade of its lights: red, amber, green. With a kind of big white beacon in the middle. These lights then gained in intensity, illuminating at the same time the surroundings, the road and a close swamp. The children, terrified, ran back into the house to take refuge.

I watched the object with my dad for another 2 minutes, we started walking under it. It looked like it was the width of a soccer field. It was metallic gray, very dark... I could hear a faint engine noise, really soft. And not very noticeable until it was very close.

The object stayed there for another minute. Then I was afraid it would land. As I thought about it, it flew away at the speed of a blimp... I watched it for another 2 or 3 minutes, before it went out of my field of vision. I was frightened, but I was sorry he was gone."

Dennis then contacts the sheriff's office.

"I learned that night, a little further north, lots of cars had pulled over to the side of the road as the object flew over the entire area. I then gave an interview to a newspaper and told them, "Please don't mention my name, I just want to warn the citizens that there is something hovering in our sky." I don't know if this craft is from somewhere else. But our area is between the 3 New York airports, and it's in the path of 5 small local airports. So we in this community are very familiar with everything that flies overhead. But this object did not look like an airplane at all. It didn't look like anything I've ever seen in my life."

March 24, 1983

During the night of March 24, the UFO manifested itself and showed itself ostensibly. It is without question one of the craziest moments of this wave. The daily *Reporter Dispatch* of September 11 notes: "It was like *War of the Worlds* narrated by Orson Welles, once again. Except this time, there was no need to turn on your radio. All you had to do was look up to the sky. On the night of March 24, hundreds of citizens in Westchester and Putnam did just that. Motorists pulled over to the side of the road to scan the sky. Mothers clutched their children and hid inside their homes. Between 8:30 p.m. and 11 p.m., police station switchboards were flooded with calls from curious, puzzled and hysterical citizens."

A gigantic and silent machine, covered with intense lights, flew for more than an hour over the towns of Yorktown, Somers and Carmel. Several thousand people saw it. It was close to mass hysteria.

"People couldn't believe their eyes," testifies Sergeant Vincent Puma, an officer with Carmel Police Headquarters. "They kept reporting this huge thing in the sky. It literally drove them crazy."

The object caused a massive traffic jam at the intersection of Routes 202 and 35 when motorists stopped to observe it. Some witnesses were terrified and rushed home. Others, more curious, have only one desire: to follow it wherever it goes.

Among the many testimonies collected, here are a few briefly.

Ed Burns, an IBM project manager who resides in the Yorktown Heights area, says, "If there is such a thing as a flying city, then this was a flying city. It wasn›t a small device, it was gigantic."

Bill Hele, chief weather officer for the National Weather Service, says, "I've been in the aviation business for the last 20 years, and when I saw this craft, I realized it didn't look like any known object."

John Piccone, a Yorktown resident who worked in aerospace, confirms, "The object passed over our driveway, and it looked like a V formation. One of the lights on the right side of its structure came off and moved back slightly. It was like it was watching us. About 10 to 20 seconds later, it re-entered the formation. I work on spacecraft as well as aircraft. There is no doubt in my mind that it was not an aircraft."

The police officer Kevin Soravilla, when he saw it, thought at first that it was a long distance plane in difficulty. But he quickly changed his mind: "The craft was equipped with 6 to 8 very strong lights, it was V-shaped. This thing was huge. I then thought of an airship. But after stopping, the object turned. It was then perpendicular to the ground. A blimp is incapable of maneuvering like that."

If we talk about maneuverability, this UFO behaved in a surprising, even unprecedented way. When a driver, alone on board, saw it in the distance, she discovered it a second later above her vehicle. A couple tells us that the object suddenly spun on the horizon at a dizzying speed before returning to its initial position, all in a fraction of a second... What is this craft that, parading above populated areas, seems to defy our known aeronautical laws?

We investigate

Philip Imbrogno, a science teacher and UFO enthusiast, says, "It all started in 1983. I still remember vividly that day, I was having lunch when the mailman came by and said, 'Phil, have you read the paper? It says that hundreds of people have seen a UFO over the county.' I told him I didn't know anything about it. I immediately grabbed the paper and started reading. At the time, I was a field investigator for CUFOS. That›s when Allen Hynek called me, "What the hell is going on in your sky?" I told him I was going through the paper, taking down the names of the witnesses and getting ready to interview them. Hynek replied, "Don't move, I'm coming!" I was flabbergasted. That was the beginning of a very long collaboration. From that point on, I was in frequent contact with Allen Hynek. He and I conducted a lot of field investigations. Dr. Allen Hynek was an exceptional man. He was a kind of mentor to me. Our friendship started there. He was a very discreet man, very humble. These are great qualities because he immediately put the witnesses at ease, at ease. At the beginning of the 1980's, don't forget that it was fashionable to suggest that witnesses of a UFO phenomenon were in general illuminated people, rather crazy. So people who had seen a UFO didn't dare talk about it. But when Allen Hynek interviewed witnesses, he was so respectful, so attentive, that people confided in him immediately. You felt at ease in his presence. We collected a lot of testimony from him. Allen Hynek became a true friend. I often flew to Arizona when he moved there. We worked on astronomy projects. I learned a lot from him over the years. And of course, it was with him that I investigated that exceptional wave of UFOs in the Hudson Valley."

What do the police think?

Overwhelmed, the police are at first very skeptical and reluctant. Eventually, however, they changed their minds. In the meantime, when Imbrogno asked Danbury police officers about the number of reports they were collecting, their response was scathing: "Well-rounded people don't report UFOs." To a person wanting to report a sighting, an officer at the same station replies with a sneer, "OK, go to bed and the pink UFO will go away." A bit cavalier. A Danbury officer summed up the general attitude perfectly when he said, "It can't be UFOs because they don't exist!

Not all officers feel that way. In the field, Imbrogno is assisted by Lieutenant George Lesnick, a 28-year veteran of the Fairfield Police Department. An avid UFO enthusiast, Lesnick, 56, travels throughout Westchester, Putnam and Dutchess counties, locating and interviewing thousands of witnesses. We feel like pioneers," he says. People here want an answer about these UFOs, and we do our best to try to solve the mystery..." Our investigator defines himself as a romantic, enjoying more than anything this exciting adventure, being a "UFO vigilante". Impressed by the testimonies, he declares: "This sum of observations in New York and Fairfield allowed me to meet the most credible witnesses. I have met judges, doctors, scientists, lawyers, professors, businessmen, police officers, aeronautical engineers, and meteorologists, all of whom are convinced that they have observed something truly strange over their heads."

First explanations

The first hypothesis put forward by the State Police is that of several microlights flying in formation. These ultralights would be equipped with special lighting. This theory is however questionable because most of the sightings take place at night. However, flying microlights at night is strictly prohibited. Moreover, flying in formation for these unstable machines, sensitive to the slightest gust of wind, is very risky. It is almost impossible that a group of microlights can remain in perfect formation, be stationary for long minutes, or turn synchronously as the UFO described by many witnesses. Finally, the last detail, a group of microlights flying in concert would certainly produce a devilish racket comparable to "a squadron of lawnmowers". But the triangles and boomerangs of the Hudson Valley are almost all silent.

Second hypothesis: military aircraft. According to the Schenectady *Gazette* of November 29, 1983, the UFO was a plane bringing back from Pasadena, California, cadets from the U.S. military academy after a match between the Navy and the Army. Surprising, because the UFO was seen in several places, several nights in a row. This plane would thus walk tirelessly above the Hudson Valley? Seeing that this explanation was not convincing, the Brewster and Carmel police officers adjusted their fire.

New theory: it would be in fact military planes taking off from Stewart airport - former US Air Force base - and going south, in New Jersey. Not knowing the route well, the pilots would have followed the road network to avoid getting lost, especially the *Taconic Parkway* (a well-lit north-south highway) where the UFO was spotted many times. Here again, this poses a problem. Can we imagine that the US Air Force would allow military aircraft piloted by inexperienced men to fly in formation over densely populated urban areas? And how is it that this UFO was seen flying north, east and west, when a formation of planes leaving Stewart Airport for New Jersey must travel south?

The hypothesis of microlights and military aircraft being not very admissible, the forces of order do not however disarm. The New York State Police announced, triumphantly, that they had finally solved the mystery of the UFOs. It would be a group of 4 to 5 small civilian planes flying in formation, setting up a hoax to fool the local population. These pilots from the town of Stormville obviously like to make jokes. Private K. C. Evans confirms this. He says he followed these lights emanating from several planes until they landed at the Stormville airport. After meeting with these pilots, he told *Reporter Dispatch*, "Basically, it›s four or five guys who like to do formation flying every week. And they get a kick out of reading the UFO sightings that appear in the press the next day. That's their thing, even if they don't really want to admit it. I could provide you with the names of these pilots because they are not breaking any laws." This explanation is being picked up massively by the country's media. It is even said that these pranksters call themselves "the Martians". It is undeniable that some merry men, adept at acrobatics, play UFOs from time to time. But some witnesses say that they are easy to spot. According to them, their little demonstration has nothing to do with the maneuverability and appearance of the large UFO observed.

However, the main police departments adopt this explanation, because they think it reassures the public. So no more worries, good citizens, sleep easy. An Asbury Park daily newspaper, dated September 13, 1984, confirms: "Obviously, we all know that UFOs are not piloted by extraterrestrial creatures watching us... But these UFOs do serve a useful purpose. They briefly divert our attention from the very real concerns of our planet. And they will, over the next few months, feed the conversations of future cocktail parties."

However, one object kept haunting the skies over the area. Beginning on March 24, it was seen regularly along the Hudson Valley, then in the Kingston area, then in New Paltz, near Hook Mountain, and finally in Rockland. It is also seen in northern Westchester, Putnam and southern Dutchess counties. It is found peacefully everywhere from southern Manhattan to eastern Danbury. Those who saw it vehemently rejected the official hypothesis. After seeing the massive object in the sky, Joanne Williams, a building inspector in Torrington, told a reporter for the *Hartford Courant*, "This explanation of planes flying in formation is a load of crap!"

A high resolution video

Date: July 24, 1984.
Location: Brewster, Putnam County.
10pm.

Robert Pozzuoli, vice-president of an important electronics company, lets his dog loose in the garden. Suddenly, he sees strange lights in the sky. He immediately calls Lori, his wife, and asks for his camcorder. He then takes stock of this strange phenomenon and films it.

Once the sequence is projected, we see a disk-shaped object with a series of 6 lights on its circumference. The object passes behind a tree. When it reappears, it looks different. The lights are multicolored and a red light flashes while escorting it. This video is first acquired by the ABC television channel. Their technician said upon viewing it, "I have never seen anything like this before. Every time I watch it, I get goosebumps. It's weird."

The video was then sent for analysis to Dr. John Baker of West Coast University in California. This specialist is formal: it is not about aircraft in formation. But what is it then? He doesn't know a damn thing and refuses to continue his investigation.

In 1985, as part of its program *American Undercover*, the famous television channel HBO devoted a report to observations of the Hudson River. For this, it entrusted the video to the *Jet Propulsion Laboratory* in Pasadena, California. An expert in computer development, Dr. Al Hibbs, is in charge of analyzing it. To do this, he uses the laboratory's computer, a multi-million dollar machine that has been used to process images of Mars, Jupiter, Saturn and Uranus taken by the Voyager and Viking space probes. Result: Hibbs is unable to identify the object in the video, it doesn't look like anything known!

While many take the film seriously, others scoff at it. Pozzuoli philosophically states, "People can ridicule me, I know I've seen something I can't explain. If it's not of this world, I'd like to know where it came from."

If it is impossible to determine with certainty its origin, on the other hand we know that after having been filmed by our witness, the UFO immediately took the direction of the nuclear power station of Indian Point.

The object filmed by Robert Pozzuoli

Source

Reporter Dispatch, White Plains, July 14, 1988.

Above a nuclear power plant!

This is probably the most striking and astounding observation of this entire wave.

Date: July 24, 1984.

Location: Indian Point nuclear reactor site, located on the Hudson River in Buchanan, New York.

The personnel of the power station had already observed a UFO - a craft of a hundred meters from one side to the other -, on June 14. On July 24, it happened again. This time, the UFO, with impunity, violated the high security space of the power plant, a space that no plane is allowed to cross without proper authorization. Carl, one of the security guards, recalls, "It all started when a guard called out, "Hey, the UFO is back!" Hearing this, we all ran to see it. There were 5 of us then, including 2 leaders... I found myself about 150 meters from the object when it came closer to the power plant. It looked like an ice cream cone. You could see that it was a solid object about the size of 3 soccer fields. At one point, it came directly overhead, and we were looking at it from below. It was still moving, but very slowly. I could have walked and stayed at its height, it must have been moving at less than 10 miles per hour."

The object was then positioned, less than 10 meters away, above the only reactor in operation at the power plant. That night, a wind blew up to 55 km/h, a detail that allowed us to exclude the hypothesis of a formation of microlights or small civil aircraft.

Here is how, after interviewing the main witnesses, investigator Philip Imbrogno summarizes this amazing visit: "On July 24, 1984, at 8:10 p.m., the object was filmed in Brewster, a town in New York State. This is the first high-resolution video that could be made of the object. 15 minutes later, the UFO headed west... And it went straight to the site of the nuclear reactors of the Indian Point power plant. 12 police officers and security guards witnessed what happened then. I should point out that this is military territory, under heavy guard, which houses nuclear reactor No. 3. The officers were in shock when the object appeared. A state of alert was immediately triggered. Their first impression was that a large aircraft was going to collide with the reactor. Hence the panic! But as the object got closer, they suddenly realized that it was not a conventional aircraft. They wondered, "What the hell is

   UFO: The 12 files that the Pentagon cannot explain

that thing?" The object then positioned itself and came to rest just above Engine #3, the only engine that was operating at the time to provide power to the New York City subway system. The officers walked under the object. They were able to observe it very closely. The UFO was gigantic, larger than a soccer field. And bigger than a C-5A, the world's largest plane with a 65-meter wingspan. It obscured the entire sky. According to witnesses, the base of the object was made of dark gray metal. Circular openings could be seen, like hatches, large enough to drive cars through. The object was completely silent. At that moment, the commander made the decision to shoot the object. The men grabbed their weapons. But just as they were about to open fire, the commander received an urgent call. He was then ordered, "Do nothing!" Simultaneously, the entire security system protecting the reactor failed. The motion detectors went out. The alarm system stopped working. An agent manning the cameras was able to film the object. I interviewed this man and he revealed that he was forced to tilt his camera 180 degrees in order to film the entire UFO. The day after this apparition, the officers were summoned early in the morning. A man dressed in civilian clothes was waiting for them. This man confiscated all the reports concerning the UFO, the radio recordings, the videos of the surveillance cameras. Then the commander addressed the men and said simply: "Nothing happened last night! Is that clear?" "

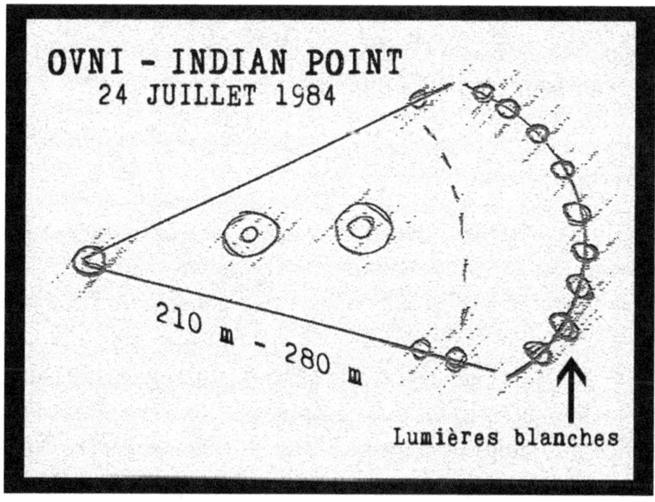

Sketch from the description of the Indian Point security personnel

A jam-packed conference

If the high authorities, embarrassed, claim that nothing is happening, the public, on the other hand, is crying out for an explanation. Philip Imbrogno and Peter Gersten, Peeskill's lawyer, decided to organize a meeting-conference around the Hudson Valley sightings. The date was quickly set: it would take place on August 25, 1984, from 10 a.m. to 10 p.m., at the Henri H. Wells Middle School, located on Route 312 in Brewster, on the border between Connecticut and New York State. A program was quickly put together: Budd Hopkins (abduction specialist), John Keel, John Fuller and Whitley Strieber attended. The cream of the ufology world gathers to discuss the phenomenon. But our organizers are anxious because the room still holds 500 seats. Even if they try to gather as many witnesses as possible, will they succeed in filling it?

As soon as the doors opened, it was a rush! At 10 o'clock, all the seats are occupied. The citizens arrive en masse. The huge parking lot is jammed. People pile in as best they can to listen to the speakers and witnesses. A large part of the audience remains standing. By noon, more than 1,500 people have already turned out.

Even more surprising, more than 75 journalists attend the conference. Some big newspapers are represented like the *New York Times* or the *Chicago Tribune*. Television stations like ABC, CBS and NBC sent reporters. The video of Bob Pozzuoli was broadcasted. 10 TV stations asked for it. It was a historic moment. This conference, which lasted until midnight, remains one of the biggest ufological events ever organized in the United States.

The witnesses confide in us

Following this conference, tongues are wagging. Philip Imbrogno can then paint a more precise picture of the phenomenon. He explains: "In short, the witnesses describe the same thing: an object the size of a soccer stadium, triangular in shape or sometimes like a boomerang, depending on how it appears. This object does not make any noise. It has red, green and orange lights. This object is gigantic. It is often followed by smaller, independent objects that dive into the lake. Many witnesses also saw red lights coming out of the huge UFO. These lights followed cars, people. It was as if they were taking pictures, collecting information and then re-entering the huge craft. The witnesses all described the same thing, the same object. We had testimonies from police officers. They told us that they left their posts in a hurry and started chasing this UFO. It was like a scene out of the Spielberg movie, *Close Encounters of the Third Kind.* I was able to interview more than twenty of these policemen. They were all stunned by what they saw. It shook up people's beliefs. Those who didn't believe in UFOs, when confronted with this triangle, now believe in it with all their might. They all told us that this thing, this object, was neither a mistake with something known, nor a plane. It was a gigantic spacecraft. Finally, many witnesses have provided us with a disturbing detail: this object is able to disappear in a flash and then reappear."

The investigator sees the UFO

On March 21, 1985, investigator Philip Imbrogno saw the UFO in his turn. It hovered in the air above Interstate 95, in Bridgeport, Connecticut. A real shock. He says, "The lights were rigid. There was no sound. It looked like an orange boomerang. We tried to follow it in our car and almost had an accident. People were looking up at him, frantically slamming on their brakes. The whole area was in a panic."

Before that night, Imbrogno was not convinced of the existence of UFOs, even though he had spent 10 years investigating sightings by others.

"Usually, a team of investigators never gets to see the UFO they are working on. But in this case, we saw it. That's when I was 100% convinced that we were dealing with a phenomenon that did not correspond to human technology. I'm not saying it's extraterrestrial. I'm just saying I don't know where it came from."

Meetings of the third kind

For some, the strangeness of the phenomenon goes even further. Indeed, some witnesses report seeing, accompanying the UFO, enigmatic beings. Philip Imbrogno, circumspect, notes that sometimes, in addition to the observations, "something mysterious" happens. Some facts seem difficult to believe. And yet... Here is a perfect example.

Date: October 1987.
Location: Candlewood Lake in Fairfield and Litchfield counties.

Our witness lives in Brookfield, on the west side of the lake. Here is his testimony: "It was mid-October, around 6 p.m., I was coming home from work. I had just driven down Candlewood Lake Road when I thought I saw a plane flying low in the sky. The object passed over the trees, but I didn't hear anything that would suggest a crash. However, it really disturbed me. I then turned off onto the airport road and as I started up the hill I noticed 4 cars parked without lights, most of them on the side of the road. I flipped on my headlights and my car came to a stop. I suddenly had no battery, no radio and no headlights."

Our witness then gets out of his vehicle. He approaches the motorists who are discussing on the side of the road. There are three men and a woman. Very excited, these people explain to him that a huge machine passed above them and made their cars stall. The object, triangular in shape, was completely silent. It was bright, with white and orange lights. It obviously descended behind the nearby hill to the west.

"It was getting dark and I could make out a glow in the woods. I wanted to go and see but no one wanted to go with me. I thought maybe it was a small plane that had crashed and I wanted to go check it out. I grabbed my flashlight and headed into the woods. I went about a quarter mile before I reached the hill. The glow was getting stronger and I knew there was something on the other side. As I climbed, the glow turned dark red and then an off-white."

When he finally reached the top of the hill, our witness saw a strange illuminated object. Considering the distance, it is difficult to distinguish the details. For that, he progresses more, with difficulty, through a very dense vegetation.

"I had to descend to reach a gap. I was stunned when I saw a dark triangle-shaped object hovering among the trees. It was very strange, because it was not flying above the trees, but in the middle of them... like a ghost! I mean, a craft with such dimensions should have broken branches and its engines should have blown the trees around. But there was nothing but silence.

"I wanted to get a little closer to it when I heard some noise coming from there. I then saw this figure wearing some kind of suit approaching the object. I immediately hid behind a bush. This man - if he was indeed a man - went straight to the object and looked in my direction. He was of medium height. His jumpsuit was dark with metal-like stripes glowing around his arms and waist. I didn't see his face, but I'm sure he was wearing some sort of helmet. I sensed that he knew I was there and I had thoughts in my head that I shouldn't come any closer. I was more than willing to obey. As I watched, this being raised its hand as if to say goodbye and

UFO: The 12 files that the Pentagon cannot explain

disappeared in a flash of red light. The object then faded away as if someone had turned it off."

Shocked by what he has just experienced, our witness runs back to his car. At the risk of being considered crazy, he realizes that he will not be able to tell this story to anyone.

"When I got to the road, there was no one left except for one man. He told me that the cars had restarted and the others had left. He himself had been "chosen" to stay to make sure I returned. He asked me if I had seen anything. I told him no."

A letter re-launches the investigation

In 1987, J. Allen Hynek, Philip Imbrogno and Bob Pratt published a book on these sightings entitled *Night Siege: The Hudson Valley UFO Sightings*. A must-read.

A few weeks later, an event reshuffles the cards. We remember that the video made by Robert Pozzuoli in July 1984 was analyzed by several experts. This without really official conclusion. However, at the beginning of 1988, a letter made public by the press and emanating from a division of the US Space Agency (the American space agency) reopens the debate. Signed by Lew Allen, director of the *Jet Propulsion Laboratory* of Pasadena (California), this document assures that the lights seen on the video in question "are attached to a unique and rigid device, such as a "ship"".

This made a big noise and swept aside the hypothesis of microlights and civilian planes from the Stormville airport flying in formation. The newspapers then dared to use headlines such as: "The Hudson UFO: not planes! This was enough to re-launch the investigation.

This document is of course taken seriously because the *Jet Propulsion Laboratory* is a private division of the *National Aeronautics and Space Administration* (Nasa). Nothing fanciful, therefore. Robert MacMillian, a spokesman for the *Jet Propulsion Laboratory*, was immediately contacted and confirmed that the letter was genuine and had been written by Lew Allen, the director. But MacMillian adds, suddenly cautious, that the opinion expressed in the document is only a "supposition" and that no further analysis will be made.

This makes Philip Imbrogno jump: "I can't believe they didn't do more analysis. Scientists are curious by nature. I think they've done more thorough research."

The press relays the information while revealing that the UFO of the Hudson River is becoming more and more discreet. It seems, for some time, to be deserting populated and urban areas... to haunt the water points and reservoirs of the country. Knowing that the State of New York - the 3^e most populated in the United States - has nearly 7,000 lakes, he has plenty to explore.

Source

Reporter Dispatch, White Plains, February 21, 1988.

Conclusions

What is this triangular object that - in a frantic concern of exhibition - flew over highways and houses? Endowed with an unprecedented maneuverability, we saw it appear and disappear in a flash. Or, in the middle of the sky, it tilted on its side and turned, in front of the stunned witnesses, "like a fairground wheel! Moreover, its speed in flight - or against the wind - was quite lower than the stall speed of an airplane.

Neither the police, the FAA, nor the US Air Force could offer a satisfactory explanation. The FAA investigated the case and tried to locate the prankster pilots in and around Stormville, but was unsuccessful. Then it lost interest in the case. One of its spokesmen, Louis Achitoff, said in an interview: "Why should we care about a UFO? If the pilot up there has a license and is flying at a good altitude, who cares what planet he came from? No comment.

Thus, the UFO of the Hudson Valley escaped the analyses, blurred the tracks, and evaded the very moment when it was thought to be held.

Philip Klass, a well-known skeptic, gave up trying to unmask him. In the August 1983 issue of *Omni* magazine, he said, "I have been researching UFO sightings for 18 years, and so far I have not found any evidence to suggest an unknown or extraterrestrial phenomenon. It would take a lot to convince me, but this could be the first unexplained case in 17 years."

The zealous investigators - J. Allen Hynek, Philip J. Imbrogno, and Bob Pratt - who conducted a lengthy investigation concluded, "This object is not a secret weapon, nor a hologram, nor a formation of planes, helicopters, or airships, nor, we believe, anything of human design. There is no conventional explanation for the Hudson Valley UFO. We don't know what it is."

In 1989, these majestic triangles left the state of New York, to come and frolic - with equal insolence - above Belgium.

   UFO: The 12 files that the Pentagon cannot explain

Sources

Gazette, Schenectady, November 29, 1983 - *The New York Times*, August 25, 1984 - *MUFON UFO Journal* No. 198, October 1984, p. 13 - *Discover, The Magazine of Science*, November 1984 (case illustrates cover) - *The Wilton Bulletin*, October 23, 1985 - *Times*, Beverly, August 11, 1986 - *Reporter Dispatch*, White Plains, September 25 and 28, 1987 - *American*, Waterbury, November 13, 1987 - *Courant*, Hartford, December 16, 1987 - *Times Union*, Albany, December 27, 1987 - TV show *"Unsolved Mysteries,"* Season 5, Episode 1, aired September 16, 1992 - *Coast to Coast AM* Radio Show: *"Hudson Valley Ufos & the Paranormal,"* April 22, 2008 - J. Allen Hynek, Philip J. Imbrogno and Bob Pratt, *UFOs on the Hudson River*, Trajectory, 2011 - Linda Zimmermann, *Hudson Valley UFOs*, Eagle Press, 2014.

IX. UFOs: abductions in the sky

"UFOs are a genuine mystery, as puzzling and fascinating today as they were when I first accepted the idea of their existence in 1975. The only thing I take for granted is this: the more we learn about the UFO phenomenon, the more complex it becomes, and the more we realize that we know so little about it. Whatever its nature, there is a dark side to this phenomenon..."
Bob Pratt

Bruce Maccabee, an optical physicist and former U.S. Navy employee - is particularly interested in incidents involving pilots and UFOs. He says, "It is sad to learn that many aircraft crash and that pilots, crew, and passengers lose their lives every year. In most cases, it is fairly simple to attribute these accidents to mechanical failure, bad weather or pilot error. There are also a considerable number of cases where an aircraft disappears for no apparent reason while flying over a lake or ocean. But usually traces are found afterwards, such as floating parts of the aircraft or life jackets. There remain, however, a small number of incidents in which an aircraft disappears under more mysterious circumstances: circumstances involving unidentified flying objects!"

It is precisely four of these cases that we will discuss.

The ultimate flight of Felix Moncla

An early case of alleged abduction dates back to the 1950s.

Date: November 23, 1953.
Location: Lake Superior, near Soo Locks, Michigan, USA.

Shortly after 6:00 p.m., U.S. Aerospace Defense Command radar detected a UFO over Lake Superior, the huge body of water that straddles the United States and Canada. An F-89C Scorpion jet, registration number 51-5853A, took off at 6:17 p.m. from Kinross Air Force Base. Guided from the ground, it tried to intercept this mysterious intruder.

The F-89C interceptor is piloted by 27-year-old Lieutenant Felix Eugene Moncla. In the rear cockpit, 1er Lieutenant Robert L. Wilson, age 22, a radar observer, also attempts to track the UFO. The interceptor, codenamed *Avenger Red*, is flying at nearly 500 miles per hour. It had enough fuel in reserve for 1 hour and 45 minutes of flight.

As Felix Moncla describes his approach to the intruder, his radio transmission is suddenly jammed by heavy electromagnetic interference. From the base, an Air Force team follows the operation. These men see the F-89C chase the UFO for 260 kilometers over Lake Superior. But once the communication was interrupted, the controllers noticed, dumbfounded, that the F-89C was getting dangerously close to its target. On their radar screen, in an incomprehensible way, the two *blips* - these signals designating the aircraft -, merge and suddenly disappear!

The controller hastily activates a search device. We suspect that Moncla and Wilson may have ejected before the collision. They have life jackets and inflatable rafts at their disposal. But they had to be quick, because they couldn't last long in the icy waters.

All night long, American and Canadian planes flew over the lake, patrolling at low altitude and regularly launching flares. At dawn, boats joined the search while planes combed the area for 150 kilometers. No trace was found, neither debris nor oil stains. The UFO, the plane and the two lieutenants seemed to have mysteriously vanished.

The Truax base quickly sent an official statement to the *Associated Press* saying: "The plane was tracked by radar and was seen colliding with an object 110 kilometers off Keweenaw Point in Upper Michigan. It was seen colliding with an object 110 kilometers off Keweenaw Point, Upper Michigan," and the *Chicago Tribune* headlined, "Interceptor plane with two men on board disappears over Lake Superior. The case, tragic and shrouded in mystery, caused a stir.

The US Air Force sputters

At first, the US Air Force staff tried to cover up the incident. It declared that the radar operators had misread or misinterpreted the data on their screen. There was therefore no collision.

Unconvinced, the NICAP (National Committee for Investigation of Aerial Phenomena) leads the investigation. In 1958, they exchanged several letters with the mother and brother-in-law of one of the missing airmen. They also discovered that the widow of the officer, who demanded some explanations, obtained surprising and contradictory answers from two representatives of the US Air Force.

- 1re explanation: while trying to identify a low-flying airliner, Felix Moncla would have slipped under the aircraft in question, without paying enough attention to his altimeter. He hit the water with his wing and crashed. The NICAP investigators are outraged: "This doesn't make sense. When spotting an unknown craft, standard and defensive procedures require the interceptor pilot to first shine his powerful headlights on it and then contact it by radio. No jet pilot would try to slip under an aircraft flying so close to the water. Nor would he need to, since all aircraft have identifications painted on their sides or on the tops of their wings."

- 2de explanation: the F-89C exploded at high altitude and no other aircraft was involved in the incident. This second version was obviously improvised in the emergency because the first one, by all accounts, was considered ridiculous. Here again, for the investigators, the explanation is absurd. If the F-89C did indeed explode at high altitude, why were no bodies or debris from the wreckage ever found? In an accident of this type, fragments of life jackets, rafts or parachutes invariably rise to the surface.

The US Air Force lies

In 1960, NICAP investigators sent a questionnaire to ATIC, the U.S. Air Force's technical intelligence service. One of the first questions asked was, "What are your findings concerning the Kinross incident where an F-89 interceptor disappeared while tracking a UFO? Were only body or aircraft fragments recovered?" The answer, obtained on June 1er 1960, was very brief: "ATIC has no knowledge of this case." Two weeks earlier, on May 16, 1960, Major L. J. Tacker, spokesman for the U.S. Air Force, had claimed the same thing in a letter addressed to investigator Richard Levine. This is surprising when one knows that the disappearance of the jet and of the two pilots was confirmed in November 1953 by Captain Robert C. White, head of information for the North American Air Force.

It is also the first time that ATIC has contradicted a senator. In fact, during a Congressional inquiry, Senator Byrd stated: "The Kinross incident in November 1953 was an unfortunate accident in which no UFOs were involved. The pilot successfully identified a Canadian company plane. Conspicuously, the F-89 encountered some problems on its return to base and ultimately crashed into Lake Superior. Senator Byrd received a complete dossier on the incident from the US Air Force. And copies were also sent to the chairmen and other members of the Senate Armed Services Committee. So why the lie?

From hypothesis to hypothesis...

Senator Byrd's version, in which the alleged UFO was in fact a Canadian airliner that had deviated from its flight path, was quickly dismissed. Indeed, the Canadian airlines insist, "None of our aircraft that day flew through that area."

Kinross Air Force Base then proposed a new explanation: the so-called UFO was a military aircraft belonging to the Royal Canadian Air Force. But after investigation, Captain Robert White, a press office officer at the Pentagon, concluded that the object seen 112 kilometers from Keweenaw was never identified. While claiming that there was never a collision, he revealed that the U.S. Air Force was completely unaware of the nature of the intruder. He said that the F-89C never intercepted a Canadian or similar aircraft. And that Moncla and Wilson did not make any distress calls before disappearing.

Another version was put forward: Felix Moncla, who is said to have suffered from vertigo, would have been taken ill and would have lost control of the plane which would then have crashed into the lake. This is enough to make a lot of pilots laugh. Just aberrant. Moncla would have engaged the autopilot while waiting for his discomfort to pass. And in the worst case, co-pilot Wilson would have been perfectly able to take over from him momentarily.

A sad hoax

Major Donald Keyhoe, who investigated the case, notes in his book *Strangers in Space*: "A letter came to me a little later from Moncla's mother. She said, "I suppose the Air Force has its reason for keeping the truth from us, but it is hard on a mother. God bless you for what you are doing." Filed in 1953, the accident report was never released." Under the U.S. Freedom of Information Act, or FOIA, and following a request made on December 27, 1993, this report will finally be made public.

The "Kinross affair" gradually sank into oblivion. But then, unexpectedly, it resurfaced in 2005. Adam Jimenez, a spokesman for the *Great Lakes Dive Company*, claimed that a team of divers had just spotted the wreckage of the F-89C on the lake bottom. As evidence, he posted underwater scans of the aircraft on the company's website. While searching for the remains of the *Cerisoles* and the *Inkermann*, two French anti-mine ships, they came across the sunken aircraft in 1953 with their Sharc2 sonar. From these scans, the team would have determined that the wing and nose of the jet were "sunk" in the lake bed, but that the canopy and fuselage were both intact. And, last but not least, the team also spotted an "unusual" object about 60 meters from the plane. The object," says Jimenez, "appears to be large and teardrop-shaped. It is exactly 64.77 meters from the F-89C. And the scan shows an interesting detail: a long trail behind it, as if it had crashed. [...] We can confirm that this object is metallic. We have distinguished a mark, like an impact, at the height of the missing wing of the F-89C Scorpion. It is possible that this missing wing is under the mysterious object". This was enough to create a big stir in ufological circles. However, the company's website quickly disappeared without a trace. And this exciting sighting story turned out to be a sad hoax.

Unanswered questions

Even today, no explanation for the disappearance of the F-89C is fully satisfactory. Many questions remain unanswered. For example, how can we explain the interference that interfered with Moncla's radio communication with the control tower? Was it due to magnetic interference emitted by the UFO? Or was it simply caused by the bad weather and the meteorological front that was progressing over the lake? It should be noted, however, that no radio communication problems were experienced by the F-89C search flights piloted by Lieutenant Mingenbach, Lieutenant Nordeck and Captain Bridges. These US Air Force officers crossed the same weather front very shortly after Moncla and Wilson.

One testimony also remains troubling: that of Lieutenant Mingenbach, who claimed to have picked up a radio transmission about 40 minutes after the F-89C disappeared. He said it sounded like an accidental transmission from Lieutenant Moncla. He almost certainly recognized his characteristic Southern drawl. Can we imagine then that the F-89C did not crash after it disappeared from radar? If so, what could have happened to the plane and the crew?

A documentary, directed by David Cherniak in 2007 and entitled *The Moncla Memories*, retraces the Kinross affair, summoning however strange "memories" from beyond the grave and a hypothetical extraterrestrial hybridization. For informed readers only.

In the Moreauville, Louisiana cemetery, a stele is erected in memory of Felix Moncla. The memorial plaque reads, "In loving memory of Gene, Felix Eugene Moncla Jr. 1ᵉʳ Lieutenant, U.S. Air Force, born October 21, 1926 and disappeared November 23, 1953, while intercepting a UFO near the Canadian border while flying an F-89 aircraft." Amazing, isn›t it?

Sources

The Capital Times, Madison, November 24, 1953, p. 1 - *The Fresno Bee*, November 26, 1953, p. 52 - *UFO Investigator*, vol. 1, no. 10, July-August 1960, p. 1 - *UFO Investigator*, vol. 1, n° 12, April-May 1961, p. 3 - *BUFOI Magazine n° 4*, March-April 1965, p. 32 - Donald Edward Keyhoe, *Les Étrangers de l'espace*, France-Empire, 1975, pp. 225-227 - *The Standard*, Warrnambool, Australia, October 22, 1986 - *UFOs: The Global View*, proceedings of the 6e international congress on August 16, 17 and 18, 1991 in Sheffield, England, p. 29 - *MUFON UFO Journal No.* 462, October 2006, pp. 3-13 - *Daily Press*, Ashland, November 20, 2003 - *Capital Times*, Madison, October 26, 2006 - *Capital Times*, Madison, April 26, 2007 - *Wisconsin State Journal*, Madison, October 23, 2008 - *Phenomena* No. 35, March 2012, p. 21 - *Phenomena* No. 76, August 2015, pp 4-5.

The Case of Captain Coyne

This story made a lot of noise. It quickly became a classic of ufology. Considered to be solid, it involved 11 witnesses, including 4 soldiers. This encounter in mid-air was classified among the 20 most credible UFO encounters ever reported in the United States.

Date: October 18, 1973.
Location: about 10 miles southeast of Mansfield, Ohio, south of the Great Lakes.
It is about 23:05.

After taking off from Columbus, a U.S. Army Bell Huey UH-1H helicopter ambulance is returning to its base in Cleveland. The aircraft belongs to a U.S. Army Reserve unit, the 316th Aeromedical Detachment based at Cleveland's Hopkins Airport. On board were four reserve soldiers. Lieutenant Arrigo Jezzi, 26, a chemical engineer and co-pilot of the aircraft, is at the controls and occupies the front left seat. Behind him is Sergeant John Healey, 35, a police officer and air doctor. Also in the back is Robert Janacsek, 23, chief mechanic. Finally, occupying the front right seat is Captain Lawrence "Larry" Coyne, 36, flight commander, reservist and Army veteran. A pilot since the age of 17, Coyne is what is known as a seasoned pilot.

The 4 men went to Columbus for routine examinations. Their return is under ideal conditions. Everything is calm. The helicopter is flying at an altitude of 750 meters. It is a clear, starry night. The outside temperature is 6° C. The aircraft flies over the fields and hills of the Mansfield area. The moon, in its last quarter, spreads a soft pallid light.

Suddenly, Sergeant John Healey sees a red light to the west that doesn't look like the lights of an airplane - by the way, at this time of day no aircraft is supposed to cross their flight corridor. He watches this for a brief moment and avoids talking about it. It doesn't seem to be a concern. 4 minutes later, it is Sergeant Robert Janacsek's turn to locate, on his right this time, in a southeastern direction, the same red light. It seems to be stationary and looks like a marker light on top of a radio transmission tower. But suddenly the light began to melt toward the helicopter at an estimated speed of 600 knots. Alerted, Captain Coyne thought it was an Ohio National Guard F-100 fighter. Fearing a collision, he immediately took control of the aircraft and began a descent of 150 meters per minute.

A green ray

Coyne immediately contacts Mansfield Air Force Base, "This is Army Helicopter 15444, do you locate a high performance aircraft in our area at 2500 feet *[762 meters]?"* No response, as he quickly loses contact with the ground controller. Coyne and then Jezzi try the various transmission frequencies in vain. They perceive perfectly the tone of the channels, which indicates that the radio works, but they can neither transmit nor receive. Quite incomprehensible.

Suddenly, the light becomes more intense. It now looks like the landing light of a Being 727 and is heading straight for the helicopter. This is clearly abnormal. Coyne begins a descent to dodge it. He says, "That light came at us at over 900 mph. At first it was distant, pretty far over the horizon, but within 10 seconds it crossed the sky and was closing in on us. At that moment, I thought a collision was inevitable."

The crew is extremely worried. The helicopter quickly loses altitude and tries, as best it can, to stabilize itself at 500 meters above the ground.

At 500 meters altitude," Coyne says, "I gathered all my energy in anticipation of hitting this thing. It was coming at us from the right, and it was literally coming at us. I was scared because we had little time to react. And this thing was awfully fast!"

Amazingly, the light stabilized at 150 meters above the helicopter. Thank God, there was no impact! But our 4 soldiers are not at the end of their surprises.

When we looked up," says Coyne, "we saw that it was actually an object that had just stopped above us. It had a gray, metallic-looking hull and was about 18 meters long. It had an aerodynamic profile and the shape of a large carinated cigar. It was equipped with a red light at the front. This light shone at a short distance from its nose. And a green light at the back reflected off its hull."

"It was like a submarine," Janacsek said.

This strange object, totally silent, does not present any visible mark, neither portholes, nor door, nor evacuation hole, just a central dome on its upper part. It seems quite solid because it occults a part of the sky and the stars. And then something inexplicable happens: the green light at the back of the object turns into a powerful beam that illuminates the helicopter's cabin. Coyne said, "That light swung around like a spotlight. It came at us, very bright, flooded the interior of the cabin, blotting out the glow of the red lights on our instrument panel, turning everything green." According to Coyne, the object was so large that it filled the right front windshield of the helicopter.

Sucked in by the UFO?

The strange object flew over the helicopter for a few seconds and then, negotiating a 45-degree turn to the right, quickly moved away to the northwest, toward Mansfield. The men were relieved, however, in shock. The danger of a collision seemed to be over!

But suddenly our 4 reservists are confronted with the strangest and most inexplicable experience of their entire career as pilots. All of a sudden, the helicopter is literally sucked in, as if attracted by the UFO for 700 meters. Was it caught by an updraft caused by the object? Is it due to the displacement of an air mass? A plasma effect? An intention of the intruder? In any case, the helicopter starts to rise at an extraordinary speed. It is incomprehensible because the rotor of the helicopter is tilted downwards, so it should logically descend. But it seems literally magnetized by the UFO. The crew is terrified. The needle of the magnetic compass is deviated, turning of approximately 1 turn every 15 seconds.

Against all logic, Coyne turned the helicopter's rotor upwards. At an altitude of 1,150 meters, the helicopter undergoes a sort of jolt and finally comes to a stop. Inside the helicopter, everything starts to work normally again. And radio contact is miraculously re-established.

An impossible speed

Very shaken, but happy to be alive, the men regained control of the aircraft and returned, this time safely, to Cleveland Air Force Base.

Back home, Larry Coyne says, "If I had been flying the helicopter by myself, I would never have reported this incident, because what happened that night is too implausible, and to talk about it would have risked my position as unit commander."

The next day, Coyne approached P. J. Vollmer, FAA operations manager at Hopkins Airport, to find out which agency he should report the incident to. Of his meeting with Coyne, Vollmer would confide in an interview conducted by J. Allen Hynek, "I'll never forget that man when he came to me. I've known Coyne for a while, not personally, but I really appreciate his honesty and his ability as a pilot. In a case like this, I don't know anyone else I would trust more. I trust his judgment without any hesitation. I don't know what happened, but one thing is certain: a slight tremor in his voice made me sense that he was very shocked. I understood that he wanted to talk about it. He needed to report this incident, but he didn't know who to talk to."

The four reservists also felt the need to confide in each other. They told the same story to the base commander and to investigators. The FAA authorities quickly opened an investigation but did not reach a satisfactory conclusion. To record the incident, a month later, Coyne completed an *Operational* Hazard report, a document for military personnel who face risk, especially in airplanes and helicopters.

P. J. Vollmer later made the following statement to the *National Enquirer* magazine: "This is the first time we have seen such an incident with a UFO. We are wondering what this flying machine is, how it could have driven a helicopter and increased its speed from 100 to 900 miles per hour without apparent damage. And according to Captain Coyne's flight instruments, his helicopter rose, through the layers of air, at a speed that is impossible."

Even today, the mystery remains.

On October 19, the helicopter's rotor underwent a Magnaflux-Zyglo test to determine if it had been subjected to abnormal mechanical stress and could have been damaged. The results were negative.

However, after the incident, it was found that the magnetic compass on board was completely out of order. It had to be replaced.

More troubling, Coyne contacted Mansfield Airport to listen to recordings of their radio exchanges. Inexplicably, their communications could not be recorded. Nothing remained of their dialogue during the incident.

Attempts to explain

Journalist and investigator Philippe Klass, an avowed skeptic, speculated that the crew saw a fireball that night caused by a meteor shower. The investigator Jennie Zeidman, collaborator of Allen Hynek, conducted a chronological analysis of the incident, second by second. According to her, the duration of the contact, the deceleration of the object and the angle of the movements completely eliminate the possibility that the object seen was a meteor.

Moreover, the meteor hypothesis does not hold if we consider the following points:
- red, white and green lights aligned in a fixed position on the object;
- no tail was observed;
- the way of flying of the object is contrary to that of the meteors;
- the object was observed for a long time, whereas meteors, in the best weather conditions, are visible for only 30 to 40 seconds.

The affair made a lot of noise. On November 4, 1973, the *Mansfield News Journal* reported the incident. So did the *Arkansas Gazette*. The newspaper stated: "Captain Lawrence Coyne, a helicopter pilot and reservist, doesn't believe in UFOs or other such 'stuff. But after the experience he had two weeks ago, he's not so sure.

A dozen witnesses

What is disturbing and makes this incident all the more credible is that we have no less than 11 witnesses, divided into 3 groups, who observed the scene from their car or their home.

Erma C, her son Charly, her niece Carene and two other teenagers were returning from a family dinner. They were driving on Route 430. At the bridge over the Charles Mill man-made lake, east of Mansfield, they observed the incident as they parked their vehicle on the side of the road. Two of the children (13 years old) got out of the car. They saw a helicopter and a large object described as "blimp-like", "as big as a school bus" and "pear-shaped". The object was hovering above the helicopter, about 650 feet (200 m) above the trees. The object then emitted a green light. This beam illuminated the children as well as the expanse of the road around them. "Everything turned green. The trees, the car, everything!" they said. The children then rushed to the vehicle in fright. Mrs. C. immediately started the car and drove off without asking for help.

Another example: Jeanne Elias, 44, was sitting quietly at home in Mansfield. It was after 11 p.m. and she was watching the evening news. Suddenly, Jeanne heard the sound of a military helicopter, so loud and so close that she thought it was going to crash into the house. The noise persisted for "a long time. When it stopped, John, her 14-year-old son, called her from his room. A noise had woken him up. And he was surprised to find that a green light bathed the room. John then realized that "some kind of object, just above the house, was shining brightly in his bedroom.

5,000 dollars!

In 1974, *The Cleveland Press* reported, "Following a near-collision with their aircraft, Larry Coyne, a helicopter pilot, and his fellow pilots received a $5,000 check for testifying to the incident. *The National Enquirer*, a weekly magazine, felt that these pilots provided the most credible and scientific report of a UFO encounter during 1973. The magazine offers an annual $5,000 award to the first person to prove that a UFO is an alien craft and not a natural phenomenon. The newspaper›s editorial staff and a panel of scientists determine the winners of the award. Pentagon Colonel Andrew Sullivan told the *National Enquirer*, "There is no reason to doubt the honesty of Lawrence Coyne's account." However, the FAA is not keen to officially acknowledge the incident."

Epilogue

Following this incident, Lawrence Coyne became an active ufologist. In 1978, an event was widely reported: Sir Eric M. Gairy, Prime Minister of Grenada, proposed to the United Nations General Assembly that the UN establish "an agency or department to undertake, coordinate and disseminate the results of research on unidentified flying objects and related phenomena. Following this, on July 14, 1978, a meeting between the secretary Kurt Waldheim and some renowned ufologists was organized. Jacques Vallée, Claude Poher, Allen Hynek, David Saunders and Leonard Springfield presented their recent conclusions on the UFO phenomenon. Then on November 27, 1978, a 5-hour lecture was held on the various aspects of the UFO problem before a special committee of the United Nations. Dr. Hynek spoke about the physical aspects of the phenomenon, Jacques Vallée emphasized the social aspects and Lawrence Coyne (now a lieutenant colonel) was able to tell the story of his incredible adventure aboard an army helicopter. Alas, no other country supported Grenada and the story ended there.

Lawrence Coyne was thus given media coverage. We even saw him on French television, in the program "Ces Ovnis qui nous échappent", directed by Bernard Mermod and broadcast on FR3 on June 13, 1980. He declared: "When I think back to that night when I saw this object, it was as if another world opened up to me. I felt insignificant. This craft represented a technology unknown on our planet", which, one can imagine, disconcerted the US Air Force.

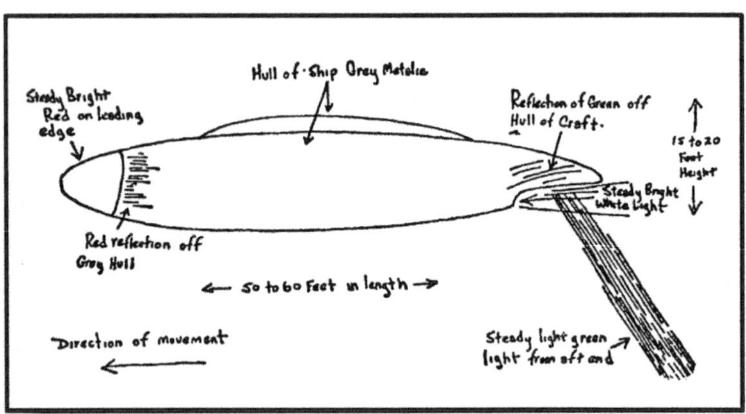

Drawing of the UFO by Captain Coyne

Sources

The APRO Bulletin, vol. 22, n° 2, September-October 1973, pp. 1-5 - *UFO Investigator*, November 1973, pp. 1-2 - *National Enquirer*, December 16, 1973 - *The Cleveland Press*, June 7, 1974 - *Phénomènes Spatiaux* n° 40-41-42, June-September-December 1974, pp. 13-16 - *Historia* hors-série n∞ 46, " Les Soucoupes volantes ", 1976, pp. 38-39 - *Ovnis, Un desafio a la ciencia* n∞ 10, February 1976, pp. 29-33 (this case illustrates the cover) - *Flying Saucer Review*, vol. 22, n° 4, November 1976, pp. 15-19 - *Fate*, vol. 31, No. 8, August 1978, p. 66 - Jennie Zeidman, *"A Helicopter-UFO Encounter Over Ohio,"* Center for UFO Studies, March 1979 - *UFO NYT* No. 5, September-October 1982, pp. 4-9 (this case illustrates the cover) - Philip J. Klass, *UFOs, The Public Deceived*, Prometheus Books, 1983, pp. 135-160 - *MUFON UFO Journal* n∞ 256, August 1989, p. 3 - *Lights in the Night* n∞ 321, May-June 1993, pp. 4-10 (this case illustrates the cover).

The last flight of Frederick Valentich

Date: October 21, 1978.

Location: Bass Strait, southwest of Melbourne, Australia. This inlet of the Indian Ocean separates Australia from Tasmania.

The Valentich family lives a peaceful life in a small yellow brick house on Avern Avenue in Avondale Heights, a suburb of Melbourne. Guido, the father, and Alberta, the mother, cherish their 4 children: Frederick, Richard and infant twins Olivia and Laura. The parents are Italian, originally from Trieste.

Frederick, born on June 9, 1958, is the eldest. At the time of the events, he was 20 years old and had a passion: flying. He spent 3 years, as a cadet, in the Royal Australian Air Force training corps. But he was rejected for the military pilot training because of his bad grades. He is now taking some courses to get his commercial pilot›s license. While waiting to fly regularly, he works in a military surplus located on Puckle Street. His boss, Dick Williams, described him as a "very dependable, cheerful, if somewhat shy" young man.

This Saturday in October is a mild day. The air is barely dampened by a light breeze blowing from the north. At 6:05 pm, the sun begins its descent on the horizon. The evening falls slowly on the Australian coast. An ideal time to fly at night as the visibility is excellent. Not a cloud in sight. And the weather service reports no turbulence.

It›s a good thing: Frederick has to make his first night flight. He has 200 Australian dollars in his pocket, entrusted to him by the Royal Air Force officers in Melbourne. These soldiers asked him, if he went to King Island, to buy a stock of lobsters from a local fisherman.

In high spirits, wearing jeans and a blue T-shirt, Frederick enthusiastically fills out the standard Department of Transportation "Domestic Flight Plan" form. Since he has a valid Class 4 instrument rating, he is, for the first time, allowed to fly at night. But it must be a *full reporting* flight, which means that he must contact the civil authorities by radio just after take-off, once he has reached his cruising altitude. As well as later, at the height of Cape Otway, when it will leave the Australian coast to begin the flight phase over the ocean to reach King Island.

Between heaven and earth

At Moorabbin Airfield, Frederick refuels a small rental plane, a single-engine, 4-seat Cessna 182L. This white and blue passenger plane, serial number 182-58572, dates from 1967. Then Frederick goes around the plane for the last checks: wings, tail, tires, propeller... Everything is in order.

18h19.

Frederick took off 44 minutes late. He took care of loading 4 bright yellow polystyrene life jackets. You never know, when he returns, people from King Island might ask him to bring them back to the mainland.

Frederick preset as many radio frequencies as he could on his communications and navigation equipment. He started by dialing 125.9 MHz because he needs to call Tullamarine's flight service when he reaches an altitude of 2,000 feet *[609 meters]*. This is standard procedure.

In the meantime, the engine runs steadily. The air nozzle makes his brown hair dance. Frederick is happy, suspended, in his Cessna, between sky and earth.

On the airport...

At Tullamarine Airport, Steve Robey, 31, is in charge of radio and radar installations. He himself has been a commercial pilot since 1968. On this night, he is a flight operator, whose job is to assist pilots when they are flying in uncontrolled airspace. He can inform them of weather changes, the possibility of other air traffic in the area or similar alerts. Robey has Frederick's flight plan in hand. The young pilot has to fly from Moorabbin to King Island and back, a distance of 480 km. It should take him just over an hour.

The night falls

Frederick flies over the town of Mornington, then along the coast, passes Torquay. It is 6:41 pm. Very quickly, the night falls and the sky becomes opaque

---

   UFO: The 12 files that the Pentagon cannot explain

black. On his right, he sees a few small lights running, lower down, on the nearby coastline. On the left, it is the dark and infinite expanse of the ocean which seems surprisingly compact.

His radio sputters. A nasal voice, covering the sound of the six-cylinder engine, asks, "Delta Sierra Juliet... Do you want to revise your arrival time at King Island? You said 9:30 p.m., but you'll obviously be there later." Frederick sits up straight in his seat, suddenly serious. "Affirmative, let's say 10:00 p.m.," he replies proudly.

Then suddenly, he flinches. He realizes that he forgot to ask for the lights to be turned on on the King Island runway. As he thought he would arrive before dark, this detail, which is not a security detail, escaped him. For a moment, in the vastness of the darkness that suddenly envelops him, Frederick feels vulnerable.

A huge metallic object

Frederick Valentich flew peacefully at an altitude of 1,500 feet *[457 meters]*. He saw Cape Otway. This was the signal for him to negotiate a 45-degree turn to his left, to leave the reassuring proximity of the coast and to face the open ocean. He then had to fly over Bass Strait for 48 miles *[77 km]* before he could reach the northern tip of King Island.

At 7 p.m., our pilot took off over the black water. But after a few minutes, a detail bothered him. Very quickly, he contacted Tullamarine and spoke with Steve Robey. Here is, in their exact chronology, the detail of their exchanges:

- 7:00 p.m. 6:14 p.m.
VALENTICH: Melbourne, this is Delta Sierra Juliet. Is there any known traffic below 5,000 feet *[1,524 meters]*?
OPERATOR: No known traffic.
V: Delta Sierra Juliet. I'm... It looks like... a big plane below 5,000 feet.

- 7:00 p.m. 6:46 p.m.
O: Delta Sierra Juliet, what type of aircraft is it?
V: Delta Sierra Juliet. I can't confirm anything, it looks like 4 big landing lights.

- 7:32 PM
V: Melbourne, this is Delta Sierra Juliet. The plane just passed overhead at less than 1,000 feet *[304 meters]*."

O: Copy that. And it's a big plane? Confirm.

V: Uh... Unknown because of its speed of travel. Is there a military aircraft in the area?

O: Delta Sierra Juliet, no known aircraft in the vicinity.

- 7:00 p.m. 8:18 p.m.

V : Melbourne, it approaches me, coming from the east.

- 19h 8 min 49 s

V: Delta Sierra Juliet. It seems to me that he is playing some kind of game. It passes over me 2 or 3 times and invariably at speeds I can't identify.

- 19h 9 min 2 s

O: Copy. What is your altitude?

V: My altitude is 4500: four, five, zero, zero *[1371 meters]*.

O: Delta Sierra Juliet, and you confirm that you can't identify the plane?

V: Affirmative.

- 7:00 p.m. 9:28 p.m.

V: Melbourne, Delta Sierra Juliet. This is not a plane. It is...

[Mic open for 2 seconds.]

- 7:00 p.m. 9:46 p.m.

O: Delta Sierra Juliet, Melbourne. Can you describe the, uh, the plane?

V: Delta Sierra Juliet. It passes. It's an elongated shape. [I can't identify it anymore than that. [Melbourne, he's in front of me now.

- 7:10:07 PM

O: Received, and what is the size of, uh, the object?

- 7:00 p.m. 10:20 p.m.

V: Delta Sierra Juliet. Melbourne, it looks like it is stationary. Right now, I'm making circles. And this thing is circling above me. It also has a green light, it's like metallic, very bright on the outside.

　　　　　UFO: The 12 files that the Pentagon cannot explain

Guido Valentich, the young pilot's father, was convinced that his son had been kidnapped by visitors from another world. On October 24, 1978, he declared to the daily newspaper *The Sun*: "Since we have no proof of his death, I think he must have been kidnapped, but I am confident that his "kidnappers" will return him to me!"

While waiting for a possible rebound, he fights on all fronts. Receiving letters from all over the world, he took the time to reply to each person. He contacted the famous French oceanographer Jacques Cousteau and asked him to explore the Bass Delta with his "diving saucer". Cousteau agreed, but never obtained government permission.

Yet Guido Valentich did not give up. He collaborates with Richard Haines, a former NASA scientist who worked with the former Apollo astronauts. Together, they questioned the witnesses and kept on questioning the Air Force. Guido grants, without getting tired, interviews to the press. And he accepts to appear in important television programs.

4 years later, on October 20, 1982, *The Sun* published an article entitled "The pilot's father is still hopeful". Guido Valentich says: "Is he on another planet? I don't know. It's hard to know exactly where he is," but he believes his son is still alive. His wife, 43 years old, shares his feeling. "Moreover, she believes in UFOs," concludes the article.

Every year now, Guido goes to Cape Otway. And scans the sky and the sea in the hope of getting a sign of his beloved departed.

For the family, in the absence of recovered debris, the thesis of the accident is considered improbable. It is true that in the event of a crash, the Cessna should have broken up when it hit the surface of the ocean. Debris would then have been recovered. The aircraft's wingtips, rudders and elevators are light and float as a priority.

Guido Valentich died in April 2000. He never stopped searching, investigating, looking for explanations about the unacceptable disappearance of his son. The Australian daily *Herald Sun* of October 11, 2000 revealed that, as he was dying, Guido Valentich clung to the idea that Frederick was still alive. He said, "I don't expect to meet him where I'm going.

Many assumptions

All over the world, people tried to explain the disappearance of the young pilot.

- For some, Frederick Valentich would have been involved in drug trafficking. The Bass Strait is indeed used by many traffickers, going back and forth between

Australia and Tasmania. In small planes flying at low altitude, they transport their goods, suspended in nets at water level. If intercepted, they can drop everything quickly into the ocean. But it is unlikely that our pilot had to deal with such traffickers. His exchange with the control tower does not suggest such a scenario. Moreover, the description of the object - with its 4 very bright projectors - does not fit with the modus operandi of the smugglers who act in all discretion, avoiding to be noticed.

- Was our pilot flying, himself, under the influence of illegal substances? Highly unlikely. All the relatives are formal, Valentich drank very little alcohol. And he hated drugs. Gregory Reaburn, a long-time friend, confirms: "Frederick was the kind of guy who would inform the police if he saw that someone around him was using drugs."

- Suicide. This theory doesn't really fit. Frederick Valentich was obviously a happy young man. In a close and loving family, he never showed any signs of being unhappy. His younger brother, Richard Valentich, who spoke for the first time, said: "I cried for 3 days, I think I cried non-stop. His passing was a real shock to me. It caused a big void in my life. The suicide theory is totally impossible. He had a girlfriend, Rhonda Rushton, age 17, whom he loved and wanted to spend time with. My sisters were only 4 years old and he loved them and protected them like the apple of his eye! It doesn't add up. He wouldn't have left like that. There are easier ways to disappear if you want to leave your family. At least not like this! I keep thinking about what happened. And I always come to the same conclusion: I don't know. Flying was his great passion. He loved it. He spent his last years doing nothing else. It was everything to him."

- It was then imagined that Valentich had set up this scenario to steal the Cessna and then sell it. With the money he made, he would have disappeared from circulation and made a new life elsewhere. The tank of the Cessna contained enough fuel to fly almost 800 kilometers. But this remains highly unlikely, as the plane was never found. After all this time, even if it was made up, the plane would have reappeared.

- Vertigo. Disoriented, Valentich would have suddenly lost his means, and would have crashed into the ocean. Hardly credible. Our pilot was not prone to this kind of discomfort.

- A meteorological problem. Definitely to be ruled out. The Melbourne Bureau of Meteorology confirms that on that night, "conditions were perfect for a night flight. No turbulence to report. Visibility was excellent. At 10 p.m., an aircraft over King Island could clearly see the light of the Cape Otway lighthouse. This, of course, makes the theory of a loss of orientation very unlikely.

- Frederick Valentich would have been shot down accidentally by the army. A missile during an experimental operation could have pulverized the plane and its pilot. But the behavior of the unknown device, which played for several minutes with the Cessna, invalidates this hypothesis.

- James McGaha, a retired U.S. Air Force pilot, and Joe Nickell, author and investigator, believe that Valentich, deceived by the illusion of a tilted horizon, put his plane into a downward spiral, known as a "death spiral," and then crashed into the ocean. As for the lights seen by the young pilot, they were simply the planets Venus, Mars and Mercury as well as the bright star Antares.

- Finally, there remains the unconventional hypothesis of an "exotic" craft, from beyond space, which would have "abducted" the aircraft and its pilot. This would take into account the fact that Valentich affirmed that the intruder seen was not a plane. And that at that time, the radars did not detect any civilian or military aircraft.

The magnetic strip of the exchange

The recording of the radio exchanges between Frederick Valentich and Steve Robey does not help the investigator. We know that these exchanges lasted a total of 12 minutes and 13 seconds. However, the available copy of this communication is of shorter duration. Richard Haynes specifies: "The total duration of the voice recording that I was able to obtain and that I am using for my analysis is only 6 minutes 32 seconds. Either the times given on the officially released version are incorrect or my tape has been 'cut'. If segments of this authentic voice exchange have been cut, one must ask by whom and for what reason(s). This issue has been raised by other investigators; no satisfactory answer has been put forward so far."

We are certain that part of this tape is missing. An article in the *Sun*, Melbourne edition, dated July 9, 1980, reveals that 5 minutes of the recording were deleted "in the name of national security". We will appreciate that. This is corroborated by an article published on October 25, 1980 in the New Zealand *Star* newspaper.

Frederick Valentich's fiancée, Rhonda Rushton, sent a letter to Richard Haynes on August 25, 1980, stating, "The Department of Transportation told me that the government was withholding some of the information that was on the tape. Then one day a man from the Department of Transportation came into my office and, in the course of a conversation, told me that there was a minute and a half of the tape that had not been released because the government thought it would cause panic and they did not want that to happen."

A very disturbing photo

An unexpected picture will re-launch the much discussed UFO hypothesis. The evening of Valentich's disappearance, at the same place, on Cape Otway, a plumber named Roy Manifold took 6 photos of the sunset. At the time of the shooting, he did not notice anything abnormal. But when he was developing the pictures, he noticed, on picture number 5, that something seemed to emerge from the sea. And on picture number 6, a curious object hovers above the waves.

These pictures were taken at 6:47 pm, 20 minutes before Valentich alerted the Melbourne control tower about a strange apparition.

The negatives are seriously analyzed, including by the ufology group *Ground Saucer Watch* (GSW) of Phoenix, Arizona. The final analysis report states, "In image 6, taken about 20 seconds later, a cloud-like object is seen. A disk structure is visible above the general shape. [...] All modes of computer analysis were used to obtain this data, including: contrast enhancement, color enhancement, digitization, computerization and filtering...

"Close examination of the original negatives revealed that the object is not caused by a defect in the emulsion. Computer analysis revealed that the object is not a known type of cloud or weather phenomenon. In fact, digital densitometry revealed a highly reflective area at the "top" of the object, indicating a metallic structure. There is no evidence of a hoax... [...] The size of the object is estimated to be about 20 feet *[6 meters]*. Conclusion: based on the computerized image data, GSW technicians concede in good faith that the image shows an unknown flying object of moderate dimensions, apparently surrounded by a cloud-like vapor/ exhaust residue."

The Air Force and many skeptics do not agree. They suggest that it is a residual cloud, "a dying cumulus".Strange, because no cloud appears in the first 4 pictures taken at 20 second intervals...

The photo of Roy Manifold made the rounds of the international press. The opinions remain divided.

A UFO nut?

What discredited the UFO hypothesis in the eyes of the skeptics was that the journalists of the time repeated over and over again that Frederick Valentich was passionate, even obsessed by the subject. In the Australian Air Force investigation report, document V116/783/1047, we read the following: "Frederick was a firm believer in UFOs. He collected articles and information on the subject. He read the book *Chariots Of The Gods* by Erich von Däniken, as well as other books on the subject. His interest was born 6 years ago. And he was definitely convinced when he had access to confidential Australian Royal Air Force files on UFOs at East Sale and Laverton. He obviously did not share this information with his family because it must remain confidential. One night, his mother would also have seen a UFO. She called her son, and together they were able to observe the phenomenon... This happened nearly 8 months before his disappearance."

Was Frederick Valentich a UFO freak who saw them everywhere? It seems that the reality is a little more nuanced. Yes, the young pilot was interested in the phenomenon. But, after having interviewed his fiancée Rhonda Rushton on October 24, 1978, the investigator J.C. Sandercock noted in his official report: "We then discussed the subject of UFOs, which had been widely reported in the press. Miss Rushton confided to me that on Sunday, October 15, 1978, while driving in the heart of the Dandenong Ranges, Valentich said to her, "If a UFO landed in front of me, sure, I'd like to get on it, but never without you." Miss Rushton knew that Valentich kept some items concerning UFOs, but she says he was not an avid collector. He had a reasonable interest in the subject, that's all."

Many witnesses

To this day, no material proof of his death could be brought, Frederik Valentich is still officially considered as "disappeared". What happened to him is still unexplained.

It should be noted that the Bass Strait region has long been known to be an important area of UFO activity. Numerous witnesses, even before the year 1947, claim to have observed mysterious celestial objects there.

On the afternoon and evening of Frederick Valentich's disappearance, more than 20 people living in and around the Strait reported seeing a green light. This light was almost at the location where Valentich reported his encounter.

The Australian Air Force has also indicated that it has officially received 11 reports from people along the coast claiming to have seen UFOs on the night of the incident.

Among the witnesses, at 6:55 p.m., P. Farr, an Australian Air Force reserve officer, who was driving on Huntingdale Road, saw a shimmering metallic shape in the sky. Also that evening, at 11:45 p.m., John Snow, who was driving in the Barwon Heads area, heard his 11-year-old son describe a green light that was rapidly crossing the horizon.

But the most astonishing testimony came later. On October 11, 2000, the Australian daily *Herald Sun* gave a more than disturbing account. Mr. Hansen confided that he was driving that evening from Apollo Bay to Cape Otway. He was out rabbit hunting and had two nieces with him. On the way back, his niece Tracy, sitting to his right, saw the lights of an airplane with a large green light in the sky. The presence of this large green light was so unusual that our witness decided to stop and get out of his vehicle. He said he clearly saw a large greenish circular light "that seemed to fly over the plane. It was about the size of a tennis ball held at arm's length. Its color was similar to the navigation lights of an aircraft. He told his wife about his strange sighting that night. And the next day, to his colleagues at work. This was even before the Valentich story was told. This corroborates Frederick Valentich's testimony to the control tower.

Epilogue

On October 21, 1998, 20 years to the day after Frederick Valentich's disappearance, at Cape Otway, near the lighthouse, Steve Robey, who was the last person to speak to the young man, unveiled a memorial plaque in memory of the lost pilot. He gave a moving speech and told Valentich's parents, Guido and Alberta, who were present, "I know today - from having known you, and having seen the stable environment in which your son grew up - that Frederick disappeared after encountering something we can't explain even 20 years later."

Nice conclusion from one of the actors of this drama. But that only adds mystery to the mystery.

UFO: The 12 files that the Pentagon cannot explain

Frederick Valentich and press of the time (Australian Express, October 27, 1978)

Sources

The Sun, Melbourne, October 23, 1978 - *Sunday Press*, Melbourne, October 29, 1978 - *International UFO Reporter*, vol. 3, n° 12, December 1978, pp. 2-10 - *Lights In The Night* n° 182, February 1979, pp. 14-17 - *MUFON UFO Journal n°* 141, November 1979, pp. 5-7 - *The Australian UFO Bulletin*, September 1980, pp. 13-14 - Richard F. Haines, *Melbourne Episode. Case Study Of A Missing Pilot*, L.D.A. Press, 1987 - *Phenomena n°* 28, July-August 1995, pp. 16-20 (this case illustrates the cover) - National Archives of Australia (NAA), file V116/783/1047 entitled "VH-DSJ: Cape Otway to King Island, 21 October 1978 ", 319 pages).

The lost flight from Puerto Rico

Date: June 28, 1980.

Location: Mona Channel, the Caribbean strait that separates the islands of Puerto Rico and Hispaniola.

18h10.

José Luis Maldonado Torres, 31 years old, and José Alberto Pagán Santos, 22 years old, take off from Las Américas International Airport in Santo Domingo, Dominican

Republic. The 2 young pilots are flying a two-seater aircraft, model Ercoupe 415-D, registration N3808H and dating from 1947. The aircraft belongs to José Pagán Jiménez, an officer of the Puerto Rico Air Force, and father of Pagán Santos.

José Luis Maldonado Torres is a flight instructor. He has 200 hours of flying experience. José Alberto Pagán Santos is a young student pilot.

Nearly 2 hours later, the 2 young men fly over the Mona canal. The visibility is perfect. They are impatient to return home to Puerto Rico. So far, their trip has been smooth.

A strange object

20h03.

Several planes pick up an alarming radio message from N3808H: "Mayday, Mayday, this is Ercoupe three, eight, zero, eight. We are confronted with a strange object on our course, we are lost."

Iberia Airlines flight IB-976, from Guatemala to Spain, responded immediately. Asking for some details about this distress call, he gets the following answer: "Uh, we are going from Santo Domingo to San Juan. But we have encountered, uh, a strange object on our way that has made us change our route 3 times. Right now it's ahead of us, in position one hour. Our heading is zero, seven, zero degrees... Our altitude is 1600, at zero, seven, zero degrees... Our VOR is not responding, no more frequency... "

The Iberia flight IB-976 relays the message to the flight center of San Juan. And asks N3808H to turn on its transponder.

20 hours 5 minutes 10 seconds.

N3808H briefly replies, "But we don't have a transponder, sir!"

20 hours 5 minutes and 40 seconds.

Iberia IB-976 asks the distressed crew for their call sign and estimated position. The pilots respond, "Right now we are supposed to be about 35 miles *[56 kilometers]* off the coast of Puerto Rico but we have something weird ahead of us that keeps throwing us off course... I changed course for a second. [Unintelligible.] Our current route is about 300... We're still in the same situation, sir."

Then the communication with the Ercoupe is definitively interrupted. After that, we hear a strange metallic noise.

A futile search

20h07.

N3808H disappeared from the *Atlantic Fleet Weapons Range* radar. The aircraft's last recorded position was 35 miles *[56 kilometers]* west of Puerto Rico, in open sea.

20h15.

An object reappears on the radars. As it does not answer the calls, it is impossible to identify it. If it is N3808H, the 2 pilots do not send any more distress signals. Then the object finally disappeared.

In the hours that followed, a joint search was conducted by the authorities of Haiti, Puerto Rico and the Dominican Republic. Lieutenant Pagán, father of José Alberto Pagán Santos, was deeply affected by the situation and actively participated in the search. He carried out several tracking missions, including with his own helicopter, focusing on the area indicated by the last radar position. But after 2 weeks, no trace nor any debris having been found, the research is abandoned.

It is then that the lieutenant Pagán is contacted by a certain Carlos Busquets, who has connections with the FAA of Isla Verde. The man reveals him that there is a recording where his son evokes a confrontation with an unidentified flying object. Thanks to his status of police officer, Pagán can listen to this tape and is amazed. However, the FAA refuses to provide him with a copy and asks him not to talk about this case to anyone.

On July 18, 1980, Lieutenant Commander M. R. Adams sent a letter to the Washington Bureau of Aeronautical Research stating, "To date, nothing has been found that would shed light on the fate of N3808H. The Coast Guard has suspended its search and, unless new positive information indicating the location of the aircraft and/or its crew is available, no further search will be undertaken."

The mystery remains total concerning the mysterious aircraft seen by the 2 young pilots. What is this object that forced a small two-seater plane to turn around? The small plane obviously negotiated a 300 degree turn to escape the intruder.

Epilogue

The first theory put forward was that the co-pilot was inexperienced and had probably forgotten to refuel. Then, to be much more convincing, the authorities ended up closing the case by declaring officially that the small two-seater had crashed into the open sea due to a technical failure.

This made Lieutenant Pagán jump and say: "My son was already an experienced pilot and it was not the first time he made this flight from Puerto Rico-Dominican Republic and back. Besides, our plane was in perfect condition. I was in charge of its maintenance. I had just replaced its old engine with a new one. The plane was in perfect working order. The best proof is that at no time did they mention any mechanical problem. Although the Puerto Rican authorities are well aware that our two pilots mentioned a strange object that was stalking them, they preferred to give the media this kind of "theory"."

Like Guido Valentich (Frederick's father), Lieutenant Pagán remains hopeful. He confides: "My son believed in the reality of UFOs. He had seen several. So did I. Of course, I have no certainty that he was abducted by one of these objects. But what we do know for sure is that one of them is involved in what happened. If that's the case, I really hope that one day my son will be returned to me. It's hard to say, but I have a feeling. And then, it's a small consolation for my wife and for me. I sincerely hope that one day our two pilots will be back."

Sources

Accident Report No. MIA-80-D-A079, archives of the National Transportation Safety Board of Washington - *Flying Saucer Review*, vol. 43-44, Winter 1998, pp. 6-9 - *Daily Mail*, London, November 11, 2000 - Gian J. Quasar, *Into The Bermuda Triangle*, International Marine-McGraw-Hill, 2004, pp. 43-45 - *Thimoty Good, Need To Know*, Pan Books, 2007, pp. 312-320 - *UFO* No. 251, Brazil, October 2017).

X. Betty Cash and Vickie Landrum: a bitter remake of *Apocalypse Now*

The Facts

Date: December 29, 1980.

Location: a forest near Huffman, northeast of Houston, Texas, USA.

Witnesses: Betty Joyce Cash, nee Collins, a 52-year-old businesswoman; Vickie Marzelia Landrum, nee Holifield, 57, a restaurant employee; Colby Lee, 7, Vickie's grandson.

The day after Christmas is always a time to relax and enjoy an evening with friends. That evening, Betty suggested to her friend Vickie that they go to Cleveland to play bingo. Unfortunately, once there, the two women were disappointed to find that most businesses were closed. They decided to try their luck in New Caney, a nearby town. Same scenario, the town is almost deserted and the stores are closed. Not only is it a vacation, but it's a Monday. So the merchants have good reason to stay at home. And with their families.

Dejected, and as a consolation, Betty, Vickie and Colby eat in a nearby truck stop. Then filled, they take the road of the return, bound for Dayton, their place of residence.

Driving her 1980 model Oldsmobile Cutlass Supreme, Betty takes the 1485 side road through a forest of oaks and pines near the town of Huffman. This road, heading to the outskirts of Houston, is known to be dark and lonely. It is about 8:30 pm. It's dark and the sky is partly cloudy. The rain that has fallen all day has just stopped. The engine of the vehicle purrs peacefully. The radio, tuned to the KIKK channel, broadcasts in mute some refrains of country western. Sitting in the back seat, with his nose against the window, Colby watches the shadowy landscape go by.

Vickie, Colby and Betty

Our trio travels about 20 kilometers. Suddenly Colby calls out to her grandmother and asks, "Grandma, what's that weird thing flying over the trees?" Surprised, the two women bend down, scan the sky and see indeed a luminous point that slowly gets closer. Then, as it grew, it finally took on the appearance of a colossal diamond-shaped machine.

This extraordinary machine then loses altitude and stops in the middle of the road, 7 meters above the ground. It blocks completely the passage of our stunned trio. Betty, terrified, brakes to death. Inside the vehicle, Colby screams of terror. Vickie - who is very religious - starts to pray.

Betty says to herself that she can circumvent the obstacle by rolling on the side of the road. But the ground is soggy and she's afraid of getting stuck. Vickie," she finally yells, "I can't even make out the edge of the road. I can't go backwards or turn around!"

Here is our trio, immobilized in the middle of nowhere, in front of a gigantic ship which lights up violently the surroundings, "as if the whole forest was going to blaze".

The diamond-shaped UFO measures nearly twenty meters. Of a dull metallic gray, it is "much higher than a water tower". Orange and red flames shoot out from its base. It looks like a rocket reactor. It smells like a flammable liquid, "like lighter fluid". Its light is blinding. And it emits an intense heat, very quickly unbearable.

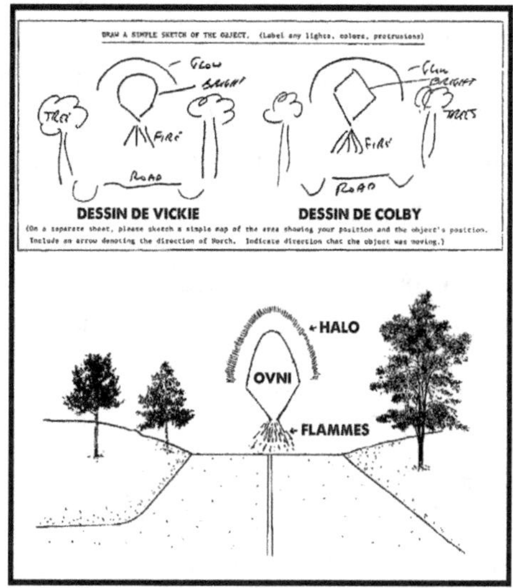

Drawings of the UFO made by Vickie and Colby. And reconstruction.

A hellish heat

Our trio leaves the vehicle. Terrified, Colby tries to flee into the woods. Vickie catches up with him just barely. The child returns to the car and takes refuge in the front seat, under the dashboard. Near the open door, Vickie is unable to move. She looks at this senseless thing for a brief moment. Then she quickly joins Colby inside, who can't stop screaming.

Betty Cash is more adventurous. Driven by curiosity, she advances, decided to see more closely this monstrosity. A hand protecting her eyes, she remains 10 minutes to contemplate it. What is this machine ? And where does it come from?

About 30 meters from the car, the UFO emitted a muffled sound, like a wind tunnel. As well as a series of irregular beeps.

The heat he gives off is suffocating, hard to bear. Inside the car, Vickie begs Betty to come back. Leaning her hands on the dashboard, her fingers dig into the melting vinyl upholstery!

Inconvenienced, Betty turns back. She tries to get back into the car. But while opening the door, she burns her hand on the white heated handle. She must use her leather jacket as a protective glove. In spite of the cold of December which reigns around - it is 4 ∞C -, the flames of the UFO dispense an intolerable heat.

This strange machine seems to be in a bad way. Each time it tries to take off, the flames of its base redouble. Finally, after several attempts, after about ten minutes, it finally rises with a huge crash and flies away in the direction of Galveston Bay. This thing," says Betty, "lit up the sky. It was like daylight. That›s when we saw that it was surrounded by a lot of helicopters." Betty and Colby count them. There are 23 of them! "I counted them," Betty points out, "to convince myself that I hadn›t gone crazy!"

The nightmare begins

The way is finally clear. Vickie says with relief, "We're safe and sound. But I'm burning up and it's so hot."Betty realizes that the car's engine has stalled. She starts again and quickly leaves this strange place, foot crushing the gas pedal. While driving, she engages the air-conditioning because the cockpit was transformed into a true furnace.

After this trying face-to-face which lasted about twenty minutes, Betty has only one hurry: to return to Dayton as soon as possible. For that, she takes the secondary way 2100. It is 21h50 when she drops Vickie and Colby at their home. Our driver then returns home, greeted by her friend Wilma Emert.

One would think that all this is now a bad memory. But alas, the nightmare has only just begun.

Once at home, Betty feels ill. Dehydrated, she drinks glass of water on glass of water. She suffers at the same time from a terrible headache and nauseas. She says to herself that by sitting down, that will pass. But then large patches appear on her neck and scalp. Her skin became extremely red. The hours passing, the eyelids of Betty start to swell until almost closing. The plates, which appeared earlier, are transformed into blisters full of a clearer liquid. Betty then suffers from repeated vomiting and violent diarrhoeas. Her ears are so swollen that she has to take off her earrings.

December 30, 1980

The next morning, Betty's condition has deteriorated considerably. Her friends are seriously worried. They fear that she will die at any moment under their eyes.

In Dayton, Vickie and Colby are also ill. Their condition is a little less serious than Betty's. Their skin, however, has turned red as if after a bad sunburn. They had stomach cramps, vomiting and diarrhea. During the following days, Vickie will empty 3 bottles of baby oil to try to soothe the sustained irritation of their skins.

On the right side of her head, Vickie loses some hair. But it grows back fairly quickly. Her scalp, she notes, has become "unresponsive". Colby has trouble sleeping. He has many nightmares and wets his bed because he refuses to get up at night in terror. He doesn't want to sleep alone anymore. It was not until the second week of February that he agreed to return to his room.

December 31, 1980

Catastrophized, Betty's friends reach Vickie and beg her to watch over her friend who is now in a semi-conscious state. They feel helpless and realized "that getting help for people claiming to be UFO victims is impossible". During this Christmas season, most doctors are out of town. And the few practitioners available refuse to take care of an "unknown" patient. People who are not part of their clientele are not their priority. Especially, when the relatives claim that the patient in question was a victim of a UFO. Believing it to be a bad joke, the doctors systematically hang up.

It should be added to that that Betty is cardiac. The general practitioners contacted, not having in hand her medical file, do not want to take any risk. However time is short. Betty, hardly conscious, is unable to communicate the name and the address of her cardiologist. What complicates singularly the situation.

Powerless in the face of the doctors' refusal, Vickie continues to care for Betty as best she can. Alas, any food or drink she gives her is immediately rejected. Something is really wrong, Vickie will say, Betty being famous for her strong appetite.

The situation becomes more and more critical. Betty weakens day after day. As a last attempt, Vickie contacts the pharmacist where Betty gets her supplies. "Excellent initiative: they find a part of her medical file. Armed with this information, Vickie immediately contacted the emergency room at *Parkway General Hospital* in Houston.

January 3, 1981

Betty is finally hospitalized in Houston. She loses large portions of skin, her hair falls by handfuls. She is so weak that she is unable to walk. Her eyelids are so swollen that she is almost blind. A nurse had to regularly apply balm to them. It will be a week before Betty can open her eyes and recognize the people around her.

Despite her critical condition, doctors say she is a compliant patient who never complains. Her cardiologist, Dr. V. B. Shenoy, confirmed this. He then ordered a battery of tests to determine the cause of her strange burns. But at the end of a series of tests carried out, no answer seems satisfactory.

At the end of 12 days, in spite of its very worrying state, one sends Betty back at home. But once in Dayton, nothing goes any more. It is then necessary, on January 25, to hospitalize her again for 15 days.

Strange symptoms

Vickie and Colby also suffer, but not as alarmingly as Betty. After 2 to 3 weeks, their stomach cramps and diarrhea eventually subside. But they still have persistent, painful skin and eye irritation. Vickie, who used to wear glasses to read, notes that her eyesight has deteriorated and she must now wear them continuously. Now her fingernails are falling off... She collects them, numbers them and keeps them in a box in the hope that a scientist can one day analyze them.

At the beginning of February, Betty left the hospital and found refuge with her mother, Pauline Collins, who lived in Birmingham, Alabama. Too weak, she was unable to return to work and needed assistance with every aspect of her life. In Birmingham, Betty is seriously taken care of and is hospitalized several times in emergency.

Our 3 witnesses present a singular symptomatology. First of all, a state of inexplicable fatigue. The least effort annihilates them. Then a loss of appetite. Finally, a lower resistance to colds and other small, usually temporary, ailments that astonish the specialists. How to explain the slow deterioration of their physical form?

So far, our three witnesses were in good shape. Colby was doing just fine. Those close to him testify that he was an active boy who loved sports, fishing, and outdoor activities.

The same goes for Vickie. She used to be a very active woman, working hard to provide for her family. She worked both in Betty's restaurant and in the canteen at the local school. Sixteen hour days were common for this hyperactive woman.

Betty Cash was also an energetic woman. She had to undergo heart surgery in 1977, but recovered perfectly. Her doctor said, "The symptoms she has had since December 29, 1980, have nothing to do with her previous heart problems. She visits us every 6 months and I can tell you that until then she was in perfect health. These symptoms did not exist before that night in December." Betty, who had planned to open a new restaurant, is forced to abandon her plans forever.

What is the cause of their physical deterioration? Is it the proximity of this UFO? Betty was directly exposed to the heat and the glare of the object during 10 minutes. Vickie between 3 and 5 minutes, Colby approximately 1 minute. Following that, here is drawn up by several specialists, the list of the induced physiological effects:

- Colby: erythema (redness of the skin), swollen and watery eyes, stomach pain, diarrhea, anorexia (sudden loss of appetite), weight loss (he went from size 6 to size 5), increased tooth cavities ;

- Vickie: erythema, photophthalmia (swollen, watery, painful eyes), significant decrease in vision, stomach pain, diarrhea, anorexia, increased immunodeficiency, ulceration of arms due to pressure sores and depigmentation, deteriorated nails that eventually fall off, hair loss, regrowth of hair of a different texture ;

- Betty: erythema, aggravated photophthalmia (swollen and closed eyes, painful and watery), asymmetrical vision, stomach pain, vomiting, diarrhea, anorexia, lung infections, severe loss of vitality and weight, lethargy, bed sores and depigmentation, significant hair loss, regrowth of hair with a different texture.

A fight is organized

If by mutual agreement, the two women had decided to remain silent ("We cannot tell what we have lived, we will be taken for crazy!"), faced with the gravity of their wounds, they end up speaking. "I ended up telling everything during my second hospitalization," says Betty. "I was afraid that one makes fun of me and that one transfers me directly in psychiatric unit. However her attending doctor confides to the investigators: "When I examined her, I said to myself that she presented all the signs of a poisoning with radiations. But I thought that was a ridiculous assumption and I quickly dismissed it. Then, when Ms. Cash told me what she had experienced, my initial diagnosis made sense."

The released word then pushes them to the fight. Vickie is the first to react. Attempting to make a statement and seeking help, she first contacted Dayton Police

Chief Tommy Waring. Two days later, Waring gave Vickie the hotline number of Robert Gribble in Seattle, a retired firefighter and director of the *UFO Reporting Center*. Vickie called him on February 2. He immediately put her in touch with MUFON, APRO and CUFOS, the three main ufological associations in the country, associations known for their help to witnesses of UFO sightings.

Betty and Vickie then contact the US Congress. But this only amplifies their frustration. They receive only one answer, very laconic, telling them that the state group supposed to deal with UFOs does not exist since years. Instead, they were told to join a cult movement based in California!

With the help of MUFON's attorney, Peter Gersten (who decided to take on their defense), Betty and Vickie set out to determine the nature of the device that had caused them so much trouble. Dozens of letters and calls were sent to officials and members of the government (including Senators Lloyd Benson, Charles Wilson and John Tower), most of which went unanswered.

Investigator John F. Schuessler, a collaborator on several space programs (Skylab, Space Shuttle) and a NASA engineer, meets Betty in Houston on February 22, 1981, and Vickie on February 28 in Dayton. Schuessler - also co-founder of MUFON and member of the Project *Vehicle Internal Systems Investigative Team* (VISIT) - is interested in UFOs. He immediately took up the case. Convinced of the good faith of the witnesses, he thought that the object seen by the two women was probably of extraterrestrial origin. "If it was a secret device experimented by the army, why draw attention to this test with 23 helicopters? It doesn't make sense." In the aftermath, he contacted Texas air bases that could house that many aircraft. A spokesman for Fort Hood Air Force Base in Killeen, which houses more than 100 helicopters, replied that none of their aircraft were flying around Houston that night. Major Tony Geishauser says, "I don't know of any other place around here where you can find that many helicopters. If something happened, I don't know what it is...There may be some super secret there that I obviously wasn't made aware of."

The father of scientific ufology, Dr. J. Allen Hynek, who recently founded a UFO study center in Evanston, Illinois, finds this "a very crucial case" because of "absolutely undeniable physical effects. He says, "Something really happened. These two women did not pull out their hair, nor did they decide to make themselves virtually blind. We have a solid case. It's very clear. We have many other UFO encounters in our files, but rarely as real as this one."

Press and media go wild

An article published in the *Weekly World News set* the world on fire. This long paper, signed by a certain Dick Donovan, headlines, "Three people are now living in pain and terror after being attacked by a flaming UFO!"

But it is a report published by the *National Enquirer* tabloid, distributed in August 1981 in all the big stores of the country, which is going to offer to the " Cash-Landrum " affair a national exposure. Not to say international.

Flairing up such a crunchy subject, the press has a field day. Betty and Vickie are solicited from all sides. With the chance of the interviews, the two women confide themselves. Very believing, Vickie Landrum admits to the journalists, that this night of December, she believed to live the realization of a biblical prediction. "All my life, I have been told that this world would end in flames. As this object seemed to split the sky in two, I thought it was the end of time. I said to Colby, my grandson, "Look closely at the center of that light. You will see a face appear. It is the face of Jesus Christ. Don't be afraid, he is coming to take us to a much better place than this."

Vickie then details the ordeal she has endured since that terrible encounter. The burns on her arms have left several whitish scars. But for the past 8 months, her burns have been rekindling when she is exposed to the sun. She and Colby now shun sunny days, which are impossible to bear. They also avoid hot water, which is too painful for their skin, and have to make do with cold water baths.

Vickie's hair has grown back, "but it's not the same. It used to be soft and easy. It's not like that anymore. I'm ashamed to even go to the grocery store because of it. But worst of all, she says, is her eyesight, which is failing drastically. "My eyes were so badly burned that I thought they were falling apart. Since that incident, I have had to change my glasses twice and each time with stronger progressive lenses. I am losing my peripheral vision and am developing a severe cataract. And Colby, my grandson, also has to wear glasses."

The famous TV show, *"That's Incredible"*, decided to deal with the case. The filming was done in two stages. On July 15, 1981, the team travels to Dayton to film Vickie at her home. Then on September 10, Vickie and Colby took a plane to be filmed this time in a studio. America begins to be seriously moved.

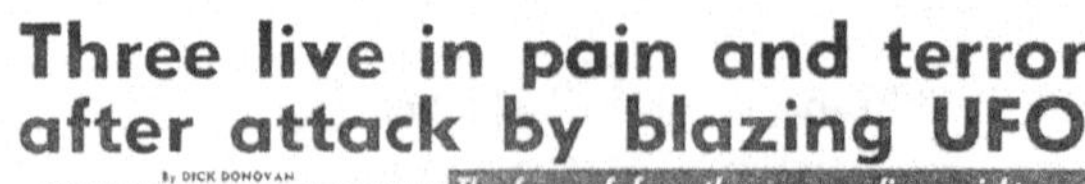

Three live in pain and terror after attack by blazing UFO

Weekly World News, March 1981

23 helicopters!

If until now the US Air Force seemed to take little interest in this affair, everything changed after the broadcast of the program "*That's Incredible*". In Washington, members of Congress said they were "disturbed" by the story. They asked the Pentagon to investigate. They were uncomfortable with the presence of the 23 helicopters in the Texas sky that night. Lieutenant Colonel George Sarran of the U.S. Army Office of Inspector General became actively involved. He contacted a large number of air bases to determine their possible involvement, but without success. Major Dennis Maire of Ellington's 136e transport unit in Houston also contributed valuable data on the capabilities of these aircraft.

UFO: The 12 files that the Pentagon cannot explain

On August 17, 1981, Betty, Vickie and Colby are received at the air base of Bergstrom (Texas) and auditioned by several military: the captain William J. Camp, the captain Terry Davis and his assistant, Pat Wolfe. Our three witnesses are formal. They clearly distinguished helicopters that seemed to escort the UFO. The aircraft were clear in the sky despite the very dark night and the moon in its third quarter. Betty confirms: "The sky was full of helicopters, she says. I even feared a collision between these aircraft that were so close together." Vickie agrees, "The noise they were making was similar to a tornado."

Colby timidly answers the questions. He draws the helicopters he saw, flying in a compact swarm around the UFO. Thanks to an identification chart, our witnesses end up designating unequivocally Chinook models with 2 rotors, Boeing CH-47. These are common US Air Force helicopters, generally used to move heavy loads or battalions of soldiers. It is noteworthy that the little boy has been terrorized by these machines ever since.

Vickie tells the military that on April 30, 1981, a CH-47 from Ellington Air Force Base landed in Dayton as part of a future Farmers Day celebration. The aircraft was piloted by Willy Culberson. When the plane flew over the city in preparation for landing, Colby was literally in a panic. Vickie decided to take him to get a closer look at the plane, hoping that it would seem less scary once they landed. When they landed in the landing zone, they found that there were a lot of people there. Indeed, the public was invited to board the aircraft and meet Culberson.

Vickie and Colby had to wait a while before they were allowed to enter the helicopter and talk with the pilot. During the tour, Vickie and Colby asked Culberson if he had ever flown in the area. He replied that last December he and other military personnel had been called to watch a troubled UFO near Huffman! Vickie jumped. She told the man how happy she was to meet him. She revealed that she was one of the people burned by the UFO. But the military man immediately changed his attitude. He refused to talk to her any further, and then pushed them out of the aircraft.

Later, when interviewed by John Schuessler on the telephone, Culberson denied having been involved in such a mission. Following calls from John Schuessler to Major Dennis Haire, Cumberson again denied having made any such statement. Only later, when confronted by Lt. Col. George Sarran, did he admit to making such statements.

The investigation is progressing at a very slow pace. When contacted, the FAA representative at Houston Intercontinental Airport revealed that 350 to 400 helicopters operate commercially in the Houston area. But alas, there are no Chinooks in that fleet. In the end, numerous calls to military installation officials yielded no answers. Fort Polk, Fort Hood, *Dallas Naval Air Station* or *England Air Force Base* in Louisiana say they have nothing to do with these night flights and know nothing. In the end, no one claims authorship of these Chinooks!

New witnesses

However, we did see them! A Dayton police officer, Lamar Walker, comes forward. He says he was off duty that night. He and his wife Marie were on their way home from Cleveland. On FM 1960, five miles north of Dayton, he did see several large helicopters moving in formation. The aircraft were flying low and appeared to be looking for something. He said he was slightly unsure of the exact date, but thought it was the evening of December 29, 1980.

Rosalie Semour and her daughter Michelle claim to have seen a large number of helicopters flying over their house that same evening. "They were coming from all directions," they said. One of the helicopters hovered for a moment over a tree that is 60 meters from their home. Michelle said it was a long green aircraft, with no glass bubble on the front like you usually see. Further away, there was a strong glow as if a craft had crashed or was down. The two women watched this intense aerial ballet for 15 minutes. The helicopters were shining powerful searchlights toward the ground, as if they were looking for something.

It was discovered that other people had also seen the UFO. That same night, 26-year-old Angie Stanley, a Dayton postal worker, was driving home from New Caney on FM 1485, about 20 miles west of Dayton. I saw, pretty far up in the sky, a really bright light," she says. It looked like two car headlights, intense and fixed on an oval-shaped thing."

Nellie Zedick, 57, says, "I was driving with my son John and his wife Toni. We were driving to Dayton. We saw this light in the sky. I stopped dead in my tracks to watch it. This thing was silent and it was going pretty damn fast. It was shaped like a diamond with a slightly rounded end. I've never seen anything like it in my life.

From his home in Dayton, Jerry McDonald, 24, a tough oil driller, also witnessed something strange that night. He says, "I heard a noise like a rumbling, and I thought it was the Goodyear blimp. But the object I saw was more like a triangular, diamond-shaped object. In the back, it had two flares that spat out bright blue

UFO: The 12 files that the Pentagon cannot explain

flames. It also had 2 spotlights and a red light in the center. I saw all of this as it passed 100 feet above my head." Two days later, Jerry became ill. For 6 weeks, his condition did not improve much.

Belle Magee, 55, a baker, was at home in East Gate, about 12 kilometers west of Dayton. Looking outside, she saw a bright light heading toward New Caney. "It was as bright as the lighting on a soccer field. But it was moving high in the sky," she said.

Two hypnosis sessions

To refresh her memory, Vickie Landrum is placed under regressive hypnosis twice by Dr. R. Leo Sprinkle, a psychologist at the University of Wyoming. The man is well known. Over the past 20 years, he has worked with 250 witnesses of UFO sightings.

"Under hypnosis, Vickie did not reveal any new details," says the hypnotherapist, "but she also did not change her story. She expressed her feelings very dramatically as she relived them. She kept pulling on her blouse and cradling her arm as if she were holding Colby against her. She said she thought it was the end of the world and that Jesus was going to come out of all that light."

Sprinkle says, however, that there is no way to know if a person is really under hypnosis. "But based on my 15 years of experience, Ms. Landrum really was. Or maybe she took some serious acting classes." He points out that a story delivered under hypnosis is not "absolute proof" of a past event. It is, however, what the person feels, "their truth," their vision of reality.

The first session took place on July 11, 1981. The following weeks were particularly painful for Vickie. Instead of helping her, it made her feel worse. "I will never experience those moments of terror again," she swore.

Difficult years

On March 18, 1982, Betty, Vickie, Colby and John Schuessler appeared on *"Good Morning America,"* a hugely popular TV show. One feels the two women very affected.

Both women have become media stars and are constantly in demand. In the press, the interviews multiply. Vickie declares: "Not for a minute did I think that this device could come from another planet. I never believed in UFOs. I still don't believe in them. You know, I'm a very religious person," she says, then confides her worst fear: "I've lived my life. But I'm afraid for Colby. I'm afraid that in the next few years he might develop some kind of leukemia. That's what I've heard from some of the doctors, like Dr. Rank from Wisconsin and Dr. Shoney. It depends on the amount of radiation he was subjected to that night... That's my primary concern. They have to tell us what that object really was. Then we will be able to help my grandson."

Meanwhile, the boy develops "blisters the size of his thumb" on the inside of his knees.

The damage suffered by our witnesses is not only sanitary. They are also economic. Betty Cash is almost ruined, the medical expenses cost a fortune. Moreover, too exhausted, the two women are unable to work.

Betty Cash is concerned about her increasing vision loss. "I have never worn prescription glasses before. Since that meeting, I'm on my third pair!" Then to confide, "I would be much better off if I were dead."

In July 1982 and March 1983, John Schuessler told the press: "This event deeply traumatized our three victims. They are now partially blind. And that's only part of their medical problems. Not to mention their hair loss, diarrhea, excessive tooth decay, and wounds that recur and reappear regularly... All three are actually showing symptoms of severe radiation exposure. He adds, "I think the military knows very well what happened. In any case, there are two plausible hypotheses. Either the device came from elsewhere. Or it was a secret military prototype that suffered severe damage and the helicopters were sent to retrieve it and clean up this disaster."

A year later, Betty developed breast cancer. On March 29, 1983, she had to undergo a mastectomy at St. Vincent's Hospital in Birmingham. The doctors gave up treating her with radiation because her skin had become "as thin as paper".

Colby's nightmares

The McDonalds fast food chain and the *Houston Chronicle* newspaper are holding a contest for children. The principle is simple: to win a trip to Washington, D.C., all you have to do is write a story about something that happened in your life. Colby - clandestinely - decided to enter. He sent a text entitled "The endless nightmare", which perfectly sums up these times of questioning and disarray. Here is what it says: "It was on the night of December 29, 1980 that this nightmare began.

My grandmother, my aunt Betty and I had gone to New Caney. It was on the way back that it happened. There was a very large object in the sky as we were driving down a very dark road. It came closer, it was huge and very bright. It was shaped like a diamond. As it flew over the trees, fire was coming out of it. We had to stop. I tried to run away at first but finally I got back in the car. My skin got all red from the heat he was giving off. We all got a lot of blisters. It was worse for Aunt Betty. We all got really sick. Our hair fell out. The newspapers tried to help us by trying to find out what the object was. They couldn't. It's hard for me to smile now. Sometimes when I think about that night, I wake up and cry into my pillow. There were lots of helicopters that night, with big rotors. Maybe one day I will find out what it was and my nightmare will end. This is a true story. I lived it."

While Colby did not win the trip, John Schuessler notes, "This 7-year-old boy won our hearts. So we redoubled our efforts to finally put an end to his nightmare."

Rational explanations

In an article in *Time* dated 15 April 1991, we learn that the American Department of Strategic Defense had invested 24 billion dollars in the creation of ballistic missiles, under the code name *Timberwind*.According to the paper, signed by journalist Philip Elmer-Dewitt, these devices, equipped with a nuclear reactor, emitted great heat during their travels while spreading highly radioactive residues in the atmosphere. Under the name of *Project Rover*, more than ten of these prototypes were manufactured and tested... Were our three victims confronted with a test of this kind? It is impossible to know because this type of operation is carried out in the greatest of secrecy. However, it is important to know that these clandestine actions, in the heart of the regal state, paradoxically take place illegally. And they entail significant risks.

The highly skeptical Philip J. Klass of Washington, author of four books on UFOs, who has studied the subject for 22 years, says the "Cash-Landrum" case is a set-up. He believes that both women were originally in poor health and made up the whole story so that the government would cover their extensive medical expenses. Cash and Landrum said they were used to such remarks. I know exactly what I've been through," said Betty Cash. Come on, I wouldn't have pulled my hair out by the handful. And I wouldn't have burned myself to a blister and then lazed in bed for months."

A man named Stewart Campbell, who lives in Edinburgh, Scotland, believes that our trio was deceived by a planet. He says we should have known exactly what time our victims left the New Caney truck stop. For he believes the sighting took place around midnight rather than around 9 p.m. I can assure you," he said, "that a star very low on the horizon can produce the effects reported by Mrs. Cash and Mrs. Landrum, with the exception of heat. *It* would seem that this detail is important!

Finally, the hypothesis was put forward that our trio had in fact mistaken a billboard for a UFO. As big as a water tower? Spitting flames? Emitting deafening beeps? And surrounded by a flight of helicopters? To each his own opinion.

We erase the traces

During an episode of the television series *"Unsolved Mysteries"*, John Schuessler, when asked about the "Cash-Landrum case", made a surprising revelation: "I first conducted several interviews with Betty and Vickie. Then, together, we went to the site of their sighting. They provided very precise details of what had happened. And how it had happened. They were able to show me the exact spot where they had stopped on the side of the road in front of the craft. There were tracks that showed that. They also showed me the place where the object, coming down from the sky, had stopped above the road. Indeed, one could see that a part of the road had been subjected to a very strong heat. The pavement was burned. It was obvious, it was obvious. A few weeks later, people went to the site, removed that section of asphalt and replaced it. Witnesses to this operation reported seeing trucks that had no markings on them. Men then cut out that section of the road, poured a new layer of asphalt, and drove away..."

Are we trying to erase what could be considered as evidence? This will be confirmed by several people. Notably a certain Larry, who notes on the show›s website: "This happened in Huffman... About 2 kilometers from my house. When I was a kid, my school bus used to go down that road and drive right on that particular marker. It began to fade in the 1990's, but was still visible. They replaced the piece of asphalt several times in an attempt to cover that mark. The funny thing is that after tarmacking that portion of the road, a few days later the mark would reappear across the asphalt..."

Source

Unsolved Mysteries, season 3, episode 18, aired in February 1991.

A tough fight

Betty and Vickie did not give up. Regarding their injuries, military officials at Bergstrom Air Force Base in Austin, Texas, suggest that the two women - "provided they find a lawyer willing to defend them!"- to file a lawsuit against the U.S. government. They did so. But this appeal is rejected. They appealed. It was rejected again.

With the help of their lawyer and *Citizens Against UFO Secrecy* (CAUS), Betty and Vickie decided to take their case to federal court. In January 1984, their lawyer asked for $20 million in damages. On September 3, 1985, the case is examined by the *United States District Court Docket Call*. But in the end, Judge Ross Sterling decided that the case would not be heard.

Nearly a year later, officials were heard, swearing that the object seen by our witnesses did not correspond to any known military device. Conclusion: the Government has nothing to do with it. The army either. Here is what these influential people declare.

Robert W. Sommer, NASA expert: "At no time has any of the objects described by the plaintiffs been possessed or used under NASA control."

Colonel William E. Krebs, tactical chief of the U.S. Air Force, an expert on the testing and evaluation of any Air Force aircraft capable of flight: "No such aircraft is in the possession or use of the U.S. Air Force and is not in its inventory. I have never seen or heard of such a craft associated with military exercises."

Vice Admiral Robert F. Schoultz, deputy chief of the U.S. Navy: "None of the flying machines described by Ms. Cash and Ms. Landrum are owned or operated by the U.S. Navy."

And finally Richard L. Ballard, of the *Aviation Systems Divisions*: "I have compared the description of this object with the inventory I have of all of our military's aircraft capable of flight. No similar aircraft are in the possession or use of the U.S. military."

Following the comments of these experts, the judge decided to close the case. On August 21, 1986, the plaintiffs were definitively dismissed and the case was closed. Move along, there's nothing to see! At the time, John Schuessler, the main investigator in the case, was furious: "Judge Ross Sterling considered that these reasons were sufficient to close the case. This means that he will not meet with Betty Cash, Vickie or Colby Landrum. And he won't be looking at any of the documents and evidence that their lawyers have." What a strange attitude.

If the justice system and the army - very embarrassed - look the other way, America is passionate about this burning story. The media coverage of our two victims continues. Vickie Landrum and Betty Cash both appeared on the television show *"UFO Cover Up: Live"*, hosted by Mike Farrell. Again, they talk about their encounter with the UFO, their serious health problems and the grueling legal battles that followed. Betty, elegantly dressed in black, confides: "I have cancer, I had surgery in March 1983. The doctors don't know if they were able to remove everything. Some days I am fine. One understands that each day that passes is a victory for Betty. She survives, riddled with pain. Added to this is a deep sense of injustice and abandonment. "I'm so angry and disappointed in the United States government," she says. Host Mike Farrell was sympathetic: "How can I blame you, Ms. Cash? As for you, Ms. Landrum, thank you for coming to Washington. You are both incredibly brave people." And the whole country is moved.

Betty and Vickie now harbor a distrust of their country's institutions and authorities. The *Birmingham News* of January 29, 1989 reports: "The bumper sticker on Betty Cash's Oldsmobile Cutlass perfectly sums up eight years of her life. It reads, 'UFOs exist. Not the Air Force." Betty Cash says this slogan has become central to her philosophy since her confrontation with a diamond-shaped object that spat orange and yellow flames and lit up the sky. "We thought it was the end of the world," she says from her mobile home on Morgan Martin Lake. "I've had many scares in my life, but never like the one I experienced that night!"'"

Despite some voices insinuating that this is all a scam, Dr. Bryan McClelland of Birmingham, Betty's treating physician, agreed to speak to reporters: "Mrs. Cash has all the symptoms of radiation poisoning. It looks like the injuries of the victims who lived five and five miles from the Hiroshima epicenter. A biopsy of Ms. Cash's skin, performed in 1981, actually revealed radiation dermatitis."

Ruined and living in seclusion, Betty Cash explains that her medical expenses amount to more than 1.5 million dollars. Despite the uproar of the press - which now speaks of a "cosmic Watergate" - the government plays the card of apathy, opacity and indifference.

For Vickie, times are also tough. Still living in Dayton, she says that whenever she goes out, people stare at her, make long detours to avoid her and call her *The UFO Lady*. Colby, now 17, was mocked so much that he eventually fell into a deep depression. Vickie refused to allow him to be interviewed, but provided reporters with excerpts from his diary: "I don't get laughed at as much as I used to," Colby notes. But I'm tired of it. My eyes are in bad shape. Every time I go out, I have a reflex to look at the sky. It's become a habit and I wonder what's up there. Many nights I wake up and wonder if other kids have gone through what I have..."

A sad end

In 1998, after spending years investigating the Cash-Landrum case, John Schuessler published a book entitled *The Cash-Landrum UFO Incident*, a reference book on this fateful encounter.

18 years to the day after her observation, Betty Cash passed away on December 29, 1998. She was 71 years old. It was an end of life of sufferings. Not a month passed without Betty being hospitalized or treated for various complications. Followed by 15 doctors, she was regularly placed in intensive care units. Thanks to the skills of Dr. Bryan A. McClelland, of Alabaster, Alabama, Betty Cash was able to survive a few more years, becoming for many American citizens both a martyr and a tireless fighter, fighting to the end of her strength against the silence of the institutions.

Vickie Landrum outlived him by about ten years. She passed away on September 12, 2007, 7 days before her 84th birthday .[e]

Sources

The APRO Bulletin, vol. 29, no. 8, 1981, pp. 1-4 - *Daily Courier*, Conroe, February 22, 1981 - *Weekly World News*, March 24, 1981, p. 19 - *UFO Report*, Winter 1981, pp. 16-19, 54-56 - *MUFON UFO Journal* No. 158, April 1981, p. 3 (this case illustrates the cover) - *Globe*, April 28, 1981 - *National Enquirer*, August 11, 1981, p. 23 - *Corpus Christi Caller-Times*, September 13, 1981 - *The Birmingham News*, January 29, 1989, p. 22 - *Unsolved Mysteries*, season 3, episode 18, aired February 6, 1991 - *Chronicle*, Houston, September 15, 1991 - *UFO Magazine*, vol. 13, no. 8, October 1998 (this case illustrates the cover) - *MUFON UFO Journal* no. 370, February 1999, p. 9 (Betty Cash is on the cover) - *Alien Hunters*, season 2, episode no. 8, case 80103: *"Alien Fallout",* aired January 14, 2009.

XI. Colares: deadly encounters in the Amazon

This is a solid case, with a body of evidence that is difficult to dispute. At the end of the 1970s, the Brazilian Northeast became the scene of unprecedented, disturbing, even tragic events. A great number of cities were affected: Vigia, Belém, Ibitumba, Condeúba, Tapará... But it is especially in Colares, a small Brazilian island located in the Amazon River delta, that these astonishing confrontations were concentrated.

It all began in July 1977, when luminous objects of all shapes and forms took over the sky. The panic quickly takes hold of the population. And the Brazilian armed force, the FAB, must then intervene.

The place

Located in the state of Pará and in the Nordeste region, Colares is an island of 290 km^2, isolated from the mainland by the Guajará-Mirim river. It has about 6,000 inhabitants, while the municipal seat has 2,000. The population comes from the communities Mocajatuba, Fazenda, Jaçarateua, Arari or Guajará. These communities are mainly composed of fishermen. Life is rather harsh. Poverty is endemic. Electricity is only available between 6 and 9 pm, supplied by a diesel-powered generator. The houses are often rudimentary. Most of the inhabitants of Colares have very limited access to education. Many are illiterate.

Brazil in 1977

Since 1964 (and until 1985), Brazil has lived under a right-wing military dictatorship. The government in place maintains its authority in a brutal way.

In order to fight against the left-wing opposition and guerrillas, during the 1970s, Brazil applied the Condor plan: an action carried out by all the totalitarian governments of South America (Argentina, Chile, Uruguay, Paraguay, Bolivia). This campaign of assassinations and torture was carried out with the complicity of the North American CIA.

Brazil, then hit by a financial crisis, saw poverty and insecurity increase. The rural provinces survive, abandoned. In the Northeast, 6 million peasants live without land, while 15,000 people own half of the total land area. The writer and journalist Eduardo Galeano noted in those years: "The northeast of Brazil is currently the most underdeveloped region in the Western Hemisphere. Before adding: "It is on the fertile coast that endemic hunger prevails. Where opulence is most ostentatiously displayed, misery is most acute...". The high corruption of the military does not help the matter.

Source

Eduardo Galeano, *The Open Veins of Latin America*, Plon-Terre humaine 1981.

First appearances

It all began in July 1977, when some inhabitants reported the sudden appearance of mysterious celestial objects. These objects were seen in the villages of Curupati, Urumajó, Itaçu or Viseu (on the bank of the Gurupi river). The Brazilians affirm that these objects paralyze them with a luminous ray and suck their blood. That's why they call them *Chupa-Chupa* (*chupar* means "to suck" in Portuguese).

Alerted, the local authorities, at first, do not pay much attention. They attribute all this agitation to a phenomenon of "collective hysteria". Sergeant Sabino do Nascimento Costa, in charge of the police of Viseu, is not interested. The mayor of Colares, Carlos Cardoso Santos, laughed: "These are totally fanciful stories," he said. For JosÈ Giambelli, priest of the village church, "[it's] just a product of the crazy imagination of this rural population! There is nothing concrete in it. It's just gossip that has been peddled for three months by stupid people who live on the other side of the river!"

However, the testimonies are accumulating. Fisherman Benedito Gonçalves dos Anjos Siqueira and his son, Simão Manoel Raimundo Siqueira (17 years old), are living a trying face-to-face: "10 days ago, we were fishing on the Gurupi River, near Ilha Nova," says Simão. Around midnight, I was looking at the sky, the moonlight was very beautiful. Suddenly I saw a star moving up there. It was very bright, much brighter than the others. It looked like it was pulsating, as if it was sending out intermittent streams of light. I warned my father. It was then that it headed straight for us. Since we had heard about these *Chupa-Chupa*, we untied our net and paddled to the shore. There we hid in the bushes. We ran away, because we didn't want his light to reach us. My father, terrified, buried his head in the ground. He didn't want to see anything. I looked at the object. It was very yellow. It came down and stopped about 4 meters above our boat. It was shaped like a tambourine, but a little bigger. It seemed to be made of metal and had no windows or openings. For 10 minutes it swept the whole area with a searchlight, as if it was searching the place for something. The glow was so intense that it produced a blinding glare on the river water. Then the object gained height again and finally moved away in the direction of the Zé da Granja farm."

Anastácio Costa confirms this by recounting the nightmare that his friend João de Brito, who lives in Vila de Piriá, just experienced: "A few days ago, my friend João was hunting. It was 11 p.m. when he decided to lie in wait for a prey among the bushes. He had just spotted an animal when, all of a sudden, something appeared in the sky and shot a beam of light at the animal, which collapsed. João was unable to run away. Then the light was directed at him. He had the impression that it drank all his energy. He thought he would die. The flying object was cylindrical and João could distinguish voices coming out of it, speaking in an unknown language. Then the thing flew away, leaving João now without any strength. He felt so weak that he had to be hospitalized."

What is happening in the sky of the Nordeste? One sees more and more these cylindrical objects that some baptize *camburões*. But it is the testimony of a teacher, María Goretti, which makes then react the authorities. When this one, upset, declares: "A cylindrical object and of an intense brightness lit my house and all the surrounding zone", her deposition - emanating from a person considered educated and respectable -, is then taken seriously.

Accumulating testimonies, the local journalists lead the investigation. The July 17 edition of the daily *O Estado do Maranhão* reported: "The appearance of a UFO over the town of Pinheiro caused amazement and panic among the local population. Some people claim that this object approaches the inhabitants to paralyze them and draw their blood. The existence of these UFOs is no longer in doubt. A cameraman from a TV station was even able to film one of them... "

The alarm is launched. The news quickly spreads to the region and then to the country. It is in the sky of Colores, in the north of the city of Belém, that these *Chupa-Chupa* improvise a crazy dance and literally unleash themselves on the population.

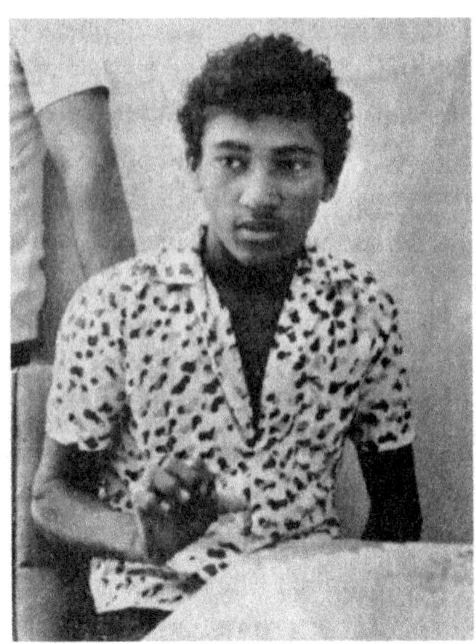

Simão viu a "luz diabólica".

Simão Manoel Raimundo Siqueira

UFOs in question

The objects seen are, for the most part, spherical in shape. We also report objects of cylindrical aspect. Some, rarer, are in the shape of fish or Y.

The observations are done mainly at night.

Most of the observed objects move from the sky to the land. Or from the ocean to the continent. Some of them dive or emerge from the waters of the river.

During their nightly evolutions, these UFOs mainly fly over small coastal and rural communities.

These objects paralyze the inhabitants by pointing a green ray at them. Then a red ray seems to take small quantities of blood from these victims.

Having a paralyzing action, these light rays can pass through the roofs and walls of houses.

The inhabitants call them *Foco* ("fire"), *Luz Vampira* ("vampire light") or *Aparelho* ("device"). But it is under the name of *Chupa-Chupa* that they are most often referred to.

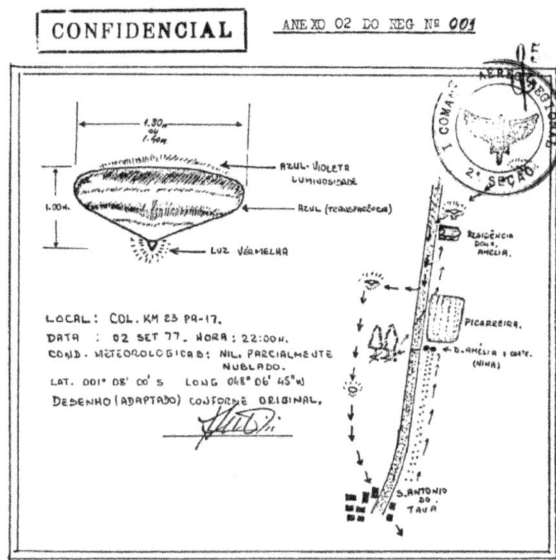

Example of UFO seen in Colares

Injuries inflicted

The victims of these *Chupa-Chupa* are usually adults of both sexes. The injuries are not inflicted casually. However, FAB members note that 2/3 of those affected are adult women.

The lesions observed in affected individuals consist of first-degree burns, 2 to 10 centimeters in length, most often located on the thoracic region.

Women are usually affected on their left breast. Men on their left leg or arm.

Burns are not accompanied by blisters. And they do not resemble the classic burns caused by contact with fire, boiling water or very hot elements. They are more like radioactive burns, like those produced by cobalt. This without any infectious process.

There is little pain in the affected area. Victims feel a slight burn that passes within a few hours.

2 days after the injury, the victim's skin peels off. At this point, you can see closely spaced dots on the skin, like stitches or needle sticks. These stitches usually disappear within 72 hours.

A few days after the incident, hair loss and scaling of the epidermis are noted in the affected areas.

After confrontation, *Chupa-Chupa* victims complain of asthenia (weakness of the lower limbs) and dizziness, aches and pains, tremors, lack of courage, drowsiness, hoarseness, hair loss, scaling of the injured skin and frequent headaches. This symptomatology has been noted by the treating physicians.

Blood tests performed on some victims indicate low hemoglobin and reduced red blood cells.

A state of panic

At the end of July, the panic reaches Colares. These *Chupa-Chupa* terrorize the population which flees to take refuge inland. The life of the island is stopped. To take the measure of this real trauma, here is the testimony of Ana Célia de Oliveira, reported by the investigator Fabrice Bonvin: "At night, people made big fires in the open air to try to prevent UFO attacks. Because of the sightings, the schools were closed, as was the police station. The daily 6 p.m. masses were all cancelled. Women and children stayed indoors while the men stood guard. No more fishermen went out to sea, there was nothing left to eat on the island. Also, people systematically moved in groups. From 6 p.m., when it started to get dark, people would gather in the houses. At that time, we had electricity until 9 pm. Among the UFO overflights, I remember one sighting where I heard a man shouting for our attention. I opened the door and observed several UFOs flying in formation and then dispersing in the sky. The islanders were firing their rifles into the air to scare the UFOs away. On one occasion, a UFO flew over the village at a height of just 50 feet."

Faced with the gravity of the facts, the prefect of Vigia, then the mayors of Vigia and Colares send a letter to the first regional air command of the aeronautics of Belém, the COMAR. They ask for the help and intervention of the army. While waiting for an answer, the mayor of Colares provided firearms to the villagers so that they could defend themselves.

"I have never forgotten the panic on the faces of the people who said they were attacked by these lights that came down from the sky and made their blood flow," *recalls* journalist Carlos Mendes. Dispatched to cover the events by the newspaper *O Estado do Pará*, he estimates that he interviewed 80 victims.

Captain Hollanda intervenes

The army finally decides to intervene. It entrusted this mission to a man it considered providential. Entered in the legend under the name of Hollanda, this captain of the Air Force is in reality called Uyrangê Bolívar Soares Nogueira de Hollanda Lima. Interviewed in 1997 by the journalists of the Brazilian magazine *UFO*, he confided that his interest in UFOs goes back to his childhood.

In 1952," he says, "I was 12 years old and I was at the window of my house, in BelÈm, when very large objects appeared in the sky and caught my attention. There was a bright light over the whole city. The next day, the story was published in the newspaper. It was said that these objects had stopped over a scout federation during a swimming championship. In any case, everyone saw them. That's when my interest in this phenomenon began, long before I joined the army. And long before the Prato operation. I have always believed in extraterrestrial life and the possibility that "they" have the curiosity to observe us. We are a planet with intelligent life that should be of interest to aliens."

He explains: "Until then, my activity consisted in watching over the security of the state. And to keep an eye on anything that might compromise national security. It had nothing to do with UFOs or aliens. However, I was already aware of some sightings in the Amazon. But these UFOs were not considered an external threat. To many, they were just a dubious phenomenon. Some officers - probably most of them - saw UFOs as an improbable thing and didn't care."

Captain Hollanda knows perfectly these Amazonian jungle grounds. He has, in this hostile environment, tracked down rebel factions to the dictatorship, fighting, in his words, "against the actions of terrorists and communist parties that tried to infiltrate the country". He is said to be a determined, pragmatic man of impressive culture. A tough guy, in short.

This is how it all began for him: "I was not in Belém at the time," he says. Although I was assigned to Belém, I was taking a course in Brasilia. When I returned, I introduced myself to the head of the second section of COMAR, Colonel Camilo Ferraz de Barros. He then asked me, "Do you believe in flying saucers?" This was rather surprising. I didn't even know that research on the subject was underway. And when I said yes, he said, "So you're in charge of this case. "He sent me a file with some material. That was the beginning of the operation I was going to order. Even though it didn't have a name yet. I also think that it happened because the commander of the 1st COMAR, Brigadier Protásio Lopes de Oliveira, at that time, was very interested and believed in unidentified flying objects. Otherwise..."

Captain Holland

Operação Prato

Hollanda confides: "I was the one who decided to call this mission: *operação Prato* ("Operation Plate"). It was my idea. I gave this name because Brazil is the only country in the world that designates UFOs under the term "disks". In France, they call them saucers, which means plates. The Portuguese call them "flying dishes". In Spain, they are *platillos voladores*, and the *platillo* is also a dish. In short, even the Russians talk about dishes, never about discs, as we do in Brazil! And since in the Armed Forces, an agent must name certain operations by a code name, this mission could not escape the rule. The goal of the operation was that it could not be identified. It could not be called "Operation Flying Disks". That's why I chose the term *prato*.

"When I returned from Brasilia, I knew that agents had been sent to investigate these UFO sightings. We had been seeing them for a while in the area of Colares, this island attached to the municipality of Vigia. The mayor of the town had sent a letter to the commander of COMAR saying that the UFOs were disturbing the fishermen. Some of them were no longer able to carry out their activity because these objects were flying over their boats. Sometimes, some UFOs even dived very close to them, into the rivers and the sea. The local population did not sleep anymore, they stayed awake all night. The men lit fires, knocked on cans, shot off large fireworks to try to keep the invaders away. It was the panic that prompted the mayor to contact the army for help. The brigadier general ordered me to investigate these events.

"We were a team and I was the boss. We had five agents from the second division of COMAR. And then we were getting a lot of information from people on the ground who were seeing these lights. They helped us a lot. Sometimes I would split my team into 2 or 3 observation groups in the woods. Of course, we were in constant contact with each other, *via* the radio.

"Our goal? Let's just say I really wanted to get proof of this. I wanted to get to the bottom of this mystery. Everyone was talking about these lights and objects that the locals called *Chupa-Chupa*. The Air Force needed to know what was really going on since these objects were violating Brazilian airspace. It was my responsibility to find out what they really were.

"Who were these invaders? I thought, 'Maybe it's the feathers of an owl reflecting the moonlight. Or something like that... I went there to get to the bottom of it. For at least 2 months, when I came back from my mission, I kept telling my commander that we had not discovered anything. That was during the first two months of the Prato operation, during which I didn't see anything that would change my mind. Sometimes I would stay in the jungle for a week and only return on Sundays to spend some time with my family. Each time I returned, my commanding officer would ask, "Did you see anything? "I would invariably reply, "I saw some strange lights, but nothing extraterrestrial." In fact, we were observing flashing lights, flying low, but nothing really peculiar.

"We had a precise methodology. We always noted the name of the person who had lived the experience, the place where it happened, the date, the time, etc. We described in detail each fact collected. We would describe in detail each fact collected. If 3 cases took place on the same night, we heard from the 3 witnesses successively. Some of the descriptions were banal, others were really strange. Sometimes we recorded reports of things that we could not prove to be true, such as dematerializations of house walls or entire roofs.

"The first woman I interviewed in Colares, for example, told me things that seemed absurd. We had left Belém by helicopter, just to interview this victim who had been attacked by a *Chupa-Chupa*. I could first see that she had a mark on her left breast, a brown spot, as if it were a burn. And there were 2 dots that pierced her epidermis. She told me that she was sitting in a hammock putting a child to sleep. All of a sudden, the environment around her started to change temperature. Of course, the lady thought it was strange. But she had no idea what would happen next. Lying down in the hammock, she saw that the roof tiles started to turn reddish, the color of embers. Then they became transparent and she could see the sky through them. It was as if those tiles had turned into glass. She could see the sky and even the stars. Through this hole in the ceiling, the woman also saw a green light shining in the sky. It was a UFO. A red ray came out of the object, hit the left breast of this inhabitant who immediately felt numb. It is strange that most of the time, people are hit on the left side.

Captain Hollanda finally sees them

Two months of investigations, of wild camps, of compulsively scanning the sky. And few results. And then suddenly, leaving the clandestinity, the phenomenon seems to want to show itself and to measure itself with the military of the FAB. Something has just changed. Captain Hollanda testifies:

"It was indeed strange. They, whoever they were, knew for sure where we were and what we were doing there. It even seemed that they were looking for us, because when we least expected it, they appeared, right there, above us. We had just arrived a month ago, and as soon as we were settled in these places, which were known for their appearances, space probes kept coming to observe us. Sometimes the soldiers moved. These objects escorted them. They accompanied us almost all the time, as if they were aware of our movements.

"For example, in the case of Baía do Sol, something special happened. At that time, the school year was ending and many people stayed on the beach at night. There were at least 100,000 people at the water's edge that weekend. However, an object came right at us, in a very dark place, where there was only us. Why did it come towards us in the dark when there were so many people nearby on the beach?

"As Baía do Sole is a very favorable place for UFO sightings, we started to frequent this area quite regularly. Friends from the National Information Service (SNI) wanted to accompany us on some of our missions. These agents just wanted to see, with our team, these things fly. They knew that we were doing a serious job... That day, with Milton Mendonça, a photographer, we arrived in Baía do Sol, around

6 pm, and we set up our photographic equipment. We then stood in a dark and secluded place, to watch what might happen. However, for personal reasons, I had to return earlier in the night. I had to reach Belém at 8 pm because I had an appointment. Around 6:30 pm, 3 luminous points appeared, aligned very high in the sky, flying at high speed. I know enough about planes to say that the speed of these things was well above average. The dots were flying in a west-east direction. At 7:00 pm, 2 more strange objects, flashing, still in a line, appeared one behind the other, but this time moving in a north-south direction. The SNI agents were still not there. However, we had made a date to meet at 6 p.m. to share this vigil. So I waited a little longer. Then I started to dismantle the equipment. Finally, the guys arrived. They asked if anything had happened while they were away. I joked that I had made an appointment with the UFOs at 6:00 p.m. and that they had also shown up at 7:00 p.m., because these objects appear every hour. One of the agents then asked a silly question, "What time is he supposed to show up for another one?" I replied that I didn't know, that we weren't waiting for a streetcar that met strict schedules. I also told the men that if they wanted to see UFOs, they should stay there all night. Just then, as we were talking, one of them called out, "Look at that, now. Up there." And there the Brazilian hero shook on his base. For there was a huge ship right there above us. It was a dark, black disk, at an altitude of about 150 meters. It was standing exactly where we were, totally still. A light in its center was changing from yellow to amber. And it made a sound like an air conditioner. It sounded like the clanking of a bicycle chain as you pedal backwards. This thing was huge, maybe 100 feet in diameter. We watched it for a long time. Then it emitted a strong yellow light that lit up the ground. This was repeated about 5 times, at regular 2 second intervals. Off, on, off. It was a progressive light, not illuminating like a flash. But it was simultaneously increasing and decreasing. We had the feeling that anything could happen. It was dark. We were in a very isolated place and no one knew our position. Well, just us and "them" *[laughs]*. We were all amazed! I had never seen anything like it. And yet it had been 2 months since our operation had begun. We had never seen a ship like that before. It was so unusual that we did not even think of taking out the camera that we had just put away. Besides, it was in its box and it would have taken a long time to take it out and assemble it. We just stared at the thing, terrified. This amazing thing that lit up everything around us, with a very intense yellow light that sometimes went out, and sometimes came on... Although this observation was of great beauty, I was terrified. I felt helpless."

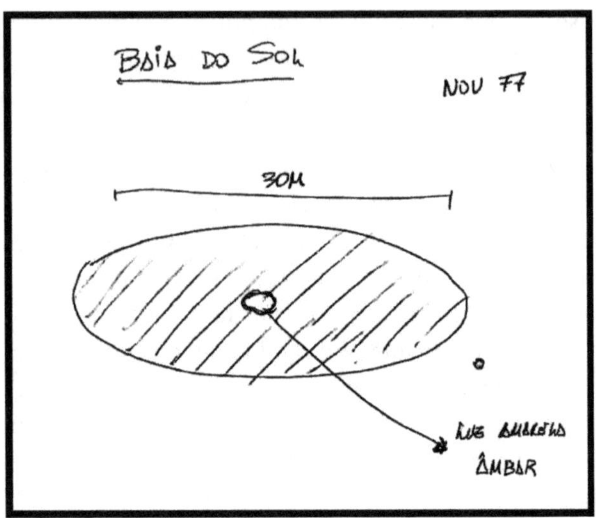

UFO seen by Captain Holland

40 victims and 2 deaths

Driven by panic, the women and children leave the island to take refuge with their families, inland. The dentist, the teachers and even the commissioner also fled. Despite this sudden exodus, the 24-year-old doctor Wellaide Cecim Carvalho de Oliveira resists and decides to stay at her post. However, she remembers her arrival on the island: "I landed in Colares in a tragic way. The tide was low and the ferry could not cross the Guajará-Mirim, the river that separates the island from the continent. I was accompanied by a friend from the area. Unable to cross the river, we had to use a canoe. As we were about to reach the other side, just as we were about to get out, the canoe overturned. I almost drowned because I can't swim. It was my friend who helped me. And then, while accosting on the island, we fell on a mangrove. We were stuck in the mud up to our knees. This caused me to have seizures that lasted about 6 months. Let's just say I was shipwrecked at my workplace..."

Hard landing. But determined, our doctor quickly took command of the health unit, a very basic establishment with 1 registered nurse, 12 nurses at her command and 1 dentist. Dr. Carvalho assumes the functions of both doctor and director of the establishment.

During more than 6 months, it looks after the usual bobos of the fishermen of the corner. They are generally accidents due to the stingrays of which the beaches are infested. Or parasitosis caused by the consumption of raw fish.

Then suddenly, many patients show up, asking for help and claiming to be attacked by celestial lights that stalk them. Doctor Carvalho is doubtful. At first, she puts it down to hallucination or drunkenness. But strange thing, all these islanders present the same symptoms:

- low blood pressure,
- burns, like sunburns, on the face, throat and chest, appearing as purplish spots
- small perforations inside these burns,
- local loss of sensitivity,
- asthenia with a very low hemoglobin level.

Finally intrigued, she placed these patients under observation for 4 or 5 days.

I treated about 40 people," she says. Mostly adults. At first, I thought these people were either crazy or that it was a popular belief. I even thought it was witchcraft. But after the fifth case, I began to take it all seriously. I took a closer look at the victims' injuries and saw things that didn't exist in my medical books... For a long time, the police chief, the priest and I were the only professionals in Colares. When the UFOs appeared, many people left the island. Only 3 professionals remained on the island. There were no more stores open. We had little to eat except eggs and cassava flour. The fishermen did not want to fish anymore because they were afraid."

The victims follow one another in the summary room of the health unit. Confronted with a real epidemic of burns, the doctor notes, without really understanding, the great fatigue felt by these men and women aged between 18 and 50.

Among these 40 victims, 2 will die. Dr. Carvalho remembers. One morning in September 1977, at 7:30 a.m., a woman was waiting for him at the door of the dispensary. Very agitated, she told him that she had just been attacked and burned by a *Chupa-Chupa*. She then opened her blouse and showed a large red spot on her left breast with small perforations. I was trying to calm her down," she says. I told her it was nothing serious and that she shouldn't let it bother her. I gave her 5 milligrams of diazepam; she could barely lift the glass of water to her lips. She complained that she was having trouble breathing. She felt dizzy and weak. I later realized that these were typical symptoms, along with the headaches and a decrease in red blood cell count.

"Three hours later, I was called to her home in an emergency. I found her in a deep coma, her body completely rigid, losing her breath. She had no fever and had not vomited. I tried to drive her to Belém in my car, a green Volkswagen Beetle, but I didn't have enough gasoline. So she was taken there in a car from the prefecture. I waited for news. A few hours later, I received a medical statement and a death certificate from the Renato Chaves Forensic Institute indicating heart failure as the cause of her death. She was a 44 or 45 year old maid..."

Then she adds: "The man who died, on the other hand, was younger. He was a 32-year-old fisherman. He had the same burns on his chest. The document from the Government did not specify the cause of death. There was no autopsy because the air force was not authorized to perform one. Both people died the same day they were burned. The man died at his home in Colares about two hours after I spoke with him."

Burned animals

According to Dr. Carvalho, "there were also attacks on animals. Animals were targeted more often than human beings. Generally, we found dead animals that had no hair or feathers left. At dawn, some would go into convulsions and die. When they had not been recently attacked, they looked burnt, dry and scorched, with eyes wide open, as if they had been placed alive in an oven. The area around the attack scenes smelled of scorched hair. No one had the courage to eat these animals, even though we were hungry and had nothing else to eat. No one even tried, because we were terrified. That's when we started to fish for crab..."

"The animals attacked were usually ducks, chickens, pigs and cows. As well as dogs that went right into the light emitted by the objects to see what it was. The form of death was always the same: the next day they were found dry and with their eyes wide open. I estimate that the *Chupa-Chupa* attacked many more animals than humans. This may be information that ufologists don't know, because I never thought it was interesting."

The doctor sees a UFO

For a scientist, these stories seem hard to believe. Until one day...

In November 1977, I saw a UFO," says Dr. Carvalho. It was about 6 pm. I was coming back from a patient's house, accompanied by my housekeeper. Suddenly, she began to pull on my dress, repeating: "Doctor, doctor...". I looked at her and she immediately fainted. At that moment, looking up to the sky, I could see the most beautiful and fantastic thing in my life. It was a cylindrical object that emitted a very bright light and flew very low over the street, dancing, making majestic loops. At its ends, there were lights. On its upper part, a dome of red color. Its lower part was purple. As it moved, the UFO seemed to leave a trail of light that quickly disappeared. At first I thought it was going to land on the beach. But then it suddenly started to rise straight up into the sky and I saw it disappear into the firmament. I could not make out any windows or openings on the surface of the object. I followed it with my eyes in a state close to ecstasy, so beautiful was this vision. The people near the beach ran to barricade themselves in their homes. This panic being contagious, I also started to run while supporting my fainting maid... Even today, when I close my eyes, I see this object reappear. I have forgotten many things in all these years, but this I will never forget."

A baby and a little dog

The *Chupa-Chupa* continue their strange saraband in the sky of Nordeste.

Date: October 29, 1977.
Location: Tapiapanema, a hamlet of 4 houses located on Mosqueiro Island, along the Pratiquara River.
6pm.

Sílvia Mara Trindade, 17, lies next to Benedito Campos Trindade, her 24-year-old husband. They are resting from their daily work. They are alone because that evening the rest of the household has gone to the village of Mosqueiro, 16 kilometers away.

The night has just fallen. In the surroundings everything is calm and silent. Suddenly, through a gap in the window covered with a piece of plastic, the couple notices that an oval, silver object emits a greenish light, in the form of a flash. This light enters the room where they are and reaches Sylvia, 5 months pregnant, putting her in a kind of trance and numbness.

Panic because it's one of those *Chupa-Chupa that everyone* talks about! Worried for his pregnant wife, Benedito flies to her rescue. He takes her in his arms to move her away from the window. But he is also touched by the beam of the UFO. I felt strange," he says. I couldn't talk anymore. And Sylvia fainted*!*

The nightmare does not end there. Two "creatures" enter the house, holding a golden object, like a battery-operated lantern. These creatures focus again on Sílvia›s body, especially on her left arm and wrist. Reached by the light, the veins of the girl swell and seem to leave her body. Benedito calls for help. While screaming, he carries his wife in the living room and tries to hide her behind a wall.

Alerted by the cries, José do Nascimento Sobral, their neighbor, runs over. Armed with a shotgun, he shoots at the two "creatures", succeeding in making them flee.

Benedito and Sílvia took refuge at Sobral's house, 500 meters from their home. The young man recovers some strength. But Sílvia is in such a state that there is not a minute to lose. She seems to be at her worst. Benedito loads her in his boat. And while rowing, he has to cover about fifteen kilometers to reach the hospital of Mosqueiro. The journey lasts a good hour. Suddenly the UFO is back! It follows the young couple, follows him at a distance of 8 meters and directs its ray on the surface of the waves. It is completely silent. Then, as strangely as it appeared, it moves away abruptly while flying over the trees of the jungle and disappears.

When she arrived in Mosqueiro, Sílvia was taken care of by the doctors. She was found to have a bruise on the inside of her left elbow. She was so weak that she had to stay in hospital for several days. 2 months later, it is the drama: she loses her baby!

As a result of this ordeal, Benedito had a nervous breakdown, frequently crying whenever he mentioned the subject. Although we can't admit it, Osmarina, his mother, thinks that it caused him "a mental weakness". His wife never fully recovered her health. Separated from Benedito, she now lives alone. This unfortunate encounter caused another victim: a little dog named Vitória who belonged to Maria

Raimunda de Souza (18 years old), a neighbor. Benedito remembers: "I could hear Vitória barking while I was taking care of Sílvia. Maria, her boss, ran to her. An object passed over the animal and with a beam of light hit it on the head. The little dog fainted. Vitória then stopped barking and feeding. No one heard her bark anymore. And she died three or four weeks later."

Maria Raimunda de Sousa is terrified by what she experienced and refuses to talk about it. Since then, she spends hours, leaning against the window of her house, looking at the sky, fearing that it will happen again.

Sílvia Mara Trindade and Benedito Campos Trindade

And humanoids...

During this wave of 1977, testimonies reporting the presence of ufonauts or humanoid creatures (as it was the case here) are rather rare. However, the daily newspaper *O Estado* reported the strange observation of João Batista Souza, owner of the Fazenda Nova Meliá, in the countryside of Maranhão.

July 17, 1977.

Dawn has not yet broken. Suffering from insomnia, João Batista Souza decides to take a walk around his property. As he was walking, he suddenly saw a fireball flying over his property, 200 meters away. Frightened, he took shelter behind a bush and witnessed the landing of the sphere. The object, according to him, looked more like "a straw hat". A door opens and a small creature of about 1 meter in height emerges. In his left hand, the intruder holds a kind of lantern that emits a violet light. In the other hand, it carries something that the farmer is unable to identify. It is impossible to distinguish the face of this humanoid who is wearing a helmet with antennas. But what shocks our witness most of all is that the body of this being is completely covered with hair!

A blond humanoid

November 1977, another encounter with a humanoid. A pilot drives his car on a track not far from Colares. The night has fallen, thick, oppressive in this jungle territory. Suddenly, our witness sees a disc-shaped object descend from the sky and land behind a clump of trees. Captain Hollanda, who was watching the area and collected this testimony, says: "At that moment, the pilot was alone on the road, the darkness was total, and the man was totally terrified! It was then that he saw a figure heading towards him. It was in fact a blond "man", of great size, who approached the car and plunged his glance in that of our witness. Horrified, our pilot then started to cry. The blond-haired stranger shook his head, examined the vehicle›s license plate, turned on his heels and finally disappeared into the thick vegetation of the forest. A few moments later, a disc-shaped craft took off and climbed up to merge into the darkness of the night."

Source

Timothy Good, *Unearthly Disclosure*, Arrow Books, 2001.

The UFOs of Colares

Hollanda, a key witness to this *Chupa-Chupa* wave, states:

"The appearances of these objects were almost daily. They were very active. We concluded that there were 9 types of UFOs. We were able to identify and classify them. Some were probes, others were huge ships from which smaller objects emerged. All this is very well documented in our reports.

"To record all this, we had professional Nikon cameras, with telephoto lenses from 300 to 1,000 millimeters. It was difficult to handle them. They were extremely precise and sensitive. Any mistake, any wrong move, and you lost your target. But it was first-rate equipment. We also had camcorders and tape recorders, in case any interesting sound could be recorded.

The reports with drawings, photos, sketches and the rest were prepared, classified, transmitted to the commander and deposited at 1ᵉʳ COMAR, in a room reserved for them. After that, some went to Brasilia, as I was told at the time. However, as far as I know, the higher echelons remained skeptical. Some colleagues even joked about the facts."

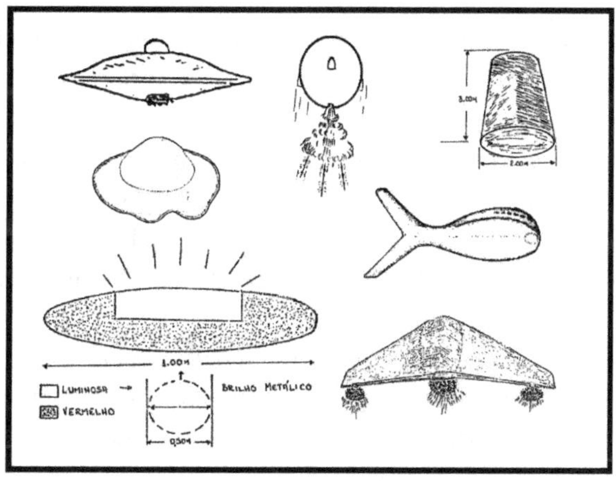

UFOs seen in the sky of Northeast Brazil

Oanis!

In Colores, fishermen are certainly harassed by celestial objects... but also by Oanis, unidentified aquatic objects. Captain Hollanda testifies: "First of all, fishermen reported to me cases of unidentified devices under water. Frankly, I didn't believe it. However, a few weeks later, I myself observed a blue light flying close over a boat before diving into the depths of the mouth of the Amazon. It was then that I realized that the fishermen were telling the truth. They indicated that there was no splash or noise when the UFOs entered the water, like a blade splitting the waves.

This is confirmed by Rósio de Oliveira, a 34 years old fisherman. He made 9 sightings between November 4 and 28, 1977. Interviewed by investigator Bob Pratt, he said: "The UFOs came from everywhere: from the sky, from the bay, vertically or horizontally. The Air Force was present and used a radio, telephoto lenses. Frequently, the UFOs hovered over the samaumeiras, the tall trees that grow in the tropics, as if they were clinging to their branches. At the time, the trees did not seem affected. It was only a few years later that they started to die mysteriously...

"We also observed 3 or 4 objects coming from several directions merging into a larger object. And all this in the greatest silence. Another time, we saw UFOs coming out of the water near Ponta do Machadinho. They were 8 very intense lights of yellow, red and white color that emerged from the water, one after the other. Then, these lights flew over the bay, and then they dived back into the depths, exactly from where they had emerged."

Researcher Vitório Peret, who formed a long friendship with Hollanda and participated in many nights of vigilance in Colares, says he had the chance to watch two videos shot by the military in the areas of Baía do Sol and ChapÈu Virado. Here is his testimony, published in October 2013 in issue 204 of the Brazilian magazine *UFO*:

"The first recording I saw was 12 minutes long. But we only saw 22 seconds of it. In the film, we saw an extremely bright UFO moving at night in the bay of Marajó, at a very low altitude. According to the calculations of the military, it should be 5 meters from the surface of the water. This object then approached a small boat. The fisherman inside the boat was afraid and jumped overboard. Then, the object changed its flight angle and entered the water in a vertical position, known in aviation as a "knife".

"The second video was much more spectacular. It was in black and white and filmed this time at night. An unidentified craft made a reverse maneuver: first it appeared under the surface of the water, as if the water was boiling. Then, it emitted a whitish luminosity and a few seconds later, it was seen emerging from the water. This scene strongly impressed all the people present of which the general Alfredo Moacyr of Mendonça Uchôa. The general compared the nose of the ship to that of the Concorde airplane which, at that time, presented the most advanced aerodynamics of the commercial aviation. Then, displaying its tapered tip, the craft began to slowly emerge. As it overcame the resistance of the water, it became brighter and brighter. Then it rose, and diagonally glided toward the horizon before melting into space, without making a sound. It was spectacular!

"Afterwards, I participated in UFO vigils with Hollanda. It was at the end of 1979, 1 year and 7 months after the end of the Prato operation. We continued to conduct investigations in the area and we also made some sightings. I myself saw UFOs diving in the waters of Marajó Bay. In the company of Hollanda and other soldiers, I experienced the most beautiful episode of my life when an object, coming from the horizon, made a fantastic flight, very low skimming the surface of the water. It stopped for about 2 minutes. Suddenly, it made a quick maneuver as if it was climbing the steps of a ladder to stop again. And finally we saw it descend vertically and enter the water quietly, very gently. This machine was magnificent, of orange-red color. It had a lenticular shape and reflected the first rays of the sun. This happened in 1981, one morning very early, at 5:05 a.m. exactly.

Face to face with the military

December 1977.

Hollanda says, "Anything could have happened to us, I don't make a mystery of it. It could have happened in the woods, in the jungle, on the beach, anywhere. We were on a military operation and we had to endure everything. Anything was possible in the performance of our duties.

"We didn't have any guns at any time. I never thought of taking a gun, even in case... We never thought of needing one. Even in the preparations for the operation, when we were discussing logistics, food, transportation, communication, it was never mentioned.

"I only once considered that this phenomenon could be dangerous. Something very strong happened, so much so that I was afraid that a kidnapping might occur. I told very few people about it. But I told my friend Rafael Sempere Durá what happened. For exposing myself to something so dangerous, he scolded me severely. He said angrily: "You irresponsible nutcase! I am your friend and I forbid you to do such a thing."

"The fact was really serious. During Operation Prato, we were aboard a ship anchored on the bank of the Jari River when a huge object approached us. At

---

first we saw a bright yellow light, like a sun. It was impossible to see its exact shape because it was too bright. Then it went out. Then we could see that this object had the strange shape of a football, pointed and wide, measuring about 100 meters. A translucent device, with small windows along its length. But it was impossible to tell if there was someone inside, even though the object was moving very slowly, and this was obviously intentional. This happened between 11 pm and 11:30 pm. It was many years ago, but I remember the date. After this episode, we commented, "What a weird thing!" Then around 1:00 or 1:30, the UFO came back. This time it was no longer the color of the sun: it was a very strong blue. It followed the opposite bank of the river. It was 70 meters away from us. This blue monster, although it emitted a very strong glow, could be looked at directly without hurting your eyes. There was nothing but this bright light. It was amazing. We stood up to look at it. I was really scared, because it was very close, just across the river... This object stayed still for about 3 minutes. During this time, we watched it in silence. Suddenly, the light went out and we could see what was behind it. It was the same "football", standing 100 meters high, motionless and without windows. Was it the same UFO? I don't know. Everyone was frightened. One of the people present even asked, "What now? If these guys come to take us away, what do we do?" Everything was new to us. And nobody knew, at that moment, what could happen."

Another version. According to the Brazilian ufologist Ademar José Gevaerd, who would have collected the confidences of Hollanda, "this one described, while he was with a commando on the river Guajará-Mirim, on the way back to the camp, a cylindrical ship of 100 meters high that practically landed on the other bank. From the top of the craft, a door opened, an alien creature emerged and floated to where they were. Hollanda suspected that it was precisely the contact with this alien on the banks of the Guajará-Mirim River, in mid-December 1977, that would have been the determining factor in the closure of the Prato operation. He stated that after reporting the fact to his superior, Brigadier Protásio Lopes de Oliveira, commander of the 1ᵉʳ Regional Air Command (1ᵉʳ COMAR), he received the order to close the mission.

UFO: The 12 files that the Pentagon cannot explain

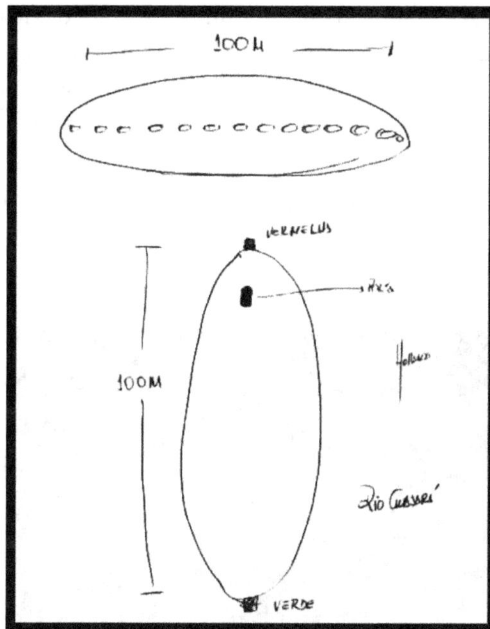

Drawing of the UFO by Hollanda

The United States takes over

Indeed, shortly after this observation, the Brazilian Air Force put an end to the Prato operation. It will have lasted 4 months in total and will be taken again, in an unofficial way, by the American government which is interested in it very closely.

The high authorities asked Hollanda to remain silent. However, he said: "When I informed my superiors of the visual contacts we had had with the UFOs and their occupants, things changed. In fact, as soon as it became clear that these objects were real, the investigation ended.

Hollanda, bitter, never approved of the decision. "But," he says, "I simply obeyed orders." Before adding, "I suspect that Brazil and the United States are signatories to a secret program called *Projeto Uno*, to which other Latin American nations are also affiliated. Don't forget that it was the United States that alerted us to the presence of unidentified flying objects in our airspace".

Nearly 500 photos, 16 hours of images filmed in super 8 mm and super 16 mm, as well as a 2,000-page report were given to the Brazilian General Staff. This was not followed up or officially concluded. According to the investigator Vitório Peret, the material of the Prato operation will probably never be released. Part of it has been destroyed and many images and reports are no longer in the hands of the Brazilian Air Force officials. It is, according to him, very likely that everything was communicated and transferred to the United States, as the Pentagon was very interested in the events of Colares.

Photo from the files of the Prato operation, taken on December 10, 1977 in Baía do Sol

Hollanda leaves the scene

However, research continued on the spot, but independently. On many occasions, Hollanda participated in UFO vigils. At the suggestion of General Uchôa, a small study group called *Projeto Alpha e Omega* was created and not officially registered. Vitório Peret was one of its 8 members.

What else did these new investigators discover? Not much, in fact. However, Hollanda had his hypothesis. For him, these objects came from elsewhere. He added: "In my opinion, these UFOs were not hostile to the population, they were only collecting biological material. The green ray paralyzed, the red one had the function of extracting blood. I myself said to people: "Do not use weapons! Don't attack them! Obviously, you can consider the emission of these blood-sucking rays

UFO: The 12 files that the Pentagon cannot explain

as a form of violence, but it is nothing but a collection without hostile intent." I think they wanted to make an antidote, a vaccine, a serological solution that would inhibit any incidence of disease in their alien organism. They were doing this from blood or material taken from humans."

Hollanda, who had remarried Cecília Maria Vianna de Aguiar, seemed to live, after 36 years of military activities, a quiet retirement in his house of Cabo Frio. But, on October 2, 1997, at 11 pm, he was found hanged with the belt of his dressing gown, leaving children from his two marriages. According to his relatives, he was depressed and had already made three other suicide attempts. For others, he had been "suppressed" for having revealed important defense secrets. This obviously adds mystery to this already intriguing episode.

Anyway, since his tragic death, Brazilian ufologists have not ceased to pay tribute to him, as well as the whole world ufological community, praising his invaluable contribution.

It must be said that Operation Prato remains a unique example of investigation into these mysterious celestial objects. For the Brazilian ufologist Ademar José Gevaerd: "Operation Prato was the largest military mission ever carried out to investigate UFOs in the world." Thiago Luiz Ticchetti, president of the Brazilian Commission of Ufologists (CBU), confirms, "What impresses me the most is the fact that we investigated something so incredible and, even today, we are not able to explain what happened."

And what happened to those blood-sucking *Chupa-Chupa*? According to Vitório Peret, "Today, these luminous objects are still seen by the residents of the interior areas. They are seen quite often, but without the same aggressiveness as in the past. The events are identical to those of the past, but these vessels no longer emit the rays or beams of light that caused so much panic and inflicted so much damage on the victims. Today, the inhabitants of the area have become accustomed to the frequency of the sightings and are no longer afraid, although they do not like to talk about them. Anyone who would like to film or photograph these strange lights would easily succeed, as these events always take place in the area.

Sources

Jornal O Liberal, July 11, 1977, p. 24 - *O Estado de Pará*, 1er November 1977, p. 12, and November 2, 1977, p. 2 - *O Estado de Pará*, March 21, 1978, p. 14 - *UFO documento* n∞ 2, August-September 1991, pp. 6-32 - Jacques Vallée, *Confrontations*,

Robert Laffont, 1991 - Daniel Rebisso Giese, *Vampiros extraterrestres na Amazônia*, Falangola Editora, 1991 - *Flying Saucer Review*, vol. 39, n° 3, autumn 1994, pp. 8-13 - *Flying Saucer Review*, vol. 4, n° 2, Summer 1996, pp. 5-10 - *Top Secret* n∞ 6, 2003, pp. 22-26 - *UFO* n° 101, Brazil, July 2004, pp. 8-26 - Bob Pratt, *UFO Danger. A Call to Vigilance*, Trajectory, 2010 - *Nexus* n∞ 83, November-December 2012, pp. 84-95.

XII. UFOs and pilots: a step of two in the sky

This pas de deux in the sky, between UFOs and pilots, is ancient history. This old couple occupies a prominent place in the ufology chronicle, and this since its creation. Let's not forget that in 1947, a young 32 year old pilot, Kenneth Arnold, unwillingly named the phenomenon "flying saucer". And he legitimized it by embodying it semantically.

Then it was pilots, civilian or military, who were the first to report the appearance of unconventional flying machines, thus opening the contemporary era of these famous intruders. Certainly, there was a time when talking about UFOs was not easy. First of all, because no one possesses or masters the language. And that the most daring of these sky crusaders were quickly threatened with sanctions, deprived of their flight license and systematically submitted to a psychiatric evaluation.

However, as early as the 1940s, these mysterious celestial objects took shape in the testimonies, however disturbing or subjective they may be. And, among the most reliable reports, we must cite those of the pilots. These personnel, trained to survey our skies, know how to recognize any object or singularity crossing their flight corridor. And they have sophisticated and powerful detection equipment.

Last but not least, military pilots are the guarantors of a nation's air safety. Reputed to have both excellent eyesight and solid reflexes, one could not dream of better sentinels. Yet, for decades, most of them, when confronted with an unidentifiable radar target, kept silent. For fear of ridicule. And of the reprimands, as we have seen, inflicted by their hierarchy. Fortunately, times are changing. Since June 25, 2021, and the submission of the Pentagon's preliminary report, the U.S. government has decided to take seriously the reports of unidentified flying objects provided by military pilots. The Director of National Intelligence is now encouraging all flight crews to report these UFOs, the government's term for UFO sightings, in order to collect additional data. This is a radical about-face from the previous position of the high authorities, which often implied ignoring or even discrediting the phenomenon.

As a tribute to these valiant pioneers, here are two cases that disarmed, at the time, the Pentagon officials.

The Thomas Mantell case

Date: January 7, 1948.
Location: Franklin, a town in Simpson County, Kentucky, USA.

That day, since 1:15 p.m., dozens of Maysville residents reported the presence of a strange object in the Kentucky sky. This intruder, sometimes stationary, emitted an astonishing red light. 20 minutes later, residents of Owensboro and Irvington, still in Kentucky, called the police to report a similar object, "circular and measuring between 75 and 90 meters in diameter".

At 1:45 p.m., the object in question, which was quite large, flew over Godman Air Force Base in Fort Knox. Sergeant Quinton A. Blackwell, the control tower operator, immediately contacted his superiors. Several officers - including Colonel Guy F. Hix, Commander-in-Chief - were able to observe it through binoculars. The intruder was described as "a parachute with the sun reflected on its silk", "a round object, much whiter than the nearby clouds" and "an ice cream cone with a reddish top". Colonel Hix said, "It was very white and looked like an umbrella. It was a quarter of a full moon. Through the binoculars you could see like a red edge at its base and top. It stayed there, stationary, for over an hour and a half."

Reinforcement was immediately requested. A squadron of four Mustang jets from Marietta AFB, Georgia, headed for Kentucky, responded immediately and volunteered to close with the aircraft.

The leader of this squadron is Captain Thomas F. Mantell. He was 25 years old and a seasoned pilot who distinguished himself during the Second World War, notably during the Normandy landings in June 1944. He was one of the first pilots to bomb the Cherbourg peninsula. And after a particularly perilous mission over the Netherlands, he was awarded the *Distinguished Flying Cross*, a service cross rewarding heroism and extraordinary achievements in aerial flight.

Mantell is followed by 3 other pilots. One of them, Lieutenant Robert Hendricks, was not with him: "We were told that a strange object was standing up there. We were told that there was a strange object up there, and we were told to go up to it and try to identify it. I didn't see it. I didn't see it, but my colleagues obviously saw it. Tom (Mantell) kept gaining altitude. I had to return to the base because I was running out of oxygen.

Mantell and his 2 wingmen decide, them, to take the UFO in hunting. A breathtaking chase begins. Mantell directed his aircraft towards the target and began a spiraling climb to 14,000 feet (4,267 meters). There, at the controls of his P-51 Mustang, he finally spotted the intruder. Our pilot told the control tower: "I see the object, it's above me, I'll try to get closer. It looks metallic. But the UFO kept gaining altitude. Then, full throttle, Mantell goes up in straight line, following it, determined not to let it go.

The other two wingers - 1er Lieutenant Albert Clements and 2nd Lieutenant B. A. Hammond - followed their leader as best they could. At an altitude of 4,800 meters, Lieutenant Clements put on his oxygen mask. Worryingly, the air began to get thinner. Especially since Mantell and Hammond, initially left for a flight at low altitude, did not embark the adequate equipment.

The pilots continue their perilous ascent. Over the town of Bowling Green, their altimeter read 20,000 feet. Clements had trouble spotting the target: "I could make out a very small, bright object, so distant that I couldn›t tell its shape, size and color. It stood to the left, below the sun." Mantell suggested his men follow the object for 10 minutes, climbing to 25,000 feet *[6,958 meters]*. And if this UFO proves impossible to reach: return as a group to the base.

But at 22,500 feet, fearing they would run out of oxygen, Clements and Hammond decided to abandon the hunt. They tried to reach their leader, but got no answer. Clements confided that the last vision he had of his leader was "his plane going straight up to the sun.

Funny show

In Franklin, local resident William C. Mayes witnesses a strange and disturbing sight. He saw a plane circling high in the sky. Then suddenly, the plane starts to dive. During its descent, it emits a terrifying noise which amplifies. Then it explodes before it even hits the ground. No flame will be visible.

Mrs. Carrie Phillips, busy on her farm in Franklin, suddenly hears an explosion nearby. She rushes to the window and in a daze, sees a plane crashing in her yard!

The accident

Fearing the worst, the US Air Force launched an investigation at 5 p.m. But they soon learned the sad news: Captain Mantell's plane had crashed near the town of Franklin, less than 140 meters from a house belonging to the Phillips family. The U.S. Air Force contacted the local police, and police officer Joe Walker arrived at the site and had it sealed off.

When Walker discovered the extent of the damage, Captain Mantell's body, partially decapitated, was pulled from the wreckage. Having been found strapped to his cockpit, it is clear that our pilot made no attempt to parachute out of the wreckage to avoid a sudden death. The exact time of the accident is established by Mantell's watch, which stopped at 3:18 p.m. on impact. An affidavit signed by Harry W. Booker, county coroner, attests to this. And according to the instruments on board, the plane would have climbed to an altitude of 9,000 meters.

Sadly, the wreckage was scattered over an area of about 1.5 kilometers. It will take some time before the tail, a wing and the propeller are finally found.

The US Air Force takes a back seat

The same evening, the *Louisville Courier* newspaper ran the headline "Captain Mantell and his F-51 aircraft destroyed after chasing a flying saucer". The excitement was palpable throughout the country. Imaginations were fired up. Explanations were demanded.

For the US Air Force, embarrassed by this tragedy, the official hypothesis is that Thomas Mantell lost his life while pursuing the planet Venus, which he would have mistaken for a flying object. But this explanation, invariably served for each UFO sighting, has difficulty in convincing.

At the head of *Project Grudge* (a US Air Force program charged with studying the UFO phenomenon between 1949 and 1952), Edward J. Ruppelt discovered that this explanation had been proposed by a Pentagon major, presented as an expert, but ignorant of the realities on the ground. In 1952, at the instigation of an intelligence colonel, Edward Ruppelt decided to reopen the "Mantell file". This time he turned to a real expert, the US Air Force consultant J. Allen Hynek. This one, rather sheepish, admits having blown the explanation of Venus to the major to ease the tensions and regrets it. Especially since at 3 pm, in clear weather, Venus is hardly visible. And that this January 7, there was a lot of fog.

Ruppelt then proposed a second hypothesis. According to the descriptions of the witnesses, he thinks that Mantell would have followed a Skyhook balloon, a high-altitude balloon that could go up to 21 kilometers, designed to collect information on the upper atmosphere. These devices, used at the time in the greatest secrecy by the Navy, were made of polyethylene and filled with non combustible helium. It was indeed discovered that a Skyhook balloon was launched the day before, on January 6, from Camp Ripley in Minnesota.

The press is still not convinced. It notes: "The US Air Force does not take into account the fact that Mantell described a metallic object. And how do you explain that this balloon could move at speeds much faster than a jet, then stop for a moment and then take off again just as fast?" Scientists then answer that the material of these balloons can, depending on certain angles of the sun, take on a metal appearance. And that they can, according to the winds of the high atmosphere, reach a speed of 640 km/h, carry out strange displacements, like negotiating sudden changes of course or remaining completely stationary.

In the end, the famous Project *Blue* Book states: "It is the opinion of the Air Force Technical Intelligence Command that Captain Mantell lost consciousness due to a lack of oxygen. His aircraft then continued to climb to an altitude where it lost power and was unable to stabilize. The aircraft then began to turn to the left, and as the wing and nose collapsed, it plunged into a long, steep spiral. This uncontrolled descent, at excessive speed, ultimately caused the aircraft to disintegrate. We believe that Captain Mantell never regained consciousness. This is due to the fact that after the crash, his canopy lock was still in place, ruling out any attempt to abandon the plane. The UFO was somehow directly responsible for the death of this experienced pilot, flying at high altitude without adequate oxygen.

2 hypotheses were advanced concerning the nature of the UFO. Either Venus, one of the most luminous celestial bodies in our sky. Or a large balloon used for experimental flights at high altitude and known under the name of "Skyhook."

On the other hand, for Major Donald Keyhoe, no doubt, Mantell did pursue an extraterrestrial saucer... He would thus be the first martyr of ufology.

Balloon, planet or UFO? Everyone will make their own opinion. Whatever the case, Mantell›s "unattainable star" remains formally unidentified to this day. And one answer remains unanswered: why did this seasoned Icarus want to fly higher and higher, beyond the limits of possibility and safety? One of his close friends

---

decided: "The only thing I can think of is that he went after something he considered more important than his life and his own family."

National Guard pilot Thomas F. Mantell, Jr.

Sources

The APRO Bulletin, vol. 3, n° 2, September 15, 1954, pp. 8 - Edward Ruppelt, *Face aux soucoupes volantes*, Éditions France-Empire, 1956, pp. 48-59 - *UFO NYT*, January-February 1983, pp. 12-16 - *MUFON UFO Journal* n° 217, May 1986, pp. 9-13, 17 - *MUFON UFO Journal* No. 264, April 1990, pp. 18-19 - Jerome Clark, *The UFO Book*, Visible Ink, 1998, pp. 351-356 - Project *Blue Book* Files, National Archives, Washington, Microfilm roll T-1206-2.

Risk of collision over Texas

Date: July 17, 1957. Location: Amarillo, a city in Texas, USA.
22h15.

Cruising at an altitude of 6,000 meters, TWA flight 21, from New York to Phoenix, is humming. The aircraft, a 4-engine Constellation, has just flown over the city of Amarillo, in northern Texas. The visibility is perfect, close to 25 kilometers. Commander G. M. Schemel contemplates hundreds of glittering houses in the folds of the landscape. This vision is soothing. The country is slowly falling asleep.

On board, too, everything is quiet. Some of the 34 passengers are already asleep. In the cockpit, the co-pilot was checking the instruments when, suddenly, the lights of an unknown aircraft, appearing from nowhere, materialized less than 1,500 meters from the plane.

Everything goes very fast. This mysterious ship is hurtling towards the plane at a prodigious speed. Commander Schemel has no other solution than to crash-land. The UFO passes over him, grazing the plane, in a shimmer of red and green lights.

In the back, it's panic. The passengers were screaming! Schemel quickly righted the plane, handed over the controls to the co-pilot and rushed to see the extent of the damage.

Among the passengers, it was a disaster. As most of them had removed their seatbelts, they were violently thrown to the ceiling. Then, when the plane stabilized, they fell back in a heap, one on top of the other, randomly from the seats and the gangway.

Mary Clark, an elderly woman with a nicked scalp, bled profusely. She lay moaning on a pile of hats and luggage on the floor. Seven other passengers and the stewardess Dorothy Rekow were slightly bruised. And several people broke down, in the grip of a real nervous breakdown.

Back in the cockpit, Schemel took control of the aircraft and contacted the Amarillo airport. He asked for permission to land in a hurry. "Send me doctors and an ambulance!" he demands. The elderly woman was immediately evacuated for emergency treatment. The stewardess, injured by a falling suitcase, bravely resumes her post.

The next day, the near-collision of flight 21 with a UFO spread like wildfire. Faced with requests for explanations from journalists and the public, the US Air Force refused to give an explanation. It asserted that "this mysterious object was in fact an ordinary aircraft that Schemel and his co-pilot did not recognize. So there is nothing unusual about it. Of course, this does not explain the prodigious speed of the intruder.

After a thorough search, the investigators of the Civil Aeronautics Department dismantled the explanation of the US Air Force. It could not, in any case, be an "ordinary aircraft" because no aircraft was present, that evening, within 80 kilometers. The closest aircraft was a USAF K-97 tanker which was cruising, at the corresponding times, very south of Amarillo. However, the staff, impatient to get rid of the problem, turned a deaf ear as usual. Move along, there is nothing to see!

However, since 1947, reports from military pilots from 60 countries concerning UFOs have been pouring in. And high ranking officers such as General Paul Stehlin of the French Air Force, Marshal Sir George Jones of the Australian Air Force or General A. B. Melville of the South African Union did not hesitate to testify. This is why the public began to take a close interest in these "saucers" that taunted trained and competent personnel. But the general staff is sulking. Not knowing what to do with this embarrassing subject, it plays dumb and uninterested while a good number of documents and reports declared confidential are exchanged underhand.

The public is demanding more and more transparency. A poll conducted by the Trendex New Poll institute reveals, on July 27, 1957, that 1 in 4 Americans now believe that these objects are real and come from beyond space.

Little by little, in a sometimes perilous flight, UFOs are becoming part of the consciousness, the daily life and the increasingly assertive appetite of the world's citizens for the mysterious and the unexplained.

Sources

UFO Investigator, vol. 1, No. 1, August-September 1957, p. 9 - *The APRO Bulletin*, September 1957, p. 3 - *Saucers*, vol. 5, No. 3, Fall 1957, pp. 12-13 - Donald E. Keyhoe, *Les Étrangers de l'espace*, Éditions France-Empire, 1975, pp. 32-33.

Acknowledgements

Special thanks to Gilbert Attard and Patrice Seray for their generosity and their precious documents.

Many thanks to Marie-Laure, Chloé and Richard, Robert Dulbecco, Carlos Sottomayor, Franck Istasse, Virginie, Nour and Fayçal Anseur, Hortense Dufour, Marie Coppola, Johan and Estelle, Sioux and Kalie (love you!), Alain Pierre, Jean-Claude Moireau, Pascale Lafargue, Carla and the Harfouche and Venant families, Pierre Lagrange, Yves Bacou, Josette Janoyer, and all those who have encouraged me since.

Infinite gratitude to Bob Bellanca and Jean-Charles Gérard.

A warm and cosmic hug to Paola Harris.

www.ingramcontent.com/pod-product-compliance
Lightning Source LLC
La Vergne TN
LVHW051154060726
842526LV00014B/3199